SEMINOLE

SOME PEOPLE NEVER GIVE UP

TINA SIEMENS

Tina (Katharina) Siemens P.O. Box 211 Seminole, Texas 79360

SeminoleTheBook@gmail.com

Website: SeminoleTheBook.com

Printed in the United States of America

ISBN: 978-1-79040-623-4

AudioBook edition 2019. Voiceover talent: Wes Malik.

Originally published in Legacy Edition hardcover by Tina Siemens in 2019.

First Trade paperback edition in 2019.

Author Consultant and Editing: Company 614 Enterprises, LLC.
Cover Design: Alfie™
Text Design and Composition: Rick Soldin
Sketches: Todd Schafer
Photos from Tina Siemens Family Collection and used with permission
Author Photo: Alejandra Dodge Photography

Dedication

To God: Who made all this possible and made me a daughter of His Kingdom through salvation!

To my wonderful and loving husband, John: Bless you for your continued support and encouragement.

To my sons, Jonathan and Chris, and their lovely wives, Tina and Christy: Mom loves you!

To my parents: Thank you for giving us an opportunity for a better life in Seminole, Texas.

To our grandchildren and future generations: May you always know your roots. Never give up. Endure!

To Dad: I'm so glad you followed Great-grandpa's advice to get us to a land of opportunity!

To my siblings: For putting up with me all these years when I talked and talked about writing a book. (It's finally done!)

To Bob and Vicky Clark: For putting your lives on hold and helping with our immigration journey.

To Bo Brown: For being the lawyer who willingly got involved in this immigration mess.

To the late George H. Mahon: As Chairman of the Appropriations Committee, he made sure our bill moved through the House and onto the President's desk. He didn't give up despite have several opportunities to do so.

To the late Senator Lloyd Bentsen: For getting a bill passed through Congress which changed our lives forever.

To President Jimmy Carter: For having the courage to sign a private bill into law and granting us our citizenship. I will spend my remaining years giving God Glory and paying back this country for that life-changing act.

To Pappy and Laura Hoffman: For being true friends to me.

To Shelby Concotelli and Candy and Dean Boyer: For helping me get involved in our beloved community; for your support and friendship.

To Susie and Tina: For helping me make a 2016 New Year's resolution to write this book.

Writing a book about my heritage has been surreal. I'm forever grateful to Michael Gray, for his keen insight and ongoing support in bringing my story to life. It's because of his effort and encouragement that I have a legacy to pass on to my family.

—Tina Siemens

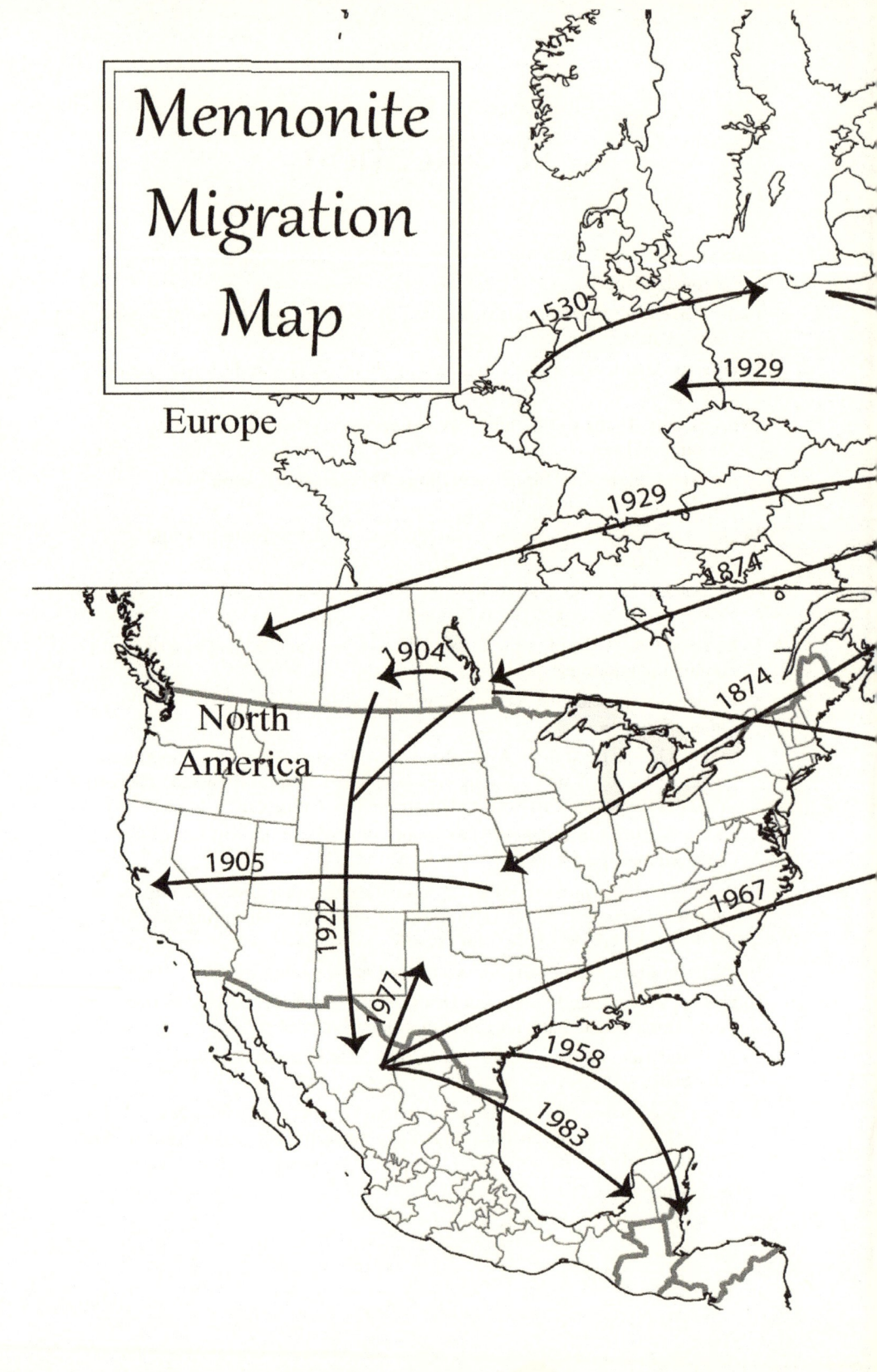

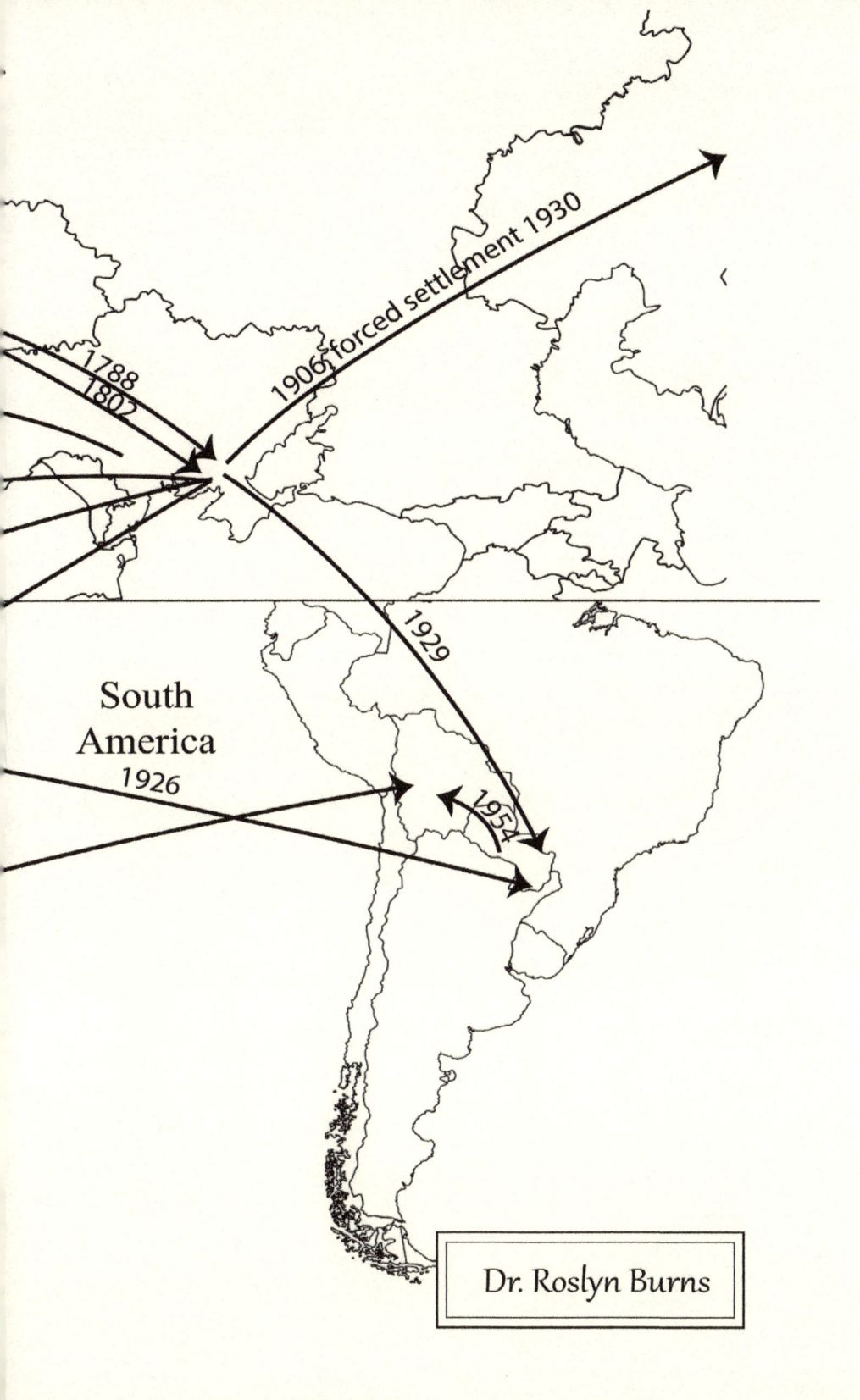

1788
1802
1906 forced settlement 1930
1929
South America
1926
1954
Dr. Roslyn Burns

Contents

Note to Reader

When I sat down and thought about telling this incredible story, I ran into several obstacles. First, I had to get all the names in order. And believe me, there were a lot of them. An unfortunate reality of Mennonite life is name similarity. Thousands of Mennonites share the same last names like Reimer and Schmitt. To make matters worse, there are a small number of first names used, such as John, Jacob, and Katharina. If a family has a little boy, John, who dies, the next boy they have is often called John. It makes reading a Mennonite story all the more difficult.

The next hurdle I had was getting the dates and timeline straight. Then I had to do a great deal of research, gathering information on a wide variety of subjects. Somehow, I survived.

Then, when I decided to tell the story in first person, I couldn't find a way to do it well. This was particularly evident with events that occurred before I was born. And describing the character's emotions while in first person proved too much for me. That's when I discovered this genre of writing called *creative nonfiction*. It allowed me to take factually accurate events and tell them in a literary style. I was able to use historical figures and pull information from ancient documents and put together a decent plot. However, I had to create some fictitious characters to tell the historically accurate events. If my great-grandparents took a seven-day train ride from Canada to Mexico, I created porters and other travelers for them to interact with so the story would be readable. And readability was my number one goal. I could have written a documentary-style encyclopedic book with no fictitious characters, yet it would've been read by only family (doubtful), friends (extremely doubtful), academic professors (possibly), and researchers. Thus, I decided to go this route.

So, what does all this mean for you, the reader?

It means that even though this is based on a true story, it's not a documentary or a *60 Minutes* exposé. Memories of my family and notes they made may not be accurate. They could be mistaken. I also found that when I researched an event, many times there were different versions and viewpoints (like Matthew, Mark, Luke, and John). I had to pick the one that made the most sense to me. I have done my best to be accurate. So, I ask that you give me grace on this and enjoy my story about a remarkable people and a wonderful town!

Principal Characters

Mennonites

Rempel Family – *Traveled from Canada to Mexico*
Jacob Braun Rempel
Judith Wiebe Rempel – Wife
Jacob Wiebe Rempel – Son
Helena Rempel – Daughter
Abraham Wiebe – Ältester and father of Judith Rempel

Rempel Family – *Grew up in Mexico*
Jacob Wiebe Rempel
Katharina Giesbrecht Rempel – Wife
David Giesbrecht Rempel – Son
Jacob "Jake" Rempel – Son

Rempel Family – *Left Mexico for Texas*
David Giesbrecht Rempel
Anna Friesen Rempel – Wife
Elizabeth "Beth" Rempel – Daughter
David Rempel – Son
Katharina "Tina" Rempel – Daughter
Aganetha "Nancy" Rempel - Daughter
Jacob Rempel – Son (Born in the U.S–Texas)
Henry Rempel – Son (Born in the U.S–Texas)

Others
Henry Friesen – Brother of Anna Friesen Rempel
Jacob J. Friesen – Father of Anna Friesen Rempel
Elizabeth Funk Friesen – Mother of Anna Friesen Rempel
Peter – Good friend of David Giesbrecht Rempel
Wilhelm Burg – David's guide to Canada
Mr. Schmitt – Traveled and lived with David Giesbrecht Rempel
Mr. Harms – Worked with David Giesbrecht Rempel
Dueck, Dyck, Bergen, and Reimer – These very common names
    refer to many different people

Politicians

Bob Clark – Mayor of Seminole (Married to Vicky)
Marcus Crow – County Judge of Gaines County
George "Chairman" Mahon – Congressman from Gaines County
area and Chairman of the House Appropriations Committee
Lloyd Bentsen – Senator from Texas

Attorneys

Bo Brown – Lubbock
John Shepherd – Seminole

Henderson Family in Seminole

Tommy Nabors – Former Tenth Calvary clerk and Father to Mae
Beth (Nabors) Henderson
Samuel Henderson – Owner of Henderson's Hardware,
Implements & Harness
Mae Beth Henderson – Wife to Samuel Henderson
Melvin Henderson – Son of Mae Beth and Samuel Henderson
Rose Henderson – Niece to Mae Beth and Samuel Henderson

Seminole Businessmen

Charles Simpson – Land speculator and fiancé of
Rose Henderson
David Bane – Partner of Charles Simpson
Eddie Fulghum – Geologist and boyfriend of Rose Henderson
Bill Smith – Traveled to Mexico to speak to Mennonites
Seth Woltz – Real estate agent
Laura and Pappy Hoffman – Owner of Hoffman's Well Servicing
and clients of Anna Rempel
Mr. Bates – Owner of H&D Grocery Store

Chapter One

February 1569
Asperen, Gelderland
Low Country (present-day Netherlands)

"Quickly," Dirk Willems whispered. "I must act quickly."

He glanced back at the tiny opening in the door. It was clear. "Yes, the rooster has not crowed—he is still sleeping. Now's my chance."

He was alone, so there was no reason to speak out loud. In fact, he had every reason to keep his mouth shut. Months earlier, Dirk Willems had been placed in this residential palace-turned-prison for rejecting Catholicism and baptizing people into a new faith. Most of the ceremonies had taken place in his home, away from the prying eyes of the Spanish. That was where they had captured him, sentencing him to torture and death.

For the tenth time, Dirk inspected the crude rope he'd made from rags tied in knots. He was unsure if it would hold him. Then he grinned. "I hardly weigh anything," he said to the face he had sketched on the wall. "I've been thinking that my constant hunger was a punishment. But I see now that God has been planning everything."

He suppressed a laugh. "I doubt this rope would have held me when I was first imprisoned. But now? I will be free in a matter of minutes."

He crept to the outer window and looked out. The land was completely dark with barely a hint of a dull gray sky forming in the east. This was it. No more time to waste.

Hastily, he looped his rope through a steel eye in the floor—one used to secure prisoners. "Yet another part of God's plan. The same device that holds me down for torture, I now use for my escape."

Carefully and slowly, he squeezed through the window opening, clinging to the doubled-up rope. As he lowered himself down from the second-story window, he smiled wider, thinking how the rare visitor had smuggled in a few rags each time he'd come. Adding the rags dropped by guards, with two or three from the rubbish left by other prisoners—dead ones now—he had created a suitable length of rope. Two of the rags had blood on them from one of his torture sessions. Rather than touch them, the guard had left them behind. Dirk suppressed another laugh. *Blood from my own suffering! Only God could plan so well.*

Dirk hit the hard ground, cold from the harsh winter that covered the region. Releasing one end of the rope, he pulled on the other until he had the entire length loosely wrapped over his shoulder.

"I'm free of that," he whispered. "But the wall is where I may fail."

The wall was four stories high, made from large blocks four feet thick. It was designed to repel attackers rather than keep in prisoners. The guards seemed to think no prisoner was willing to jump four stories to a certain death in the moat that waited to swallow them whole. Of course, they didn't count on his rope made of rags.

The steps, he thought, lowering a hand down to the ground to feel his way to the wall. *I know they're here somewhere.* His breath fogged up what low light there was. He could tell he was getting closer to the wall as it grew much darker. If he waited a few minutes more, the sky would lighten and he could find the steps. But he didn't have the time. Darkness was a necessary part of his plan.

Dirk hit the wall with a thud and stopped. The steps were near—he knew that. Yet he had a choice: go left or right. He chose right.

Tripping over the first riser, he felt his way up. The steps got easier to see as he climbed higher. At the top, he could easily spot the two guard towers, spaced equally away from him. He knew they were occupied, but the guards were likely fast asleep. He was counting on it.

Scanning the top of the wall for a steel eye, he found none. There was no need for one on the wall. With no option, he tied one end of the rope to a piece of wood, jamming it behind an archer's gap. He hoped his weight on the rope would hold the wood in place.

"God, I pray you are with me. I know Jesus walked on water, but if you allow me to get down from the rope, I have no idea how I'm going to cross the moat."

Gripping hard, he eased his thin body over the wall and began lowering himself down. But with only one strand, he could feel the rags straining. If he took his time, they might rip. With no choice, he loosened his grip and slid faster, hitting the ground with a hard thud that could have woken a guard.

He lay there for a few seconds, gazing up at the sky. A few stars were still visible, coming into focus as he caught his breath and regained his senses. He let go of the rope to feel for injuries. *Nothing. Thank the Lord*, he thought, slowly sitting up.

He pushed his back against the wall—the same wall that had been holding him prisoner—and lifted himself up. He could barely see the moat and prepared himself for the icy cold water. *Surely*, he thought, *if I don't clear the moat, I will freeze to death in its water.*

"If so, God, then that be your will."

He stuck his right foot out and waited for the water to envelop his leather shoe. It hit a solid surface. Dirk allowed himself to shift more weight onto his foot. Nothing made sense. He should have been sinking in the water. Instead, it was a miracle. God had laid a bridge for him to cross the moat.

He placed his left foot on the water and even that stayed dry. Seconds later, he was scooting across the moat—its surface frozen by the cold temperatures. He could do nothing but smile. Not only had God brought the harsh winter, but his reduced weight kept him from going through the ice.

"In suffering, so shall I be free," he said, much too loudly. "It's a miracle from God!"

Just as he set his feet on the far side, a man behind him called out. "You, there. Halt!"

Dirk twisted his head to see a guard emerge from a narrow door at the base of the wall. Running along the dirt strip, the guard yelled, "Stop! I command it!"

Dirk pulled himself up the low bank and could see nothing but freedom ahead. "God, I will live another day to carry out your divine will."

As he started to run, he heard a distinctive crack behind him. "Help! I'm drowning. Please help me!"

Dirk ran ten more paces and stopped. Without a doubt, he knew the guard had fallen through the thin ice and would drown in seconds. In the briefest of moments, Dirk Willems thought of all he believed. Forgiveness. Being born again. Helping his fellow man. Before he could take one more step, he turned around and went back to the moat.

"Help me!" the guard cried, his waist slipping below the ice as he clawed at the smooth surface in front of him. He could imagine the cold water filling the guard's boots, soaking his pants, making him heavier. Dirk Willems had been under a death sentence and was escaping it. Yet this man would take his place.

"I cannot let you die," Dirk said as he slipped across the breaking ice and grabbed the man's outstretched hand. "Jesus died for my sins, and I will not allow you to die for me. There is the presence of my savior in you."

The man held fast to Dirk and pulled himself to thicker ice. Lying flat on his stomach helped spread out his body weight and avoid cracking more ice. Refusing to let go, Dirk pulled the man to the far side of the moat—the freedom side.

"Are you okay?" Dirk asked.

"I think so," the guard replied, breathing heavy. Dirk could hear the lingering panic in his voice.

"Hey, you there. Stop!"

Both men turned and saw the *carcelero*—the warden—waving from the other side of the moat. "Do not let that man escape! You have taken an oath as an officer of the peace. Arrest that man!"

The guard, still holding onto Dirk, gazed into his eyes and said nothing. Dirk felt his grip loosen, waiting for Dirk to hit him or jerk his arm free. Dirk did nothing. As seconds ticked by, he resigned himself to being recaptured.

An hour later, he was in a more secure cell—one with no window and four guards.

The *carcelero* pulled the rope tight. This one was not made of rags, but strong hemp. Dirk felt it bite his wrists.

"You have been condemned to death," the *carcelero* said. "Do you have anything to say?"

Dirk squinted at the crowd. Many of the onlookers had their arms folded. "You may kill me today, but you will not kill my faith. I have been born again and accepted into our Lord's loving arms. I forgive you, for that is what my Lord commands."

The *carcelero* spat at Dirk's feet. "You Anabaptists are all the same," he proclaimed loudly. "You reject the true Catholic faith—the Pope—and follow your own god. That crazy man Menno Simons will lead you nowhere but to death. He's already there, waiting for you. Go and join the rest of your *Menno*-nites!"

"You can't kill all of us," Dirk replied confidently. "We are leaving this land—the Low Country—and will find a place where we can be left alone, to worship God in the true way—the righteous way. Wherever we go, however long it takes, we will find a place we can call home. That is what I'm dying for."

"Maybe that's true," the *carcelero* said. "But *you* won't be going anywhere except to ashes. Isn't that what you believe? Ashes to ashes?"

He struck a flint and ignited the kindling at Dirk Willems's feet. "See if your god saves you now. Oh, and I didn't clamp your tongue—so you can beg for mercy and renounce your faith when your god does not save you."

"Never!" cried Dirk.

"We'll see."

The wind shifted, blowing the flames away from Dirk. It appeared as if the fire would die out, but the embers were too hot. This only made it worse, prolonging the execution.

"Oh, my Lord. My God!" Dirk cried. "Oh, my Lord. My God!"

As the flames licked at his feet, a man from the crowd moved to the front. He was the guard Dirk had saved three months earlier. Dirk saw the man's expression. It was one of compassion.

The guard looked around at the fifty or so other guards and realized it would be fruitless to attempt anything. Instead, he stood there with the rest of the crowd, listening to Dirk suffer and plead to God, over and over. "Oh, my Lord. My God!"

By the seventieth cry, it was finished. Dirk Willems had given his life for the fledgling Mennonites and their deceased leader—Menno Simons.

And, for God.

Chapter Two

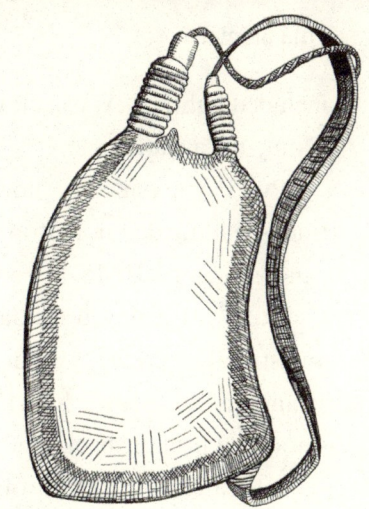

November 1875
Texas – the Llano Estacado

The horses were strung out farther than Lt. Ward liked, almost a half mile or so. He considered sending Sgt. Bingham to pull the men together but decided against it. They were all dog-tired, and their horses were ready to drop. No sense in pushing them too hard. With no water for the last day or so, who knew which horse might fall? If that happened, they'd be in a tight spot. Then he'd have to make some serious decisions—some *command* decisions.

The troop was headed west by northwest, and the late afternoon sun was heavy on his eyes. He raised his hand to shield the sunlight and spotted a rider coming toward him. It was one of his scouts, Pvt. Bobby Payne, cantering back on that bay he loved. The army wanted only dark horses, but they bent the rules when a man insisted on using his own horse. Payne was one of those men.

Lt. Ward's mare was too exhausted to close the gap between them with a trot, so he let her continue walking. He didn't have the heart to kick her, especially since she'd consumed the last of his canteen from his bare hands the day before. He remembered the crazed look in her eyes as she slurped it up—like someone was going to steal it. He'd wanted to drink it himself, but he knew if his horse died, he was done for. There was no way he could walk the 400 miles back to Fort Clark.

Lt. Ward's scout was almost within shouting distance. He hoped the scout had seen something: Comanche, Kiowa, Cheyenne, or Kickapoo. Anything was better than this endless plain of nothingness, and that included fighting. At least it would take his soldiers' minds off their thirst, if only for a short time.

Pvt. Payne reined his horse up. "Sir, we spotted a draw ahead. Animal tracks leading down. Hilton is there scouting around. I'll go back and see what we can find. Maybe some water."

Lt. Ward removed his dark blue cavalry hat, now stained with sweat, and straightened the two knotted gold braids. A cold breeze tossed several strands of his brown hair about, cooling his scalp. He rubbed his jaw, smoothed his hair back, and replaced the hat.

"Be careful, Private. Probably no Comanche down there, but don't get in a hurry. They can pop up in a second and start slingin' arrows. They might even have rifles. Then we'd be in a rattlesnake nest."

"Yes sir, we'll be careful. Do you want to wait for us here or keep moving? Maybe go around the draw and stay up top?"

"We could go for another few hours, but I'm going to make camp at the lip of that draw, near them hackberries. I'll get some fires started and put the coffee pot out. I'll pray hard you find water to go in it."

Pvt. Payne smiled. "Hilton said he could smell water down there, and he's always right, you know."

"If you two find some, I'm giving you some kind of reward. After I get some coffee in me, that is. Can't be November in Texas without coffee."

The scout gave a quick salute, pulled his bay around, and kicked it into a trot. The lieutenant watched him go until his young clerk, Tommy Nabors, appeared next to him.

"Sir, are we stopping here?"

"Nah. There's a draw ahead. Tell Sgt. Bingham we'll stop at the edge and make camp. And tell him to get some fires going." He glanced up at the sky. "It don't look like snow or cold weather, but it's November. So anything can happen."

"Yes sir," Tommy replied, turning his horse around.

Two hours later, with half the sun below the horizon, the men of the Tenth Cavalry set up their tents. Several fires burned, the largest one close to the chuck wagon. Three metal grills held steaks from a cow they'd slaughtered the day before. The smell of roasting meat set their dry mouths salivating. With no water available, they couldn't serve rice or beans, but at least they had something to eat.

Tommy stared at the steaks and felt his stomach rumble. As the company clerk, he was the last to eat. That's just the way things were.

He dropped a load of wood into a small pile and went to get more. Several men were busy chopping up fallen tree limbs into pieces he could carry. There was just enough that they didn't have to chop a tree down.

"Hey, boy, you got any water in that canteen?"

It was Pvt. Dunn. He was probably the least-liked man in the outfit.

"No sir," Tommy replied. "I ran out yesterday."

"Yeah, that's what I figured," Pvt. Dunn said, snatching the canteen from the boy's horse and uncapping it. Two drops landed on his large tongue. By shaking it again, he coaxed one more out.

"That's nothin'. You ain't hidin' any water, are you, boy?"

Pvt. Jakes rose to his feet. "Aw, leave him alone. He's just a boy. He didn't ask for this like we did." He grabbed the canteen away from Pvt. Dunn and returned it to the boy's horse.

"Yeah, he did," Pvt. Dunn sneered. "He volunteered just like us. Didn't cha, boy?"

Tommy said nothing, unsure of what to do.

Pvt. Jakes put his arm around Tommy. "I'm sure your pappy sent you out here to become a man, right?"

Tommy nodded.

"Yeah," Pvt. Dunn laughed, "and he stuck you with Pecos Bill, who didn't want you. So he handed you off to the lieutenant to babysit you."

Pvt. Jakes guided Tommy to the wagon. "Don't listen to him. You know the colonel let you come with us because he scattered them Indians at Cedar Lake eastward. I guess he felt it would be safer for you out here, 'cept now he has them Indians' sacks of mesquite beans, a mountain of buffalo meat, and plenty of water while we don't have a drop."

Pvt. Jakes moved some things around in the back of the wagon until he found the coffee pot. Handing it to Tommy, he said, "Set this on a flat rock near the fire. Lieutenant thinks it helps find water—good luck or something."

The boy clutched the pot as if it were a baby, and carefully placed it on a big rock by the edge of the fire. By now, a few soldiers had made their way over, waiting for the first steaks to be served. Tommy went for one more load of wood and joined the men after he'd dropped it off.

Sgt. Bingham sat close to the fire, shaking his boots out and inspecting his socks.

"Hey, Sarge," Pvt. Jakes said, "did you hear what them Seminoles saw down there?"

The sergeant put one of his boots back on. "Yeah, they seen animal tracks leading down the draw, and Hilton said he could smell the water. That's all I know."

Normally, Tommy kept his mouth shut, but this time he spoke up. "Why do they call them scouts Seminoles? They ain't no Indians, at least none I ever saw."

He stared at Sgt. Bingham, waiting for an answer. When none came, he glanced at Pvt. Jakes.

"Don't look at me," Pvt. Jakes said. "I really don't know. But maybe old Castillo does. He's been everywhere there is to be. Here he comes now."

Castillo was the farrier for the unit and had just finished checking the hooves of several horses. With a rasp in his hand, he was looking for a steak. It was an unwritten rule that he got served first—because he'd check on the rest of the horses before it got dark.

Pvt. Jakes held up his hand. "Hey, Castillo, the boy here's got a question."

Castillo grabbed the empty coffee pot to pour a cup. "I keep forgettin' the lieutenant sets this pot out when he wants to find water. I was looking forward to some coffee too." He found a spot near the fire and lowered his thin frame to the ground. "Okay, boy, what's your question?"

Tommy cleared his dry throat. "Why do they call them scouts Seminoles? Are they real Indians?"

Castillo chuckled. "No, they're not Comanche or Kiowa or Apache, like regular Indians. You see, there used to be a bunch of different Indian tribes all over Florida, but the Creeks came in and cleared them all out. That left a whole lot of land with hardly anybody on it—except a few leftover Oconees, Choctaws, and Chickasaws.

"Runaway slaves heard they could disappear in Florida, so they went there with other slaves escaping their masters and some runaways from the islands. It was like a big hideout for everyone, so they started mingling together—coloreds, Indians, islanders, and some Spaniards.

"That's when the Spanish started calling these folk *cimarrons*—means runaways. The Creeks also had a word for them I can't pronounce. It means 'people who live at a distance' or 'set apart.' Somehow it all got combined into the word Seminole. At least that's what this educated man I worked for in Georgia told me. He had taken one of 'em in and gave 'im a proper name—like our scouts Bobby Payne or John Hilton have."

Pvt. Jakes rubbed his jaw. "So that's why Hilton looks more colored, while Bobby Payne looks more Spanish and Indian. If I die of thirst, Castillo, at least I learned something new."

Sgt. Bingham dusted off his pants. "I have to say, I don't care where they come from or what color they are because them Seminoles can sure track!"

Pvt. Jakes patted Tommy on the back. "See? Now you know something about them. I bet Lt. Ward don't even know all that."

Tommy smiled as he watched the cook hand the first steak to Castillo and the second to Sgt. Bingham.

"Sarge, are we meeting up with Col. Shafter soon?" Pvt. Jakes asked.

Sgt. Bingham cut into his steak. "Not for a few weeks. He sent us out here to see if those Comanche he run out of Cedar Lake have doubled back here."

"I wish I was with the colonel," Pvt. Dunn said. "I'd drink up that whole lake."

"I doubt it," Sgt. Bingham mumbled through a mouthful of meat. "It's saltwater. You can't drink anything from that lake."

"What?! A lake with water you can't drink? There ain't no water on this forsaken plain!" Pvt. Dunn said, cursing under his breath.

"Hush up!" Pvt. Jakes yelled, slamming his hat to the ground.

"You hush up!" Pvt. Dunn spat back. "Or you might not be around to protect that boy when some Comanche sneaks up to peel his scalp off."

Pvt. Jakes slowly got to his feet and started rolling up his sleeves. "You're bothering the boy, and you're bothering me. You hear?"

Pvt. Dunn jumped up and reached for a knife in his belt, but Sgt. Bingham slammed down his plate and got between the two men, towering over the shorter Dunn. "If you pull that knife, son, you'd better plan on killing me first. Otherwise, you're gonna be a dead man!"

Pvt. Dunn stared hard at the sergeant's face and smirked at Pvt. Jakes. Then he cursed under his breath and sat down. Tommy moved away from Pvt. Dunn as Pvt. Jakes joined him.

"You don't pay him any mind, Tommy. He's trouble. Just stay clear of him, and sleep under that wagon tonight." He guided the boy out of earshot from the others. "Listen, you know we can see forever on this plain, so there ain't no Comanche anywhere. But they could be hidin' out in that draw. If they are, they'll have to charge up towards us through a hail of bullets. If that happens, you stay under this wagon and don't get out in the open, where a horse might run over you. You hear?"

"Yes sir," Tommy said, his eyes wide with worry.

Pvt. Jakes tousled the boy's hair and went back to the campfire to collect his steak.

⋯✦⋯

For Tommy Nabors, the night was lasting forever. He found it hard to sleep. Thoughts of Comanche in full headdress charging up the draw lingered in his mind. He kept the cavalry hat on his head—angled, so he could sleep—in the belief that it would be harder for an Indian to remove his scalp. Quietly, he pulled the blanket close to his chin and stared out between the two wheels. The wagon was situated so its long side faced the draw, giving the men a chance to use it for cover in case of attack. Combined with a bright half-moon, this position gave Tommy a good view of anyone or anything coming toward the camp.

Suddenly, he heard a foot crushing some dry brush, and it was too close for comfort. His heart raced as he squinted his eyes, looking for the Comanche

24

who were surely sneaking up on him. Slowly and quietly, he shifted his back to the fire, trying to get farther away from the danger. A loud scream pierced the night as a hand ripped his hat off and reached for his scalp.

Tommy twisted his body to get away from the strong grip of his attacker. But it was too late. He was done for.

Behind him, guns cocked as the men cast off their blankets and stumbled to their feet, quickly readying themselves for a fight. Sgt. Bingham barked out orders and kicked the campfire—increasing the light to see the Comanche. He heard Tommy screaming and ran toward the wagon, his revolver ready for action.

"What's going on here?!" Sgt. Bingham yelled. "Is that you, Dunn?"

Pvt. Dunn released the boy and crawled out from underneath the wagon. "Yeah, it's me. Don't shoot. I was just scarin' the boy—keepin' him alert."

Tommy felt his head and realized his scalp was still in place. He was grateful it was dark under the wagon because tears welled up in his eyes.

"I tell you this now, Dunn, you're goin' on report!" the sergeant bellowed.

Lt. Ward came running to the wagon with a rifle in his hand. "You think that was funny, Dunn? You're doin' this while you're on watch?!"

Pvt. Dunn said nothing, trying desperately to hide his smirk.

One of the men ran over. "Lieutenant, someone's heard us. Riders are coming up the draw!"

Lt. Ward snapped into action. "Men, form a line behind this wagon. Don't shoot until I give the order."

Forty men scrambled into place with their rifles and pistols pointed at the draw. Hearing the commotion, the approaching riders reined up their horses and called out, "Scouts coming in! Scouts coming in!"

Lt. Ward jumped up, waving his arms. "Hold your fire! Hold your fire!"

A wave of relief rushed through the camp. Amidst the shadows and half-light, the Seminole scouts appeared, riding slowly and waving their hands.

"It's Payne and Hilton!" Lt. Ward cried out. "Come on in. We see you now."

The Seminole scouts slid out of their saddles and walked the horses in. Lt. Ward pulled them away from the other men and lowered his voice. "You find anything down there?"

"Yes, Lieutenant. We found at least eight wells, maybe more. The Comanche scooped out the sand and dug good holes. There's water for sure, some just two feet from the surface."

"Yes!" Lt. Ward said, slapping his thigh. "I could hug you both. At first light, let's go water the horses in three or four of those holes, and use the others to water us. I can't wait to taste it."

Payne handed something to the lieutenant. "Sir, it tastes good—real clean and fresh and cool. We even brought some back."

"What?!" Lt. Ward stared at the leather skins full of water.

"We've been carrying those extra skins from the wagon in case we found water, so we filled them all up."

"Now I know I'm gonna hug you! Give every man a few swallows. Then bring one to the fire, because I'm making coffee. No way I'm goin' back to sleep now."

The morning sun was low in the horizon as Tommy helped the cook load up the chuck wagon. Breakfast had just been served and the men readied their horses. He glanced over at Lt. Ward, who was busy pointing here and there, giving orders while tightening the straps on his own mare.

They had stayed in the draw for two days, watering the horses and letting them feed on the sweet grass near the wells. The men had rested, cleaned their equipment, and filled every container with water. Now they were ready to continue hunting Comanche.

Tommy was about to mount his gelding when the lieutenant waved him over. "You're the clerk, so take some notes for me."

Tommy pulled out a notebook, turned to the proper page, and licked the end of his pencil. "Ready, sir."

"Out of water. Men and horses exhausted when we found fifty shallow wells—three to fourteen feet deep, most likely dug by Comanche. All located in long, north/south draw. Water is excellent quality, within one point five to three feet from surface. Excellent sweet grass at the bottom. Watered men and animals at the Seminole Wells. November 21, 1875."

Tommy closed his notebook. "Is that all, sir?"

"Yep, that's it. Mount up."

"Are you really going to name them the Seminole Wells?"

"Of course I am. They found 'em. It's only fair." Lt. Ward cocked his head and winked at Tommy. "Besides, I sure ain't calling them Comanche Wells."

Tommy grinned. "Seminole Wells. That sounds pretty good."

Lt. Ward straightened the gold braids and put his dark blue Stetson hat on, shoving it down. "Thank God we persevered. I was beginning to think we were goners. Now all we have to do is stay alive so we can tell the others there's life out here. You make sure you do that, you hear?"

"Yes sir!" Tommy said.

With that, the men of the Tenth Cavalry formed a long line and set off in search of their prey.

Chapter Three

September 1921
Swift Current, Saskatchewan

J acob Rempel stamped his shoes several times on the steps of his plain, colorless house—a place where he was the boss. His word was law. But tracking in dirt was a no-no since his wife, Judith, would have to sweep it up. Sure, she wouldn't say anything because it wasn't proper. Instead, she'd sweep all around his shoes as he sat in his favorite chair trying to relax after a hard day's work. He stood there thinking of when they were first married. It hadn't taken long for him to get the message. Staring down, he stomped his feet several times, making sure it was loud enough for her to hear. Even though no dirt was dislodged, this one act made his life easier, especially with the stress he was going through. And if there was anything he needed at this moment, it was some peace and quiet.

Jacob removed his hat and opened the front door, seeing his son crawling, playing with some wooden sticks. He was named Jacob too because the Mennonites consider it an honor to name the first son after the father and the second and third sons after each of the grandfathers. They did the same for daughters, recycling the same names over and over again. Since his father had named him Jacob Braun Rempel, he named his son Jacob *Wiebe* Rempel, using his wife's maiden name for his son's middle name. This was yet another Mennonite custom. To make matters worse, there were hundreds of other Rempels and Wiebes in the Swift Current colony, with many of them bearing the first name of Jacob. Being mostly cut off from the outside world, it didn't matter much. Everyone knew who they were.

"*Komm hia jung*," Jacob said. Come here, boy. He took his fourteen-month-old son in his arms and held him up over his head. Spit drooled off his lips and fell on Jacob's overalls, only to be wiped up with a rag by Judith before it could dry.

"So, did you find anything out?" she asked, trying to hide her emotions.

Jacob knew she was anxious to hear what news the six delegates brought back with them from Mexico. He considered giving her the short version but knew from past experience that she'd find out more information from the other wives and then pester him with questions for days as she tried to confirm the truth of what her friends had said. That's why he plopped down in his favorite chair, took a deep breath, and prepared himself for the long version.

"*Jo Heea*," he said with a heavy sigh. Yes, dear. "I learned a great deal."

Judith removed her apron and sat down in a chair opposite her husband. "Well, what did they say?"

"They told us how they traveled all over Mexico inspecting lands in several states. Some of it was suitable for farming and some of it wasn't. They finally made their way to Mexico City, where they met President Obregón in his palace and had quite an experience. They explained how they negotiated for many days before receiving an agreement signed by the president himself. They even showed us the original document with the president's signature and an official seal!"

"What did it say?" Judith blurted out. They were both worried about the increasing religious prosecutions in Manitoba. It was only a matter of time before the authorities spread this disease to Saskatchewan (Swift Current)—their colony.

"I looked at it but the document was written in Spanish. One of the men interpreted it for us. He said we are welcome in Mexico and will maintain our own schools, our own teachers, and our own religion *without* interference from the government. We can also establish our own economic system."

"What about military service? Will our son be conscripted into their military?"

"No. The Privilegium made it clear that we are exempt from any conscription. The Mexican government stated they want us to settle and cultivate their land. They need more crop production after their recent revolution. They will leave us alone!"

Judith shook her head. "That's what Canada promised. Remember?"

Jacob remembered all too well. Before he was born, his family had emigrated to Canada from Russia in 1875 after the Canadian government had guaranteed the same things Mexico was now promising. Then World War I happened and everything changed. Germans were looked at differently and it didn't help that they still spoke the same dialect of Low German, or Plautdietsch as the Mennonites called it. Plautdietsch was the everyday spoken language used in homes and for trading in the lowlands. It is different from the High German used to read and write with in the mountainous region in Prussia (present day Poland) dating back to the 1500s. The Canadian government was worried about aliens coming in and corrupting their society. They began a series of reforms to make all the citizens speak the same language, attend public schools, and separate church and state. Recently, the School Attendance Act had been passed, eliminating some of their private schools. For the Mennonites, this was the last straw.

Jacob rubbed his jaw. "Yes, I remember. But according to the delegates, Germany is close with Mexico and had provided them arms for their wars. President Obregón is desperate for people to fill up their land and help feed everyone. They mentioned how our ancestors drained the Low Lands in Netherlands and in Poland and made them productive. They told our representatives that they had studied the crop production we achieved on the Russian steppes and here in Canada. That's why Mexico wants us. They really want us!"

"So what happens now?" she asked.

"We're going to sell our land in one large block and the church will hold the money. When we leave, we will hand over our passports to make sure no one changes their mind." He could see his wife's eyes welling up. "What's the matter? I thought you would be happy with this news."

Judith lifted a corner of her apron and wiped at a tear running down her cheek. "I can't stop thinking about how we are leaving this place. It's all I've known since I was born. I'm sorry, but I'm scared."

Jacob thought about getting out of his chair and consoling his wife, but this was a male-dominated society. If he held her, he might start crying and that wouldn't do.

"You learned the same lessons I did in school, about Dirk Willems and Menno Simons. We have been wandering for generations, and we will continue to wander. With the prosecutions, we must leave. As God has told us, we cannot allow our children to mix with the world. They will see nothing but evil, so we must protect them."

Judith nodded her head and wiped her eyes. Then she went into the kitchen to make supper.

———◆———

Jacob stood on the wooden platform at Swift Current, gazing down at all the Pullman cars. He had been told there were forty-five and it looked as if every available car had been hitched up to the engine. Yet his train wasn't the only one. There were five more strings of cars all being loaded up with Mennonites. Words like "escaping" and "fleeing" were whispered by the locals, and it sure felt like that.

It had been six long months since the delegates had returned. During that time, the Mennonites who were leaving had sold their land to one buyer. The personal possessions were auctioned off in the last few days. For Jacob and his family, all they had left were the bare essentials, most of which were neatly packed into a wooden cabinet that doubled as a traveling trunk. It had been in his family for generations, used when they fled the Low Country to Poland, then to Russia, and from Russia to Canada. Now, it would carry his belongings to Mexico.

He grabbed a metal bar on the side of the train and pulled himself up to one of the freight cars, the one designed to carry animals. Through the dim light and a dozen stalls, he spotted his favorite bay, Nell, sticking her nose out for some attention. Her ears perked up as she tossed her head back, snorting. Jacob placed his calloused hand on her forehead and rubbed it for a few minutes, soothing and relaxing her. When she was calm, he removed a package of carrots from his pocket and gave her one. She devoured it so quickly he barely got his fingers out of the way.

In the next stall was his work horse, Prince. He was less excitable, but still enjoyed a good petting and a carrot too. Jacob had already checked on his cows, which were in another car, and his chickens as well, so he lingered a while longer with Nell.

He pulled out his watch. The trains were scheduled to leave in ten minutes, so he decided it was time to get back to his passenger car and find his family.

"How are yours holding up?" a man said, startling him. It was Mr. Dyck.

"Fine," he replied. "Just fine."

Jacob thought about touching his hat and moving past the man but could see he wasn't finished talking.

"It's going to be a long, hard trip—seven days, they say."

Jacob gave a smile. He had to. His father-in-law was the Ältester—the top preacher—for the entire colony. Abraham Wiebe had been elected by the colonists to impart their weekly spiritual lessons from a pulpit. This status elevated Mr. Wiebe above the other men in the colony, including the other preachers below him. Being so close to the Ältester, Jacob had a higher status. More was expected from him, at least in the religious realm. Perhaps it was time for him to provide some comforting words.

"Yes. Everything is hard. That is the way God wants us to live."

Mr. Dyck didn't return the smile. Instead, he looked sick. "It will be difficult when we get there." The man was obviously having second thoughts. It was time to push him a little harder.

"You know we can't stay here with the privilegiums taken away and fines handed out. They even seized some of our brothers' property! Soon, they will be demanding our sons fight in their wars." Jacob placed a reassuring hand on his shoulder. "No, we must leave. We have no choice."

Mr. Dyck rubbed his hands together. "My wife's family is staying behind. They've moved out to the countryside where there aren't public schools. They will continue to distance themselves from the sinners and their worldly possessions. My wife wanted to go with her family, but I was pressured by the others."

Jacob knew he himself was one of those *others*. He moved his arm around Mr. Dyck's shoulder and stood beside him. "Brother, please take comfort in knowing that we are all nervous. None of us has seen the land we are traveling to. We too have sold everything we own and are taking a big risk. But God is with us. He has protected our people. Each time we moved, we survived. Certainly, He will protect us now."

A long whistle blew.

Jacob patted the man's back. "We have five minutes, Mr. Dyck. You should check on your animals, and then hurry to your passenger car."

"Yes, I should," he said. "Thank you."

Jacob slipped past him and found a handhold to help step off the cattle car. When he was sure the man had not followed him, he glanced up and down the long train, watching passengers scurrying to get on. Conductors urged the stragglers to hurry while using hand signals to communicate with each other. It was quite a sight watching an entire city being loaded on a train.

Jacob counted the cars and hurried his step when he realized he had twenty more to go. He could hop on anywhere and make his way through the interior of each passenger car to the first one at the front, but that meant having more scenes like the last one. And he didn't feel like consoling other passengers who suddenly doubted the move, especially knowing he had a special piece of luggage underneath his wife's seat, one containing the passports of all 850 passengers. If anyone wanted to turn back, they would have to find him first.

By nine a.m., six long trains rolled south from Canada carrying 5,000 Mennonites and all their belongings. Each train had ten freight cars loaded to the roof with barbed wire, lumber, carriages, and farm implements. Then there were the nine cattle cars stuffed with pigs, chickens, cows, mules, and horses. Since the Mennonites shunned worldly possessions, there was very little luggage to pack. Each family had two or three *kjistens* (chests) of kitchen utensils, dishes, and clothes resting in their stored wagons. That was it. These people lived simple and austere lives.

Jacob and Judith had their two children with them. Helena was four and Jacob was pushing two. Three years earlier, she had given birth to Anna, who tragically died six months later. Judith was also five months pregnant. That made one baby for each year of their marriage. Since any form of birth control was prohibited and they didn't go out into the world to proselytize, having large families was the only way the Mennonites grew their religion and communities.

As the train lurched for the very first time, an excitement raced through the passengers. Jacob's children crawled up to the large windows and stared out with fascination as the countryside began moving past. Having never been on a train, they found it a new and exhilarating experience.

A few miles out of Swift Current, they saw the melting snow sending rivers of water underneath the trestles they crossed. With winter coming to an end, melting snow was just about all they saw for the first few hours.

As they traveled through Canada and into North Dakota, the terrain was mostly the same. In Minnesota, though, there was less snow and more greenery. Still, it seemed like they hadn't left Canada yet.

The big changes came in the next two states. Wide open fields of turned earth in Iowa gave way to acres of winter wheat springing up from the Kansas soil. A buzz went through Jacob's car as the passengers wondered if this land resembled their new home. Jacob wondered too.

Because Judith had packed some food to save money, they ate meals in their seats and watched the landscape rolling by the window. Everything was fascinating to them.

Up to this point, the journey had been routine. The large, steam-powered engine carried its own coal car, but occasionally they had to stop for new crews and fresh food. This gave everyone a much-needed break, a chance to stretch their legs and check on their animals.

After the first few stops, the engineer realized his passengers wanted to constantly check on their animals to make sure they had plenty of food and water. To keep them happy, he increased the stops as he didn't want to be responsible for any dead animals. The Mennonites dearly loved their farm animals. They weren't so much possessions as they were essential partners in providing the food that sustained their families. Sometimes, they were more like pets.

At each stop, Jacob spent most of his time in the cattle car, feeding carrots to Prince and Nell. He inspected the stalls and cleaned out their

34

droppings. Several boys had been assigned to this task, but he wanted to make sure it was being done properly. Judith warned him to be very careful not to get any on him. He hadn't packed a lot of clothes to change into and washing their clothes would have to wait until they arrived in Mexico. So Jacob was very careful. Fortunately, the boys were doing an adequate job and he didn't have to get his hands too dirty.

By the time they cleared Kansas, the train had been rolling for three full days and the food Judith had packed was long gone, save for the kringle—thin, twisted pieces of bread—and homemade jam. This meant they had to make routine trips to the dining car, where fresh meals were served throughout the day. Because it was a Pullman dining car, the experience was extravagant.

The first time Jacob and Judith walked to supper, they saw a long row of tables on each side of the train. One row seated four and the other accommodated two. Ironed starched-white tablecloths hung delicately over the edges, adding even more opulence to the scene. The maître d' showed them to a table for four. Both Jacob and Judith slid into high-backed leather chairs that were pulled out for them, and two other waiters came bouncing down the narrow aisle with highchairs for little Jacob and Helena. Helena, however, explained she was four and didn't need one. The waiters didn't speak Low German but seemed to understand as they nodded and took it away.

Paper menus inserted into leather sleeves were handed to them, and before they could say thank you, fresh, steaming bread appeared while their glasses were filled with water.

Judith tugged on Jacob's coat and exclaimed, "Look, ice water! And the silverware!" Her eyes were wide with amazement.

Jacob nodded, wondering how many times this scene had been repeated in the last few days. If his wife reacted like this, he was sure all the passengers were dazzled. He had already heard talk about how beautiful this dining car was.

It was true that almost none of them had ever eaten out in a restaurant. For the ones who had, it wasn't anything like this. They all knew their faith required them to avoid such luxuries—a main tenet of Mennonite life. But this journey seemed to set that aside as they really had no choice. No one had brought enough food for seven long days, and they didn't have enough time at a stop to purchase more. Thus, these highly religious travelers had to *suffer* and enjoy the elegance of a Pullman dining car.

After Jacob's first meal, he noticed more and more of his brothers making daily trips to the dining car. Soon, Jacob and Judith were added to that list. They might be going to a hard life, but there was no sense in wasting the luxuries to get there.

As Jacob considered the trip so far, he could see the railroad had pulled out all the stops. After all, they had paid over $180,000 to charter six long trains. The railroad's management obviously wanted to ensure the Mennonites got their money's worth. They also knew there were at least 2,000 more who were planning on moving to Mexico—potential customers who would soon hear about their service. That's why a lot of extra amenities were provided with no complaints.

Day four dawned and found them crossing through Oklahoma before turning east. In the 1920s, train tracks didn't make a straight line from Manitoba to El Paso, their scheduled border crossing. Also, each railroad had their own tracks or partnered up with other tracks. That's why long trips often took longer than it could have taken.

When they cleared Oklahoma, they entered the panhandle of Texas. The terrain there was almost the same as Oklahoma, and not too different from Iowa or Kansas either. By noon, however, the train began a winding, steady climb upward until they reached a flat, level prairie. The passengers were told they were now on the Llano Estacado. With a Mennonite girl translating, an old conductor told Jacob's car what he knew about it.

"*Llano Estacado* means 'staked plain' in Spanish. As a conductor who's been on thousands of trains, I've heard all sorts of reasons about where that name comes from. I had an educated fellow traveling from Chicago who told me that when the Spanish first saw it from below, it looked like a large stockade, with stakes pounded into the ground and set next to each other as if it was corralling giant mustangs. Another man—a government surveyor—told me that because there ain't no hills, no mountains or any change in it, you had to set stakes in the ground to make sure you could find your way out. Then I met a passenger, a real old cowboy, who said he always had to stake his horse to the ground as he couldn't find a stone or a tree to tie his horse up. He said half of it was nothing but a sea of grass, and the other half was bare and dry as a bone. I don't know which of them fellows is right, but I do know that it's the only place on earth where you can say something and there's no echo. The words just go on forever." He shook his head. "Yes sir, a person can sure get lost out there. I'm sure there's more than one set of bones in all these miles to prove me right. Makes me glad I have this here job."

The Mennonites' eyes were wide open as they listened to the translation. When the conductor was done, they went back to their seats and spent hours gazing out at the vast nothingness. Having been used to mountains, snow, fast rivers, and vast forests, this solitary flat land was a complete shock. Jacob held his only son up to let him watch, but soon, the boy fell asleep in his arms.

Jacob felt a tap on his shoulder. "Could I speak with you, Mr. Rempel?"

It was a young man who had lost his parents in a house fire and had to take over the farm all by himself. He had recently married an older girl and was traveling with his wife's family. The young man was also part of the group that had voiced some apprehension about where they were going. Jacob led the man to a space between the cars where they could talk in private.

"What is it, Mr. Froese?"

"My wife is concerned. With each day we go south, the land is turning harder. This 'staked plain' as they called it, she sees no rivers or lakes. There's no trees nor wood for burning. She asks me how I will build a house in a land such as this. Or even maintain a farm?"

Jacob grinned to put Mr. Froese at ease even though inside, he had the same worries. But with his status, he couldn't admit it. He would try to reassure the man—or actually his wife. "I have attended all of the meetings and spoke with each delegate numerous times. They have told me the land we're going to is surrounded by mountains. There is water nearby—a river with many springs. And it rains, at times very hard. There are beautiful, golden sunsets and fresh mountain air. The ground is fertile and able to support many crops." He placed his hand on the young man's shoulder. "And this country wants us. They *need* us. We will be left alone, set apart from the rest of its citizens. The delegates have told me it is just what we need."

Mr. Froese breathed easier. "Thank you, Mr. Rempel. My wife was worried seeing this flat, bare land. I will reassure her that our land is soon to come, and it will look much better than this."

"Of course," Jacob said. "Set her mind at ease. I'm sure the land will change soon, as will her attitude."

Jacob watched Mr. Froese head back to his seat and wondered how many more of these conversations he would experience before they reached their new home.

On the fifth day, Jacob awoke and stared out the window. They had finally cleared the vast Llano Estacado and were firmly in the heart of New Mexico, heading south. Now, the land had changed, but not for the better.

"Look at that," Judith whispered to her husband. "What is that?"

"I don't know," he whispered back. "I just don't know."

It was like nothing he'd ever seen. Miles and miles of barren desert. Strange, dangerous-looking plants like cactus and agave were everywhere. It was hard to imagine anyone walking through it, let alone living and farming there. What had once been a small minority of Mennonites murmuring their insecurities, suddenly grew to a vocal majority.

After breakfast, Jacob stood in the center of his car and held up his arms to encourage everyone. "Please! You all know that our colony has purchased two hundred thousand acres of fine land from a reputable Mexican family—the Zulegas. President Obregón recommended them. You also know Mr. D.F. Wiebe. He is an honest businessman and arranged the transaction. We agreed to pay them a fair price of eight dollars and twenty-five cents an acre and we did. Surely you know we wouldn't have paid that much if the land wasn't worth it. Trust me, if brother Johann or one of the delegates was on this train, he would tell you these facts. We are not even in Mexico and already you doubt God's plan."

From the back a man yelled out, "But this state is called New Mexico. We are going to Old Mexico. If this is what new looks like, how can you be sure that it's better than the old?"

Several people nodded in agreement.

Jacob felt the panic rising up in his chest. "You must trust the delegates who have seen the land. What you see out the window, this is not our land. This isn't even our country. Wait until the train crosses into Mexico. Then you will see. The land and everything will be better. I promise you that."

It was a bold and dangerous move—one he spent hours praying would bear fruit.

They stopped at El Paso for several hours to allow authorities to check their passports, and for the men to check on their animals. El Paso was a dry, dusty city, impressing no one. Of course, the Mennonites weren't looking for a vibrant city life since they had no use for such things. Still, the land surrounding the city looked just as grim as what they'd seen for the past twenty-four hours.

Once they cleared El Paso and entered the country of Mexico, windows were lined with anxious faces, hoping for a beautiful land of milk and honey. Unfortunately, northern Mexico was the same, harsh desert. When the land barely changed, the rumblings were deafening.

Jacob whispered to his wife. "This may get worse. You stay down in the seat with our children and help console the other wives who are questioning us and doubting this move."

Judith was worried. "You don't expect violence, do you?"

Jacob's face dropped as he mumbled, "These people have entrusted us with one million six hundred fifty thousand dollars. If the land we purchased looks like this, I may be the first one they take it out on."

For the next two days, Jacob spent all his time calming the colonists. Out the windows, he was blessed with brief scenes of habitable land, which he loudly pointed out to each passenger. They saw thriving farms and trees before the desert reappeared. Just as the anger rebuilt itself, they would pass a nice patch of earth and order would be restored.

On the sixth night, Jacob went to sleep and prayed hard that by the morning, the desert would be long gone. He didn't sleep well.

"Wake up Jacob. Wake up!" Judith shook her husband hard.

He rubbed his eyes and gazed into his wife's face. "Yes, what is it?"

"Look out the window!"

He blinked a few times and gazed out west at a land illuminated by the morning sun. The desert, along with its dangerous plants, was gone. Replacing it were long, sloping plains of dark earth. On two sides, mountains with rivers glistened in the sun. Jacob glanced at his watch. They were scheduled to arrive at their destination by nine a.m., which turned his eight-thirty reading into good news.

Springing from his seat, he walked through his car making sure the passengers were looking out the window. Jacob did nothing other than give an occasional nod and smile. He got his message across: See? Just like I promised. God provides. This is a land we can make our own.

When the train screeched to a stop, the conductors came through and shook hands with the men, thanking them for their business and looking for tips certain to never appear. Wearing nervous and excited faces, the Mennonites left their home on wheels for the last seven days.

With days of leisure under their belt, the Mennonite men had a lot of pent up energy. They couldn't wait to get busy. Every able-bodied male set to unloading the cattle and freight cars as quickly as possible while the women stood at a distance, keeping an eye on the children and their meager luggage.

Jacob walked Prince and Nell down the ramp himself, allowing one of the boys to lead his cattle out. It had taken over half a day to load up these cars, but amazingly, they were completely unloaded in less than an hour. Every male grabbed whatever he could find and offloaded it to a large field next to the long train. In no time, the small station looked like a bustling field camp.

Once everyone and everything was off the train, the Mennonites waved at the train staff and watched them pull away to make room for the next train. It was in that moment that Jacob took stock of the situation.

All around was chaos. Animals and pink-faced kids ran wild. The train station itself was very small, like something out of the Wild West. There were thirteen leafless trees surrounding it, each one crowded by blonde-haired, blue-eyed Mennonite women, their scarves pulled tight over their heads, hoping to find a little shade. He saw five wooden shacks and a few adobe huts near one grain elevator. Behind that was nothing but miles of rocky desert. Licking his dry lips, he swallowed hard.

One of the delegates had been in the first train ahead of Jacob's and was already leading his group to some land just north of the station. A long train of cattle and horse-pulled buggies snaked their way to the land where they would set up tents as temporary dwellings. The plan was to have the men measure off the lots for each family's portion. When all that was done, the Mennonites would move their tents to the lots and begin constructing their homes.

Jacob took a moment to gather his thoughts. He knew he'd be working hard the rest of the day to make it to the temporary land and get his tent set up. Yet he was ready for it. In fact, he looked forward to it. Anything was better than wasting away on the train babysitting his fellow travelers.

He stared at the distant mountains and the vast emptiness before him. Clenching his jaw, he had a thought: *We were looking for a place to be left alone and it appears we've found it.*

Jacob brushed some lint from his hat and shoved it on his head. Then he clapped his hands and yelled out, "Time to get moving!"

Chapter Four

May 1923
Seagraves, Texas

The young girl leaned back on the wooden bench and straightened her powder blue dress for the hundredth time. Sure enough, a few seconds later a breeze came along and ruffled it up again. It was a game she played. Whenever she grew hot, she straightened out her blouse, sure that a breeze would come along and toss it about. And each time it did.

She sat outside the train station, alone, with a hard-shelled suitcase standing next to her feet, which were long enough to reach the wooden deck. She was tall for her age—thirteen—and no longer sat on benches with her legs swaying back and forth. That was for children.

It was almost noon and the heat was blistering. Fortunately, she was under a roof that projected out far enough to cast her in deep shade. When a breeze rushed by, it was quite pleasant, though that didn't make the waiting any easier.

"Are you all right?" a clerk said, poking his head out from the entrance.

"Yes, sir," the girl replied.

"Are you sure someone's coming for you?"

"Yes, sir. They said they'd be here."

"Okay," the clerk said, shaking his head before withdrawing back inside.

The train that had brought her to Seagraves had come and gone over an hour ago. Then, the place was a beehive of activity, with folks hugging each other, shaking hands, and climbing into their cars or trucks before heading away somewhere. She had looked all around for her aunt and uncle but didn't find them, at least she didn't think so. She had no idea what they looked like nor had they ever seen her. That made it a process of elimination. When all the people waiting had collected their arrivals and left, there was no one looking for her. That's when she got nervous. And scared.

What if they forgot? What if they don't want me?

Thoughts like these began rolling through her mind, creating larger thoughts until she had to shake her head and think about something else, like smoothing out her dress. After twenty minutes of this, she had left her bench from inside the station and moved to the outside, where she presumed they would appear—if they did at all.

Her eyes noticed some movement coming down the main street leading to the station. A woman holding a large parasol sat atop a buckboard while a man next to her held the reins to two horses moving the carriage toward the station. Her heart raced.

That has to be them.

The carriage pulled directly in front of her and stopped. The girl watched as the man jumped down and helped the woman. When they were both on the ground, the woman closed the parasol, straightened her long dress, and walked with the man up the steps to where the girl sat.

"Rose? Rose Henderson?" the man said rather plainly.

"Yes, sir," she said, standing up.

The man reached down, grabbed her suitcase, and loaded it in the carriage. Then, to her surprise, he climbed on the buckboard, took up the reins, and set the horses off in a trot, leaving her with the woman.

"Welcome to Texas, Rose," the woman said, hugging her. "Here, sit back down while Samuel feeds and waters the horses. They've been pulling for five hours and we need them rested to go back. This gives us some time to talk."

Rose said nothing, resuming her place on the bench.

"I must apologize for being late but the Midland and Northwestern Railway used to run through Seminole. Sadly, it was unprofitable and they shut it down a month ago. It's eighteen miles from Seminole. That's why we're late. It's been a long time since we made this trip by buggy and we thought it would be quicker."

Rose smiled.

"I'm sure you're wondering why we took the carriage. We have a Ford but it was making deliveries yesterday and broke down. We're waiting for a part so it can be repaired. That left the carriage."

Rose nodded.

"How was your trip from St. Louis? Did they treat you well?"

"It was fine." She decided not to say how she had kept her face glued to the window during the entire two days, taking in a world she'd never seen before, until falling asleep against the glass. In St. Louis, she had been a prisoner in her home, leaving only to attend school. She had never been allowed to have friends over or go to their house. It was a hard existence, one of endurance.

"I brought some food. Are you hungry?"

"Yes, ma'am," Rose replied. Actually, she was beyond hungry. Starving was more like it. Her eyes widened with anticipation as the woman opened a small basket she had with her. Licking her lips several times, Rose pulled back the paper from a sandwich and took a large bite, not caring what was in it. Between bites she crunched on a juicy pickle, the salt adding flavor when mixed with the sandwich.

The woman watched her attack the sandwich and said, "Did they not feed you?"

"Yes, ma'am," she mumbled with a full mouth. "But they served breakfast very early."

"Did you like the dining car?"

"Yes, ma'am, it was very nice." It wasn't nice. It was extraordinarily elegant. She had felt like the child of some rich industrialist. The people who had sent her paid for the meals so the waiter told her to just order whatever she wanted. And she did!

"I'm glad, but you can call me Aunt Mae. My full name is Mae Beth Henderson. Most of the townsfolk call me Mae Beth so you may hear them say that."

"Yes, ma'am... I mean Aunt Mae."

Aunt Mae smiled briefly. "Listen, I'm sorry about your father. It's a real tragedy, coming back from the war and having all that happen to him.

44

Were there a lot of people attending his funeral? I'm sure there were many of his fellow soldiers there."

"Yes, ma'am. The soldiers fired off their guns several times."

Aunt Mae frowned. "When he returned from the war, your mother wrote us and said he was having trouble adjusting, with the shell shock and all. She said he may have been exposed to mustard gas. Hopefully, you didn't have to see him when he was having his spells."

"No, ma'am." That was a lie. Her parents fought all the time. When he drank, he turned violent.

"That's good because oh, those electrical shock treatments are surely horrible. I hate that he had to go through that, but I have to wonder how one shock cures another."

Rose nodded. Every time he was shocked, he was calm for a few days. It was like heaven.

"How was your mother's funeral?"

"I cried a lot so I don't remember too much." When her mom died, leaving her with just him, she thought about running away, or worse.

"I'm so sorry for all you've been through. Your father's letter said the baby was a boy and he was buried with your mother."

"Yes, ma'am."

"Childbirth isn't without risks. I should know." Aunt Mae glanced around to make sure they were alone. "I need to talk to you about some things before we get in the buggy. I don't want your Uncle Samuel hearing this, and we may not have a chance to speak privately for some time."

Rose straightened up and swallowed the last bite, handing her aunt the paper wrapper. Aunt Mae put it back in the basket then smoothed out her skirt again.

"Samuel and I have a son. His name is Melvin, and he just turned ten. It was a difficult birth, and though at first he seemed normal, at five or so, we could tell something wasn't right. Several doctors examined him and told us he will never be normal. It's hard to communicate with him. He doesn't understand jokes or seem able to follow conversations. My husband has suffered because of this. And I know the fact that the doctors say we can't have any more children really gets to him. Frankly, neither my husband nor I can fully understand our son. It was a struggle for many years until Melvin could decide when he needed to use the toilet on his own. Now, he just finds things to play with and we leave him alone. I have spent time studying him and I'm not sure what he's doing. But he's our son, and we will care for him until our last breath."

Rose looked into her eyes and saw deep pain. Before she could say anything, Aunt Mae looked away and continued. "The other matter I need to discuss with you is Samuel's relationship with your father. It was very strained. Growing up, they fought all the time. Samuel felt their dad supported your father too much. Until he gets to know you better, let's not talk about your father too much. Okay?"

Rose lowered her head and quietly said, "Yes, ma'am."

"Good. Now, I don't know what life was like with your family but out here, we all have to work—every day. I will expect you to do some chores."

"Yes, ma'am, I'm used to working." Rose tried to say these words enthusiastically.

"Good. I understand you just finished up the seventh grade?"

"Yes, ma'am. I can read and write real good."

"That will help us because we run our business from Monday through Saturday. It's called Henderson's Hardware, Implements & Harness. We live above the store and I'll need your help with meals and watching Melvin. Oh, and my dad."

"Your dad?"

"Yes. He's sixty-four and can hardly see. The hearing in his left ear is almost gone so you must sit on his right side and talk to him. We thought we lost him last year, but the doctor made a powder out of aspirin, quinine, and some other ingredient and he came back. I need you to help him find his things, or if he's dropped something to pick it up. He loves to talk and should be very entertaining. I can tell you like to listen, so you should make a good match."

From around the side of the station, the buckboard reappeared.

"Let's go," Samuel said gruffly.

They stood together and patted the dust out of their dresses. Aunt Mae adjusted her large Victorian straw hat and handed the parasol to Rose.

"Here, take this. Even though it's May, the sun in Texas is very hot. You'll need this on the way back."

Rose took the umbrella and opened it up. "But what about you?"

"Oh, don't worry, dear, this hat will provide some relief. But thanks for your concern. Now, let's hop up and show you your new home!"

⋗◆⋖

It was close to seven when supper was finally ready. Everyone, including Rose, was famished. For the Hendersons, this was an hour later than they usually ate, so it was no surprise that Samuel's blessing was barely five seconds long.

Steaming bowls of food were promptly passed around as hungry diners spooned piles on their plates. Rose stared at the various choices—skillet fried chicken, black-eyed peas with bacon floating on the top, bright red tomato slices, steaming yeast rolls with fresh butter and strawberry preserves, tea, milk, and water. Several times, Aunt Mae had to help scoop out the food her father wanted.

"Dad," Aunt Mae said, "Rose here will be staying with us from now on. I hope you can fill her in with some of your stories. You know, tell her about Seminole."

"Be glad to," he said, peering through cloudy eyes in her general direction. "That's pretty much all I'm good for now."

"Please, Dad, you help out…" she said, her voice trailing off with less sincerity.

"What do I call you, sir?" Rose asked loudly.

He turned his head toward Rose. "Oh, I guess Grandpa will do now that you're family. Is that fine with you?"

"Yes, Grandpa," she replied.

"Good," he said, waving a drumstick around. "Now let me tell you a few things about your new home."

Samuel sighed loudly but Grandpa either didn't hear him or didn't care.

"Our newspaper is the *Seminole Sentinel*. We've got all the churches that matter—Methodist, Presbyterian, and the new Baptist church. We've got the First State Bank and our own movie theater. And we're the county seat for Gaines County. That tells you something right there."

Rose nodded, then remembered he couldn't clearly see her. "It sounds like a nice town."

"It is. And our county was named after James T. Gaines—a real-life signer of the Texas Declaration of Independence. After supper, I'll show my commendations and tell you more. Would you like that?"

Rose saw Aunt Mae glance at her husband, who rolled his eyes.

"Yes, that would be nice," she replied.

"Wonderful! Now let me eat all this food. If I don't go to bed with a full stomach, I can't sleep."

Before she could answer, his head hovered over his plate as both hands shoved food to his mouth from various angles. Rose got serious about her own food, although in a much more ladylike manner.

When they had all finished, the two men went to a small area that was the living room and sat next to an open window smoking cigars. Rose helped Aunt Mae with the dishes while Melvin sat at the kitchen table randomly tapping his fingers on tiny scratches in its surface.

As she worked alongside her aunt, she studied the woman who would replace her mother. A few strands of gray hair dotted her dark brown bun. Most women in St. Louis wore their hair short, with curled bangs. It was the style of the day. Out here in this land, it seemed like hairstyles were more practical.

Rose noticed her aunt's dry skin. Small sun spots freckled the back of her hands and cheeks, with a few wrinkles beginning to lengthen. If the usual weather was anything like she had just experienced coming from the train station, it was no wonder.

Aunt Mae dried her hands on a towel. "We're finished here. If you want to spend time with Grandpa, go ahead."

Rose dried her hands too, and went to find Grandpa, who had finished his cigar and was sleeping in his chair. Uncle Samuel shrugged his shoulders. When Aunt Mae came into the living room, she motioned for Rose to come back into the kitchen.

"Listen, we only have two bedrooms. Grandpa sleeps with Melvin while Samuel and I sleep in the other. Until we come up with something better, I'm going to put you on the living room couch. Is that acceptable?"

"Yes, ma'am. I'm just grateful you're letting me stay here."

"You're family!" Mae Beth said. "Of course we would take you in. Why don't you take this time to relax because I'm going to put you to work tomorrow."

"Yes, ma'am."

Melvin was still at the table playing, so she sat down and watched him. He stopped what he was doing and stared at her, cocking his head to one side and back to the other. He mumbled some words, causing Rose to go to the cupboard and retrieve an empty tin can. When she returned, he had several marbles and proceeded to roll them across the surface, trying to sink them in the can she held just off the edge. Aunt Mae heard this and came over to see what they were doing.

"How did you know he wanted to play with his marbles?"

"He told me," Rose said as a marble rolled noisily into the can.

"What!?" Aunt Mae was so bewildered, she stepped back a few feet.

"Yes," Rose said. "I sat down and he told me to get a tin can."

Aunt Mae pulled out a chair and plopped down in shock. "So you understand what he says?"

"He didn't say anything. I just understood."

<hr />

The first two days flew by for Rose. Helping with the meals, laundry, and the store, she never stopped. At least, not until after the supper dishes were put away. Then she had a few hours before going to bed and doing it all over again.

During this time, she walked through the small town, visiting the First State Bank and learning that it had recently been robbed. Close to the bank was an interesting man who ran a tanning shed. He had several fires going to help the tanning process. As they talked, he told her that the county was overrun with wolves, antelope, and other wildlife. "I wish I had more guns and men to shoot them. I'd be covered up in hides. Say, can you shoot?"

When Rose told him no, he said, "I can teach you."

She shook her head and moved on, bumping into Sheriff F.L. Britton, who was just leaving Haywood's Barber Shop. He stepped back and tipped his hat to her. Rose had been told he was also the local tax collector, a nice fit for a sheriff who dealt in force.

She liked the politeness in this town. It was very different from what she had experienced in St. Louis.

Rose continued on, past the City Drug Store, the Lone Star Hotel, and attorney N.R. Morgan's law office. When she arrived back at the store, both her aunt and uncle were completely amazed at the effect she had on their son. Melvin was calm now, and actually cooperating with his parents. When he grew upset or angry, Rose talked to him and the storm was over. One time, he was mad because a marble had rolled under a chair and he didn't have the ability to figure out how to move it or even crawl under it. Rose showed him how and he was happy again. It was incidents like this that had Aunt Mae sending up continual prayers to God, thanking Him for the miracle that He had sent them.

It was Wednesday evening and Rose was at the kitchen table listening to Grandpa tell stories. Earlier in the day, her aunt had told her that their store was finally turning a profit. Acres of cotton were being planted to take advantage of the booming economy and its need for cloth. Farmers not only purchased implements from them, but they also had the money to pay—or at least reduce their account balance. When the couple counted up the large stack of cash and put it in the safe, it was the first time Rose had seen her uncle happy. He actually smiled.

Samuel grabbed his wife around the waist and said, "I'm taking you out to a movie, little lady."

"If we're going on a date, I'll have to fix myself up."

"You do that, but please hurry. The movie starts at seven-thirty and I want to get a good seat."

As his wife went to their bedroom, he reached from behind and produced two large pieces of hard candy. "This is for each of you," he said, handing one to Rose and the other to Melvin.

"Thank you, Uncle Samuel!"

"You're quite welcome. Thank you for the hard work this past week and your ability to understand Melvin. If things keep going well, I'll take you to the movies with us next time."

"I'd love that," Rose said.

It took Aunt Mae a good thirty minutes to get ready, but when she stepped into the living room, Rose was stunned. She was beautiful. The makeup and nice dress had transformed her. Even Samuel blinked several times.

"Why, aren't you a sight for sore eyes. Let's get going, missy. You and I have a date."

She grabbed his arm. "I just hope I have a strong man to take care of me."

Rose noticed his grin as they disappeared down the stairs.

Rose walked back to the kitchen table, finding Grandpa already there. He had a John Ruskin cigar box situated in front of him, trying to open it. "I never did finish my story about Seminole Wells," he said.

"Seminole Wells? What's that?" Rose asked.

"This town. That's what it used to be called. I was here for its beginning."

"Really?"

"Yes, I was a clerk for Lt. C.R. Ward in the Tenth Cavalry when we found some Indian wells at the draw that runs south of town. He named them after his Seminole scouts. Today, they call part of the draw farther east Wardswell Draw, after Lt. Ward himself. We even got some commendations for it which I keep in this cigar box. They're my most prized possessions."

He loosened the tiny nail and lifted the lid, feeling around inside until he held up a certificate and a red ribbon with a gold medal hanging from it.

"Here. Look at this," he said.

Rose took the certificate and read it out loud. "By order of the commander of the Tenth Cavalry, I do hereby award and present to Tommy Nabors, the Indian Wars Medal for special merit and dedication to duty." She handed him the certificate back. "Grandpa, that's special. I bet you have lots of stories to tell."

Sure enough, he did. They spent the next hour going over each and every one of them, including his first years at Seminole Wells. Grandpa had seen a great deal and was able to tell Rose about the land, the animals, and the people, all hardy enough to survive on the Staked Plain. He was just wrapping up his latest story when the boy grew agitated.

"What is it, Melvin?" Rose asked, placing her hand over his. "What's wrong?"

He mumbled some words and Rose sprung from her chair.

"What did he say?" Grandpa asked.

"He says there's a fire somewhere." She ran to the living room, which had the best view. Sticking her head out the window, she could see at the far end of town the tanning shed was on fire and spreading to Haywood's Barber Shop. Flames danced on the shop's roof and bent over in the stiff wind. She ran back to the kitchen.

"The barber shop's on fire!" she cried.

"Oh my," he said. "Which way is the wind blowing?"

"From the west, and it's a strong one."

Grandpa reached out, feeling for her arm. "Listen, Rose. When the smoke and ashes get anywhere near here, the horses will get spooked and injure themselves, or worse, run away. We may never find them. I need you to calmly go down and take each horse to a metal ring that we put in the ground years ago. It's about hundred yards behind the outhouse. Tie the horses up good to the ring but give them plenty of slack so if a wolf comes by, they can defend themselves. Do you understand?"

"Yes, sir."

"Okay, do it now. When you're done, check on the fire and come straight back up here."

Rose followed his instructions. In the fading light, she was able to see just enough to find the ring. After the first horse was tied down, she made her way back for the second horse. She could see the fire spreading rapidly, ripping through City Drug Store before reaching its fiery tentacles into the Lone Star Hotel. At any second, the smoke might drift over and the horse would smell it. If that happened, he could break through his stall and even trample her. She walked as fast as she could without raising his attention. With soothing words, she untied him and eased the large horse forward, leading him away from the store.

Sure enough, he caught a whiff of smoke and skipped a few times, jerking hard on the reins. Using all her strength, she held tight to the reins and continued talking softly, guiding him step by step to the ring. As soon as he saw the first horse, he calmed down, allowing Rose to do her work.

With that done, she ran back to the store and up the side stairs.

"Where is the fire now?" Grandpa called out. "It must be close because I can smell it."

"It's burning the Lumber House. There are people everywhere dumping buckets of water on the fire."

"That's it! We need to leave. Did you see Samuel and Mae Beth?"

"No," Rose replied. "Do you want me to go look for them?"

"No. Help me open the safe and get the money out. We'll be ruined without it."

Rose helped him over to the cabinet and opened the door, exposing the safe. Grandpa got to his knees and felt for the dial, spinning it several times when his fingers touched it.

"Bring that lamp closer, dear."

Rose held the lamp as close to him and the safe as she dared. The hissing sound of burning oil didn't appear to upset his concentration. She stood over him as he tried to see through his cloudy eyes and study the dial. He spun it to the right, stopping on a number before turning it to the left, repeating the process. This went on in each direction until he reached for the handle and tugged hard.

"Oh no!" he cried. "It's not opening."

Melvin began wailing, which got Rose's attention. She looked out the window and saw the fire was one building over.

"Grandpa, we have to go now! It's about to catch the store on fire."

"Not yet. I have to get it open."

With trembling hands, he worked the combination again and reached the same result.

"Rose, you're going to have to do it. Now follow my instructions."

Down the street, someone had run into the movie theater and told patrons the town was on fire. Samuel and Mae Beth had sprung from their seats and shot outside to see that the fire was not threatening the theater. But it was racing through the other side of the street and spreading fast.

Samuel clutched Mae Beth's hand. "Run to our place and get the money from our safe. I'm going to help fight the fire. Hurry!"

Mae Beth ran as fast as she could. When she made it to the store, it was already engulfed in flames. She hurried to the stairs and found the fire licking the railings. For a moment, she thought about dashing up through the flames but decided against it. Instead, she looked all around for her father and son and Rose. They were nowhere to be found.

Alone, she stood at a distance watching the building collapse and burn. When she could take it no longer, she fell to the ground crying. Everything was lost. Her dad. Her son. And Rose too. Just when they had started doing well. The more she thought about losing her loved ones, the more hysterical she grew. It was an hour later when her husband found her there and realized she had not saved anyone or anything.

He collapsed next to her, unable to speak. Together, they wailed.

It was completely dark now, except for the light from the glowing embers of their store. As they wiped their eyes, they noticed a small figure. They tried to focus, but their eyes were still watery. The figure came closer. It was Melvin.

"You're alive!" Mae Beth screamed. She got to her feet and ran to him. In his arms he clutched a small bundle.

"What do you have there?" she asked.

"It's the company books and all the money in the safe," a voice behind him replied.

Mae Beth looked over Melvin's shoulder and saw Rose. "You're alive too! Where have you been?"

"We moved the horses out to the metal ring behind the outhouse. That's where we've been all this time."

"Where's Dad? Is he with the horses?"

"No ma'am. I had him halfway down the stairs when he pulled away and went back in for his cigar box. Said it meant the world to him. He said he'd join us but he never did."

"Oh no!" Mae Beth screamed as she fell to her knees. "Please, God, spare my father. Please!"

The next day, they found his body among the rubble, surrounding a smoldering cigar box. Tommy Nabors, also known as Dad and Grandpa, was gone.

Chapter Five

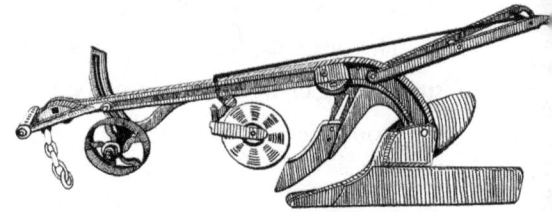

October 1925
Cuauhtémoc, Mexico – Campo 110

Jacob Rempel picked up a fistful of dirt and let it run through his fingers. The dry wind turned it into a cloud of dust, scattering it a good ten feet from where he stood. When it was all gone, he clapped the dirt off his hands, reached for his handkerchief, removed his straw cowboy hat, and wiped the sweat from his forehead.

"Papa, who does this belong to?"

The young voice startled him. He looked down to see his oldest son, Jacob, now five, holding something in his hand.

"What is that you have?"

"This," the boy said, handing a cigarette butt to his father.

"*Na oba!*" Oh my! Jacob held the butt up, inspecting it carefully. "I don't know. Where did you find it?"

"Behind the barn."

"I'm going to keep it and ask around, see who has been smoking back there. If you see someone, you let me know."

"I will, Papa. And I'll tell my teacher."

Jacob knew that was right. The children often told on anyone they saw breaking any of the rules. It was their mission—something they could be proud of. Any small infraction would be reported to the teachers, who would then report it to the preachers, or worse—the Ältester—his father-in-law. That was the last thing he needed, especially now. He watched his son run off to tell his mother what he'd found, confident his wife would redirect him to something else.

Abraham, his father-in-law, had been spending time with the boy. A few days earlier, little Jacob announced he was planning on being a preacher when he was old enough. Somehow, it had been decided. And all without consulting him—his father! He felt like he was losing control of his family.

Jacob checked his pocket watch. He had at least an hour before supper was ready. Walking slowly and deliberately so as not to arouse suspicion, he made his way to the barn, continuing past the stalls holding his horses— Nell and Prince. They acknowledged his presence, raising their heads in the hope of receiving a carrot or some other treat. Jacob had none to give. Instead, he walked to the back of an empty stall and pressed on a board, too high for any of his children to reach. Moving it in just the right way, he watched as it opened a small compartment in the wall. Jacob reached down and fished out a pack of cigarettes along with a box of matches. After hiding them in his large overalls pocket, he put the board back, grabbed a shovel, and left through the rear door.

As he walked along his land he acknowledged the distant mountains jutting up before him. The land they had settled was in the Bustillos Valley, surrounded by mountains on two sides with another far-off range covering a third side. This set up a weather pattern unlike anything they'd ever seen. It also created a soil they had not anticipated.

When they first arrived, they had pulled out their well-used, flimsy, Canadian chair plows, which were drawn by a single horse. They quickly discovered that these plows wouldn't break the hard prairie sod. Shocked at this finding, they borrowed, purchased, or invented a sturdier plow— solid steel with thick blades and a cutting disk—adding weight over the disk. They even rigged them to be pulled by two or three horses, if need be. The combination of all this finally broke through, allowing them to plow their land.

With the fresh turned earth ready, they planted seeds of flax, wheat, and oats in shallow furrows, just like they had in Canada. Unfortunately, this wasn't Canada. It was May on the semi-arid plains—or steppes, as the Mennonites called them—in the heart of Mexico, where rain was scarce. All they had were a few light rain showers, which were certainly not enough to bring the crops up. It had been a miserable start and the first of many crop failures.

A few months later, in early July, they all ran outside to see these black, angry, Armageddon-like clouds rolling off the mountains, heading straight toward the new colony. They all stood on their porches and in their fields for a good hour, pointing at the *grootet jewitta* (fierce storm). When it was close, a woman yelled out, *"Blitsen en rummel!"* Lightning and thunder! "It's like straight from the Bible stories!" Each explosion scattered animals in every direction, and children crying for their momma. Then the rain hit.

Jacob remembered seeing a small depression in the ground turn into a pond in mere seconds. The nearby pond became a lake. Two children in the neighboring Manitoba colony, playing in a dry creek bed, were instantly swept away by the raging river that rose up from nothing. It was hard to get his mind around.

The rain pounded the land for a month, washing crops and careless animals away. Each family discovered roof leaks in every structure they had.

When it finally let up, the land had turned completely green overnight. Native flowers pushed through the earth, turning the colonists' sour dispositions into smiles and laughter. At various meetings, the men discussed all this and considered it a valuable lesson: They would have to wait until after the July rains before planting a crop. If they wanted to plant a winter crop, they would have to shift their time back two months from when they had planted in Canada. It was an expensive lesson. But since they refused to communicate with farmers outside of their self-contained world, it was a lesson they would repeat many times.

Jacob reached the end of his farm—a mile-plus trek—and went behind a large pile of brush and rocks that had been put there from clearing both his land as well as his neighbor's. This pile gave him the opportunity to "hide" from watchful eyes. It was the only totally private place he had in the entire colony.

He shifted the shovel from his shoulder, leaning it up against a pile of stones. Then he took out his contraband and set to work. He'd just placed an unfiltered cigarette in his mouth and was lighting it up when he looked past the burning match and saw Mr. Dueck, his neighbor, standing there.

Jacob waved the match out and tossed it to the ground. He watched his neighbor reach into his own overalls and remove a pack of cigarettes.

When he had his cigarette lit, the two men stood there, inhaling smoke and letting the nicotine go to work.

"What's the shovel for?" Mr. Dueck asked.

Jacob exhaled a large gust of smoke. "My son found a cigarette butt behind the barn, so from now on I'm bringing a shovel with me. He might wander out here one day and there's no sense in having him find these butts here." He pointed to the ground. "When we're done, I'm going to bury all of them."

Mr. Dueck nodded, exhaling his own cloud. "I understand. As soon as my children are old enough, they'll be looking for any infractions I might commit and turn me in too. I assume Jacob is going to follow after your father-in-law."

"Probably. He's been acting like a preacher to the girls. They ignore him but that hasn't stopped him."

The two men took their time enjoying every drag of their cigarettes, the only real vice they could afford. Many of the Mennonite men smoked, including some of the preachers, but it wasn't allowed. They could be disciplined for it. And one never knew who would turn them in. That's why it was always best to do it in secret, unless they trusted someone else.

Mr. Dueck pushed back his straw cowboy hat. "I heard another family in Campo 104 left and returned to Canada."

"Yes, it's happening more and more, especially after this year's crop failure. We just didn't get the rain."

"For me, the hail was the worst. It seems like my lot got it worse than yours."

Jacob kicked a clod of dirt. "What crops came up didn't have a chance. That's when the Manitoba colony lost eight more families."

"I thought when they ordered you to return our passports in—when was that—'twenty-four?"

"Yeah," Jacob said, "the spring of 'twenty-four."

"I thought the ones who left, that would be the last of them. But they just keep going."

Jacob remembered his encounter with Mr. Dyck in the cattle car, back in Manitoba. Mr. Dyck had finally thrown up his hands and left. "And when they get back to Canada, they tell wild stories about how bad things are here, so anyone else thinking about coming down doesn't."

Jacob took one last puff and dropped his butt, crushing it out with his boot. "Life here is hard. Harder than Canada. At least the government is living up to its promise and leaving us alone. But it's a huge price to pay, especially if we starve to death."

Mr. Dueck dropped his butt to the ground. "Yeah, I sure hope we have a good crop next year or the money I have put away won't last us. I won't be able to afford a train ticket to leave, even if I wanted to."

Jacob kicked all the butts from their previous meetings into a pile. "Here, help me bury all this."

Mr. Dueck picked up the shovel and started digging as Jacob went around picking up the stray butts. When they were done, Jacob stepped on the hole, compacting it down, and kicked some surface dust over it to ensure no one found it, including one curious five-year-old.

After hiding his secret vice in the barn, Jacob went inside and found his entire family there. Helena, his oldest daughter at seven, churned milk in the kitchen where his wife stood over a stove tending to supper. Jacob, his next oldest child, played with Anna, now three. Children were the life-blood of the Mennonites. So far, Jacob had found it to be an extremely challenging process.

In Canada, Anna, their second child, died six months after birth. After Jacob was born, Judith gave birth to another girl, Anna. As was their usual custom when a child died, they recycled the name to the next child of the same sex. Thus, Anna shared the same name as her deceased sibling. Jacob's father-in-law said the Mennonites waste nothing, not even names.

When they arrived in Mexico, they had hoped the birthing process would improve. In 1924, Judith had Bernhard. A year later, she gave birth to twins: Aganetha and Katharina. Katharina lasted two months with her sister Aganetha outliving her by nine days. Thirty-eight days after Aganetha died, one-year-old Bernhard passed away. Smallpox was the culprit. The disease swept through the colony, killing a massive number of children and many adults. The coffin maker kept busy, having to add additional men to keep up with demand.

Disease was a constant threat to the colony, especially with no education as to how it spread. Even if they did know, they lacked the proper healthcare to deal with it.

For this outbreak, an infected child in the Manitoba colony continued to fetch water from a particular well, interacting with other children. The disease spread rapidly, radiating out from her campo and crossing into the Swift Current colony. There, it took away an equal number of children along with dozens of adults. One campo in Manitoba lost so many people that it shut down. The survivors there either went back to Canada or assimilated into neighboring campos. Yet the Mennonites stayed faithful to God and prayed the entire time. It was all they knew.

For many families, this was the last straw. They packed up and left. For Jacob, it was another hardship to endure.

Judith called everyone to supper. It was served and quickly devoured, as usual. The dishes were fewer than they had in Canada. Still, they thanked God for what they had and ate mostly in silence.

Jacob finished first and excused himself, going to a wooden slab that served as his desk. There, he located some paperwork, shoved it in his pocket, and told his wife he'd be back later. She already knew where he was going.

A group of men were meeting to discuss their food shortage. Jacob, although not an elected official, was part of a small group who was always invited, the connections with his father-in-law his ticket in .

He put his cowboy hat on his head and walked down the wide avenue toward the church, where they usually met. On each side were ten individual lots. The initial survey crew had laid out their campo just like the others, making every campo the same—each lot 200 feet wide and 6,400 feet deep. The only difference was when a family had some extra money and purchased two lots. But that wasn't the case in Jacob's campo as he had nineteen other families with the exact same lot size. This led to plenty of different opinions he had to deal with.

As he continued walking, he recalled the barren land when they first arrived. After assembling his tent and open-air stove, Jacob had purchased wood from the locals and set about building his house and barn in the same way they had in Canada. Thus, his house and barn were connected, but not under one roof. Before anyone's house was built, he had worked with the other men to erect the church. When that was finished, they put up a school. The Mennonites had their priorities and God was number one. He would see them through.

Jacob neared the church and saw several other men approaching, all from other campos. Saying hello to a few he knew, he went inside and took a seat on a wooden pew near the center of the church. Since he planned on saying very little, it was the best place not to stick out.

The head mayor, Mr. Klassen, and his father-in-law, Ältester Abraham Wiebe, would likely make most of the decisions because they were the strongest figures in the *Vorsteher Kommitee* (Committee of Village Mayors). Most of the men let them handle everything.

When it was time, Mr. Wiebe started the meeting off with a lengthy prayer, asking God to provide them the wisdom to make the right decisions. Then Mr. Klassen launched right in, laying out the food situation, or lack thereof. Jacob listened for a bit before tuning out most of the talk. His thoughts drifted to his own situation. He had two dairy cows in his barn providing enough milk for his family with more to either sell or turn into butter. He had a little money hidden inside the house, but definitely not enough to provide all the food they would need until the next crop came in. When they started discussing that, Jacob paid attention.

"We have resisted planting corn and beans, native crops to this area," a man from the Manitoba colony said. "I think we should give them a try." Several men nodded their heads in agreement.

A man from Jacob's Swift Current colony stood up. "We collected a great deal of natural grass from the surrounding lands when we arrived, and it took us a year to cut it all down. But that is all gone now and there's not enough grass left to feed our cows, especially with all the land cleared. We need to plant more grass to have feed for our cows." Again, several men murmured their approval.

After more discussion on these subjects and others, Mr. Klassen appeared to make the decision. "We will contact our supplier in El Paso and order two tons of wheat flour and two tons of oats. I will find out the price for the seed needed to plant the Texas strain of oats. We are all agreed not to plant the Canadian oat seed we brought with us. It's clear those oats will not do well here. We will encourage some planting of grass and sorghum to mix with the feed so the dairy cows can produce more milk. For now, we will hold off on the corn and beans. I will obtain prices on the farm equipment that has been requested. Please talk to your campos and find out if there is anything else your families need from El Paso. Bring it to me by Wednesday as I will travel to town Thursday morning and make the telephone call. With that out of the way, we have one final unpleasant subject that I will let Mr. Wiebe handle."

Jacob's father-in-law stood up. "We had a meeting with a sinner from Campo 114 and he has agreed to his punishment. As you may have heard, he was discovered with rubber tires on his tractor, instead of the metal fins. I remind all of you that it's only through struggle that your salvation is earned. The harder life is, the easier it is to be humble. And with your struggles to get your daily work done, you will have less time to explore the outside world and do things you shouldn't be doing. You should focus on your work, on your family, and on God."

Everyone nodded.

Abraham continued. "We didn't have these problems when only horses pulled our plows. Now, the machines pull the plows. When this became an issue, we decided to allow it only if the wheels were metal rims with fins added to make it more difficult for the machine to work. Thus, this sinner has agreed to remove his rubber tires and burn them. Because we have learned not to select a witness from the same campo or colony, we are sending over my son-in-law, Mr. Jacob Rempel, to watch them burn."

Jacob sat upright at the mention of his name, his heart racing.

"With that, I will say a prayer and adjourn this meeting."

Jacob lowered his head and frowned. The last thing he wanted to do was walk three or four miles to a distant campo to watch a man burn expensive rubber tires. But there was no way for him to get out of it.

When the prayer was over and the men had filed out, Abraham called him over to the side.

"Jacob, you are to go to Campo 114 and see Mr. Loeppky. He will be waiting for you after the morning meal. You will make sure he burns all the tires and then report it to me. Do you understand?"

"Yes, I understand."

"Good. How is my daughter? I haven't been by for several weeks."

"Fine." *Except for the polished dirt floor and the wind whistling through my walls.*

"Good. I would like to come by tomorrow evening and visit."

"Of course. We shall look forward to it." *We'll put on another plate since you'll arrive right before supper, like always.*

Jacob shook his hand and walked home to tell his wife the good news.

The next morning, Jacob was up, fed by Judith before the rest of the family had barely stirred. He quickly gathered his things and started off on the long walk. He wanted desperately to avoid the noonday heat.

Just as he reached the front door, his wife called out. "Jacob, would you stop at the general store and purchase a bag of salt? We are almost out."

"Yes, dear," he said, searching his pockets for some extra cash. Once he was certain he had enough, he started his journey.

A slight breeze kissed his cheeks, also pushing around the dark-brown hair peeking below his straw hat. The morning October air was nice, and not yet harsh. That would happen later in the day. The walk was mostly pleasant, allowing him the opportunity to see the families in his campo getting up and beginning their morning chores. He knew all of them well, already aware of who got up early and worked hard versus those who tended to start later. His walk simply confirmed it.

It took him about an hour to walk to Campo 114. He could've taken his favorite bay, Nell, but then he'd have to feed her a little more. And he was desperate to save as much money as possible.

At the entrance of Campo 114, he asked the first person he saw where Mr. Loeppky's place was. The lady pointed to the fourth house on the right. Jacob made his way to the front door and knocked quietly, more out of embarrassment than anything else.

A large man walked over from the barn and said, "Are you the witness?"

"Yeah, I'm Jacob Rempel, from Campo 110."

They shook hands and Jacob fell in behind Mr. Loeppky as they walked to the barn. In the corner were three tires leaning against the wall. Two of the tires fit the rear of the tractor and the smaller one fit the front. Mr. Loeppky grabbed one of the rear tires and held it out for Jacob to inspect.

"See this one?" Mr. Loeppky said, patting the tire. "It's worth a lot of money. It sure would be a shame to burn it."

The offer was vague, but clear enough for Jacob to understand. "If they somehow didn't burn, whoever reported you would simply report you again."

Mr. Loeppky stroked his chin. "Maybe not. My fields are two miles away and no one can see me out there. I got caught because I carried them back with me in the tractor instead of leaving them out there. Having these tires sure makes the work go fast. I'm able to get more done with less fuel and was even hired out to work a few others. With everyone suffering crop failure and money being tight, I sure wish I could find a way to keep them."

Jacob frowned. "Listen, brother, I could certainly use the money. But I would be in trouble if I didn't make sure you burned them. It would cost me more than you could pay me."

Mr. Loeppky lowered his head. "All right then."

He shouldered the small tire and with Jacob's help, rolled the other two out behind his barn, where he stuffed some paper inside each one and lit them. After he tossed the small tire on, black smoke soon covered the area, choking them. The two men stepped away to get some fresh air.

"This sure stinks," Mr. Loeppky said. "I can't say I've ever burned rubber before."

"Neither have I," Jacob replied. "The smoke is so thick you can't see through it. I'm glad there's some wind to take it away, although the neighbors may think your place is on fire."

Mr. Loeppky kicked the ground. "*Nee. Dee weeten waut doa aungonen deit.*" They know what's happening.

That was Jacob's cue to leave, especially since the tires were sufficiently destroyed. He tipped his hat and began the long walk back, not waiting for the man to invite him in for some food or water. He was fairly certain he wouldn't be welcome.

He had traveled about two miles when he came upon the cow pasture that all the Swift Current families shared. Besides dairy cows, the Mennonites raised other cows for beef. Most families had their cows in this common pasture.

Jacob had two cows out there somewhere marked with his own special brand to distinguish them from the others. As he drew nearer, he spotted at least a dozen men running around the field, some rounding up the herd. Jacob went to a teenage boy sitting on the fence.

"What's all the commotion for?"

The boy twisted around and recognized his questioner. "Mr. Rempel, some of the cows were stolen during the night. The men are trying to figure out which ones they were."

Jacob felt a panic building inside of him. The absolute last thing he needed was to lose two of his most valuable assets. One of the cows was going to support his family with food through the winter and the other one might have to be sold for much-needed cash. He hopped the fence and ran to search through the now-gathered herd.

It took him twenty minutes, but he finally located his two cows, breathing a deep sigh of relief. Around him, several men frantically searched for their cows. Jacob moved away from the panic and asked one of the men who seemed to be in charge. "How did it happen?"

"The tracks lead to the road over there. They took down the rails and led four, maybe five cows away. It looks like they loaded them up and took off for the slaughterhouse in Cuauhtémoc."

"Do we know who they are?" Jacob asked.

"Not yet. They could be Mennonites or Mexicans. Maybe even a combination. I'm afraid this is going to happen more and more with the tough times we're going through. There's talk of bringing the cows in each night to a corral and setting up a watch with a rotating schedule. They're saying we should put two men out here to keep each other awake or in case one is sick. If we include boys fourteen and older, we could probably limit the shifts to three or four times a year for each man. That's not too bad, really."

A man shouted in anger, slapping his leg hard. "I guess he just found out one of his cows is missing," Jacob said.

"Yeah, there's going to be more of that, I'm afraid."

I'm glad it wasn't me, Jacob thought as he turned away and headed toward the general store.

The store was centrally situated among all the Swift Current campos, and close to Jacob. A Mennonite, Mr. Dyck, ran the store, having set it up on an odd-shaped leftover piece of land that was not suitable for a farm. It was a great move since Mr. Dyck seemed to do well no matter how the colony was faring. If the crops were good, people had money to spend. When times were tight, like now, people had to buy food. That made it a highly profitable business, especially since Mr. Dyck didn't like spending every waking moment in the fields.

Jacob opened the door and shuffled in, slipping around a woman shopping for cloth.

"Hello, Mr. Rempel," Mr. Dyck said. "What can I do for you today?"

"I need a bag of salt."

"Sure, let me get that for you," he said as he walked to the back.

Jacob dug into his pocket for his money and counted out the exact amount. When Mr. Dyck returned, he pushed the bag across the counter and took Jacob's money. Instead of picking the bag up, Jacob walked around the store looking at the goods.

A few minutes later, the woman approached the counter and paid for her fabric. She smiled at Jacob as she gathered up her cloth and left the store.

When they had the store to themselves, Mr. Dyck spoke up. "I understand you were sent to Campo 114 to see the tires burn. How did that go?"

Mr. Dyck was the colony's gossip repository. Every withdrawal required a deposit.

Jacob noticed the wry smile on his face, which meant he thought that perhaps Jacob took a bribe. Jacob decided to put that potential rumor to rest. "I've never smelled rubber burn before, and let me tell you, it stinks!"

"So you saw them burn, eh?"

"Yes, I saw it."

"I heard his wife may have turned him in."

Jacob shuddered at this comment because he often wondered about his own wife. She was very close to her father. Because of this, he avoided testing her loyalty. "He didn't say, but on the way back I found my two cows and was grateful they hadn't been stolen."

Mr. Dyck picked up a rag and wiped down the counter. "Yes, a lot of that's going on these days. The mayor always blames the Mexicans, but I'm pretty sure it's the Mennonites. They know how everything is set up around here."

Jacob shook his head in disgust. It seemed that sin was everywhere. Even the isolated Mennonites weren't immune to it.

Mr. Dyck pointed to the racks behind the counter. "We have plenty of fresh eggs this morning. A bumper crop, you might say. Would you like to buy some?"

Jacob stared at the rows of eggs, certainly more than usual. "No, I have all the eggs I need back home. They're good laying hens."

Mr. Dyck slapped a pack of cigarettes on the counter. Without saying a word, Jacob handed him several coins, took the pack, and shoved it deep inside his overalls pocket.

"Well, make sure and tell your neighbors I have a load of eggs to get rid of. I'll give them a real good price."

"I sure will," Jacob said as he left the store. With the bag of salt slung over his shoulder, he continued his walk home.

A mile down the road, he saw four teenage boys riding their horses hard. They were racing against each other, something he did almost every day growing up. It was one of the few pastimes they could participate in. Over time, he'd learned to shape his horse's hooves so they ran faster. With practice and good feed, he won more than his fair share of races. It was at one of those races that Judith caught his eye. It seemed so long ago.

The boys slapped their horses' rumps, jolting off toward an imaginary finish line. Seeing this turned Jacob's gray mood into a good one. And during the last three years in Mexico, he had experienced many gray moods.

His attitude and behavior were nothing like it had been in Canada. The doubts that others had expressed on the train were beginning to take hold inside of him and grow. He felt for the pack in his pocket. Later, he thought, he'd sneak another cigarette behind the barn and all would be right in the world.

Jacob approached his house and saw the neighbor's kids playing in their yard. They were so happy not to be doing chores or dealing with all the problems adults had, he was somewhat jealous. Oh, to be a kid again!

With a smooth breeze cooling him off, he stepped up to his porch and pulled the door open. Walking into the kitchen, he could tell something wasn't right. When he saw the tears streaming down Judith's face, he knew it was bad.

"What's happened?" he asked, afraid to hear the answer.

"Our chickens. Someone stole all the eggs in the middle of the night."

Jacob stepped back and processed this information. Before long he felt a searing pain welling up in his gut, working its way to his throat. When his anger was sufficiently hot enough, he squinted his eyes and slapped his thigh hard, yelling out loud. He started to say a curse word but stopped just in time. That's when he noticed his five-year-old son watching, waiting for him to let something slip. It was hard to imagine how this day could get any worse, but it would.

Jacob was in his living room, sitting in his favorite chair, satisfied with the supper they had just eaten, when footsteps on the porch made their loud presence known. Anticipating a knock, he put down the farm tool he was repairing and got up. When the knock finally came, he answered the door.

Staring at the three men standing there, he knew it was bad news. Jacob glanced behind him and saw his wife scurrying around in the kitchen, her perpetual place. His three kids were in their bedrooms doing whatever kids did. Jacob stepped outside and closed the door. This gave him a closer view of their faces, reaffirming what he already knew. It was bad news.

"Mr. Rempel," one of the men said. "We are sorry to have to tell you but your father-in-law, Abraham Wiebe, has passed away."

Jacob lowered his head, stunned. That was the last thing he thought he'd hear. Maybe his cow had died, or someone had seen him smoking. But not this. Abraham was fit and full of vigor. It just didn't seem possible.

One of them put his hand on Jacob's shoulder. "He collapsed in his living room not twenty minutes ago. Do you want us to tell his daughter?"

Judith! Jacob would have to tell her. It would be just as bad as when he told her little Anna had passed away. Or Katharina. Or Aganetha. Or their son Bernhard. Jacob never got used to the death, nor did it get any easier.

"No, I'll tell her," Jacob said solemnly.

"We will gather up the tables and chairs," another man said, "and head over to Mr. Wiebe's house. We shall see you there in one hour or less."

Jacob watched them walk off. Even though he wanted to run to the barn and grab a cigarette, he knew he couldn't put off the news since they had to leave for singing and prayer. It had to be done now.

He went back inside, into the kitchen. None of the children were around so this place was as good as any.

Rubbing his lips, he said softly, "Judith, I need to talk to you."

She put the pot down and wiped her hands on her apron. As she did, she studied his face. Then her expression changed. "Yes, what do you want to discuss?"

"The men just came to tell me that your father collapsed in his living room barely twenty minutes ago. He's in heaven now with our four little babies."

Her lip quivered. Her hands trembled. She had experienced so much death in such a short period of time, he was truly worried for her. In seconds, tears burst from her swollen eyes and she ran to his open arms, wailing. Jacob embraced her tightly as he had many times before.

A few seconds later, the children pulled on his pants leg asking what was wrong. Jacob explained the tragedy to them, bringing more tears and crying. For five long minutes, the family cried together. Except Jacob. He could not process what life would be like without his dominant father-in-law. It was a concept that didn't make sense. Instead, he tried to be strong for his wife and children.

When it felt appropriate, he held his wife away and said, "We have to leave soon. I must get our tables and chairs ready."

She wiped her eyes and nodded. That was how he left her, standing there in the kitchen with her unwashed pots and pans and tears dripping to the dirt floor.

Out in the barn, Jacob handed his son a chair. "Put this in the back of the buggy."

Jacob didn't have many chairs, so the other families would bring theirs. Each Mennonite chair had the family's name scratched into the wood. This ensured it came back to its proper owner after big events. And a funeral of the Ältester was a very big event.

A short time later, Jacob had the buggy loaded with the wooden benches from behind their dining table, a few chairs, and his family too. They left their house and headed down the road to another campo, where the pain and misery would sink in deeper.

The Rempels arrived and parked the buggy. Judith climbed down and ran inside to comfort her mother. Already there were dozens of other families milling around. The death of the Ältester would bring them all to this place.

Several men approached Jacob and gave their condolences. With nothing else left for him to do, Jacob helped them set up the benches and chairs, which was a lot of work. The men followed a traditional layout, leaving plenty of aisle space for the mourners to move around.

Suddenly, a loud noise came from the barn. Jacob went to investigate and found two men working with some corrugated metal. They were in the process of making the display table for his father-in-law's body.

It was the Mennonites' practice to wrap the deceased in a white sheet and place him or her on two pieces of corrugated metal that sloped so the head was higher than the feet. Blocks of ice from a facility in town would be fetched and packed all around the body to keep it preserved until the day of the funeral. This design allowed the melting water to flow to the lower end of the metal sheet. From there, it dripped to a bucket waiting below. The entire setup would then be placed in the deceased's living room, for mourners to pay their respects.

As the men worked, Jacob remembered a hot summer when he was a boy in Canada and his grandfather had died. The ice had melted fast. Throughout the long night, all he could hear was the drip... drip... drip... of the water hitting the bucket. He had wondered what happened when all the ice disappeared. It was both eerie and chilling.

Apparently, other families had discovered the same problem. Sometimes, they would put this setup in their barn or feed room. One family in Mexico had done this and awoke to find a rat eating the nose off their loved one. It was a difficult situation.

At nine p.m., enough people had arrived to begin. The campo's preacher said a prayer and the singing commenced. That lasted for an hour before the crowd thinned and people went home, for they all knew tomorrow would be a busy day.

Jacob and his family went home and got right to bed, though sleep did not come easily. The next morning, they got up and had breakfast, happy that their eggs hadn't been stolen. Once again, they made their way to the Wiebes' house for the continuation of saying goodbye to the popular Ältester.

Jacob learned that his brother-in-law had slaughtered one of Abraham's calves to feed the gravediggers, who had already started. Eight boys were busy swinging picks, trying to bust up the hard earth in the cemetery next to the church. The brother-in-law had also given money to the coffin makers, who, with the large amounts of deaths going on, were still overworked. Yet they put aside their other customers to immediately begin on the special pine box coffin. It would take two to three days to make. That delay was normal since the gravediggers would take that long hammering away at the dense, cruel earth.

To pass this time, visitors came by to pay their respects. Walking around in the living room, they stared at Abraham's face for perhaps a minute or so before shuffling out and making room for another person. With a line forming, this went on all day.

Judith, her mother, and Helena stayed busy in the kitchen making food. Since there were certain traditions to follow, they had to knead a huge quantity of dough. At each funeral, the deceased's family would send two girls in a buggy to all the nearby homes and give one large piece of dough to each house to make the twisted kringle. The wife would take the dough and bake it. Kringle would then be served after the funeral to all the guests.

In addition, the women had to prepare a large feast for the funeral day. Lunch would be served before the funeral consisting of vegetable soup with *fleesch kjees*. *Fleesch kjees* were made by removing the beef slices from the soup broth, grinding the meat up, adding salt and pepper, and pressing it onto a cookie sheet, where it cooled. When that was done, it was cut into squares and served cold with ketchup.

After the funeral, a *faspa* would be served. *Faspa* was the Mennonite version of a coffee break. In England it would be called tea time. *Faspa* consisted of the kringle they had sent around to be baked, homemade buns, cookies, jams, pickles for digestion and health, coffee, and sugar cubes. The women were also responsible for feeding the gravediggers, who would certainly be hungry after digging for three days.

With the hole dug, the gravediggers became the pallbearers. They were also responsible for tossing all the dirt back in when the deceased was lowered into the grave. But before any of this could happen, a letter of notification (which was basically an obituary) had to be written by the Ältester, or in this case, a campo preacher or school teacher. The letter announced the person's death. On the back of the letter were the names of all the preachers. The man writing the letter would have his son ride to each preacher on that list and show them the letter. That preacher would then tell people in his campo about the death, and the letter would move on until everyone knew about it.

Once all of that was accomplished and the funeral day had arrived, the deceased was formally dressed. Early in the morning, several women, who were appointed by each village that had a church, dressed the deceased by attaching white sleeves and an upper body shirt, before covering the rest of the body with some cloth that was pinned all around the top edge of the coffin. For men, a black ribbon was attached around the cuffs. For a woman, they placed a black laced headpiece on her head. During the actual dressing of the body, the immediate family sat in the room mourning, knowing it was the last time they would be alone with their loved one.

For Abraham Wiebe, his funeral day had arrived. The space around his house was packed with families. Little kids ran amok as their parents found it impossible to keep them quiet.

Jacob and his family were dressed in their finest—all black—just like everyone else. They were ready to go to church for the service, which lasted for two to three hours since the other preachers gave a speech, usually about how they weren't supposed to get into worldly material things like rubber tires or that women should stick with traditional clothing.

After the last song was sung, the congregation made their way on foot to the cemetery behind the church while the body was taken by horse-drawn wagon. They sang another song at the gravesite and said a prayer. When the signal was given, the gravediggers lowered Abraham's body into the ground as more tears were shed.

By the time the dirt was halfway up the grave, Judith had seen enough. She turned away and with her mother, started back to the house. There, she and the other women would work hard to ensure the rest of the food was served properly. Jacob would wait until the people began leaving to help the men with the benches and chairs. And then, close to ten, he would make his way back to his house with his benches and chairs and family, all loaded up in the buggy. He knew by the time he put up the horses and unloaded the buggy, he wouldn't get to bed until midnight.

It didn't matter. There was no one left to watch over him or tell him what to do. With his father-in-law gone, he was now free.

Chapter Six

October 1929
Seminole, Texas

Rose Henderson smiled as she set out the clothes she was going to wear in a few hours. The centerpiece was a cotton taffeta dress hemmed just above the knee—a shocking sight to the more conservative citizens of the town. Its light orange hue combined with its purple pocket-flap accents made it the top of the local fashion scene, not to mention the coming parties.

To her friends the dress looked like it was straight from New York. They had no idea it was a 1928 edition and on clearance when she found it a month ago. She had purchased the dress during a trip to Dallas with Aunt Mae to pick out some fixtures for their new house. It too was a 1928 model.

After the fire, Uncle Samuel and some local men quickly erected a makeshift store on the burned-out site. Then they frantically filled it with whatever they could scrounge from the surrounding counties. Ed Smith, president of the First State Bank, had saved most of his structure, including the large vault that protected the town's money. Being in a good financial position, Mr. Smith was willing to take a chance on the Hendersons. After all, they had always been good customers, paying on time without a hiccup. It was a pretty safe risk.

With plenty of money available, the Hendersons brought in more equipment along with desperately needed building materials. Samuel made twice-daily runs to Seagraves to transport the new merchandise, which was gobbled up by the citizens of Seminole, many of whom had good banking relationships with the First State Bank. When Seagraves couldn't fill his store, Samuel went to Lamesa and Andrews, two cities farther away. Within days of the fire, Henderson's Hardware, Implements & Harness established itself as the center for not only buying equipment and materials to rebuild, but for exchanging information. Mae Beth and Rose handled the orders while passing on all they knew. For the first two months, none of them got much sleep.

Another key to the Hendersons' success was extending credit. Since the bank had taken a chance on them, they took a chance on the locals, letting them have the supplies by simply signing their name on a note. As the town rebounded, it paid off handsomely.

When 1924 rolled around, most everyone was back up and running. The large bulk purchases stopped. But the Hendersons found their weekly sales quite strong. That's when things shifted into another gear.

For the last several years, people hoping to get in on the Roaring Twenties purchased property and began busting up the sod. Gaines County was one of the places where this was happening. With commodities prices like cotton and corn rising, novice farmers could hardly do wrong. When people realized how close the water was to the surface, investors bought up more of the surrounding land. Before long, farms were everywhere. Then ranching took off. And all these folks needed hardware, construction supplies, and farm implements. For those items, Henderson's Hardware, Implements & Harness was the only game in town.

From 1923 to 1928, Samuel and Mae Beth, along with their son, Melvin, and their niece, Rose, lived above the store, just like before. After the fire, though, it was greatly improved and added on to. But with business being so good and cash flying in every direction, Samuel decided living in the store was no longer necessary. He purchased a nice piece of property a half mile north of town and drove to work each day in a used 1925 Buick Sedan he purchased from a rancher. He also upgraded their truck, not only allowing them to deliver entire orders in one trip, but making it easier to pick up large loads of goods and equipment from a faraway town. This saved time and kept his store filled with merchandise.

Rose had watched all this happen. It was a true miracle, one she benefited from. The Hendersons were able to pay her more and also provide her a bedroom all to herself. Because she was frugal, she saved up a good deal of money. That was how she managed to purchase such nice clothes, like the dress she was about to put on for her date with Charles Simpson. She could hardly wait.

The dress was already ironed, so all she had to do was put on her makeup and decide which earrings and necklace matched best. Rose pulled her wooden jewelry box closer and lifted out the top tray. At the bottom, staring back at her, was Grandpa's Indian Wars medal. Before he died, he had curled up in a ball with the cigar box to protect it. For days it had sat on their makeshift kitchen table until Rose finally volunteered to keep it. No one objected. She had only known Grandpa for a week, but she just had to keep something so precious to him in the safest place she had. It was her way of honoring the old Tenth Cavalry clerk.

As she applied her makeup, she studied something else of great importance: a map pinned to her wall. Charles had recently given it to her to show how much property he controlled. He was a speculator who bought up land in Gaines County for a profit. He'd already sold some of it to various farmers, ranchers, and other speculators, before going right back out and buying more.

Charles told her he was connected to a bank in Seagraves. He seemed to have an endless supply of money. He even had a sleek maroon and beige Chrysler Imperial, buying it new in Andrews just last year. He lived in Seminole at a nice rental house on 3rd Avenue and shared it with his close friend David Bane, who bought and sold stocks and bonds, things Rose didn't understand. Together, Charles and David were Seminole's most eligible bachelors, pursued by all the single women around. Fortunately, Rose had lassoed one of them.

They had met at a local fair when Charles spotted Rose sitting on a bench waiting for Melvin, who was studying the midway games. When she got up and wandered to a crafts booth, he moved in and struck up a conversation. A few minutes later, he was buying her the items she had been eyeing, and within weeks, Charles was effectively off the market.

That was over a year ago. Now, she dared to think that at some point he might pop the question. When he saw her at the bank on Wednesday making a deposit, he told her that he had made reservations at Sullivan's Steakhouse for Saturday and to dress up nice. Sullivan's was the most expensive restaurant around, so that got her wondering—was tonight the night?

On Friday, Rose made a trip to Lady's Beauty and Style Shop for a trim on her flapper bob. Her hair was thick enough to hold the perfect horizontal cut across her forehead and the vertical cuts just past her ears. With a heaping dose of Brilliantine, her hair stayed in place despite the gusting winds off the Llano Estacado. Her friends said she looked like a model straight out of a fashion magazine.

When she was done in her bedroom, she went to the living room and removed her wrap-over coat from the closet, trying it on to make sure it didn't crush her dress. The coat was secured by a large button to the side and kept her nice and warm. Although it was barely cool, she got cold easily, especially after adjusting to the brutal West Texas summers.

During this testing process, Melvin sat on the floor watching her and saying nothing. He was sixteen now and didn't need constant attention.

After being satisfied with her look, she hung up the coat and sat down on the couch to communicate with him using verbal tones and hand signals. She explained that she was going out with Charles and it would be late when she returned. Melvin scratched his ear, which meant he understood.

From her first day in Seminole, Rose and Melvin had established a special bond. She was able to understand most of his words and actions and even tried to teach her aunt, but they eventually realized that Rose had some special gift and no one else was going to be able to reach him like she could.

Because of her work with Melvin, Samuel made sure she had extra spending money even though he knew she was careful with her finances. He and Mae Beth hoped they would be able to keep her there for a long time. But when she turned into a beautiful woman and Charles appeared on the scene, they knew they were losing the battle.

Suddenly, a three-toned horn sounded, snapping her head up. The horn was followed by the roar of a powerful V-6 engine. Charles had recently told her that another Imperial had set a land speed record, traveling across the country in the incredible time of one week. Rose acted impressed even though she had no idea what the previous record had been.

She heard the car door slam and Charles bound up the steps. This was followed by a loud knock. Rose paused a second, left the couch, and made her way to the door.

As soon as she opened it, Charles yelled out, "My goodness, you are looking good tonight! Sullivan's will have to stop serving meals when I bring you in there."

Rose blushed. "Oh, stop it. Come on in. I just need to get my coat and say goodbye to Melvin."

Charles followed her into the living room and noticed Melvin sitting on the floor, watching the two of them. Reaching into his pocket, he produced a bright marble. "Here you go, Melvin."

Melvin, without changing expressions, took the marble and studied it, holding it up to the light and spinning it around in his fingers.

"Does he like it?"

Rose went up to Melvin and stared into his eyes. "He loves it. He always loves the marbles you bring."

Charles shook his head. "I don't know how you do that. I need you to look into the eyes of some of my sellers and see how low they'll go on price. I could make a fortune with you."

"If only I could do that," Rose chuckled, as she removed her coat from the closet.

Charles moved over and helped put it around her. "Where are the Hendersons?" he asked.

"They went out to a movie. We've started leaving Melvin alone and he's done well."

"I see, though I'm pretty sure Samuel isn't too happy to see me."

Rose took his arm. "Oh, they like you. It's just that he sells things and sees men younger than him making more than he does. It's different because he feels you have to work for your money instead of speculating."

Charles frowned. "Yeah, I figured as such. Although it's funny how all the farmers and ranchers I sell to seem to buy a whole lot of stuff from him."

She knew he was right but didn't want to go down that path and possibly ruin the night. So, she didn't reply. Instead, she closed the front door and walked with him to his car. Charles was short—only an inch taller than Rose—but his large personality made him seem taller.

"Hopefully, he plays with the newest addition to his marble collection while we're gone. Are you sure he'll be safe by himself?"

"My aunt and uncle will be back in less than an hour, so there's not much trouble he can get into. He'll have a special night playing with that marble."

Charles opened the car door for her. "Well, I've got a feeling this is going to be a special night for us too."

Rose felt her pulse quicken. She tried to keep a straight face as she slid across his soft leather seat and leaned back to enjoy the smooth ride.

A few minutes later, Rose and Charles were seated at a nice table with fresh bread and a dish of butter spread before them. Charles pointed to the dish. "They have a little old lady who comes in and makes this butter fresh each day. Try some, it's delicious."

Rose reached for a piece of bread when the waiter appeared next to her with an ice bucket.

"I ordered a special bottle of champagne the other day. I hope you don't mind."

Rose grinned. "I guess I'll try some—if I have to," the sarcasm obvious.

Charles raised his eyebrows as the waiter popped the cork with a flair and filled their flutes. He lifted his up and made a toast. "Here's to the best girl in Gaines County."

Rose held up her flute and acted confused. "Do I toast myself? I don't know. Is that proper?"

Charles laughed. "That's what I love about you. You're so… *original*."

They clinked glasses and took a sip. Then Charles set his glass down and grew serious. "Before I get into the topic of the night, I want to tell you what I'm up to."

"I'm all ears," Rose said playfully, batting her eyes.

"Gaines County is growing in people and money. Everyone is planting cotton and the ones who aren't are planting corn. I own or have options on hundreds of acres of potential farmland. As you know, cattle ranching is crazy. The land that doesn't sell to farmers can usually go to ranchers. And here's the best part: Humble Oil is leasing in the western part of the county. Some of my land is being leased for almost ten dollars per acre. I've already signed a few contracts with them and pocketed the money. If they hit oil—which they think they will—I'll be getting more checks. So, with all the land I control here, things are looking good. Very good!"

Rose took another sip of her champagne. She had known he was doing well. This information simply confirmed it.

Charles reached over and covered her hand. "I'm looking to build a big house on a piece of property I own on the outskirts of town. I'll drive you by to look at it later. But with all that I have, I'm missing one thing."

Rose's eyes widened.

"Do you know what that is?" He squeezed her hand tighter.

A coy smile creased her face. "An architect?"

"No, not an architect," he said, laughing hard. With his free hand, he reached into his jacket pocket, pulled out a small box, and gently placed it in her hand. "I'm missing a wife."

Rose took the box and slowly opened it. A large diamond sat atop a single gold ring. She gasped.

"Rose, will you be my wife?"

Rose nodded as tears filled her eyes, her heart pushing through her chest. "Yes... absolutely!" She put the ring on as he clasped her hand.

"I must admit I thought of asking Samuel for your hand, but I didn't think he'd say yes."

Rose touched his hand. "He'd say yes, it's just that he doesn't want you to take me away from Melvin." She gazed at the ring again. "How does it look?" Rose said, wiping her eyes and thrusting her hand out.

"Stupendous! And it should. After all, you're my fiancée now."

"And you're my husband-to-be," she said, lifting her flute.

They clinked glasses again. "Yes, and right now, your husband-to-be is hungry."

He pulled out a special cigar and signaled the waiter. When he arrived, Charles ordered for the both of them, and before long, the night slipped into an endless dream.

⟨⟩

The next morning, Rose went into the kitchen and asked if she could help.

Aunt Mae was about to say something when she caught a glimpse of the ring and grabbed Rose's hand. "Are you engaged?!"

"Yes," Rose said, beaming. "He asked me last night. I got in so late I didn't want to wake you."

Mae Beth tossed her head back. "I thought that might happen before the year was up. Wait until Samuel finds out. He left early to drop something off at the store. Are you going to church with us?"

"Of course. I'm not married yet. I'm still part of this family."

"In that case, put on this apron and give me a hand." Aunt Mae handed her a bowl of pancake mix to stir up. "How soon are you leaving us?"

"I don't know," Rose said as she tied her apron. "He said to start thinking of a date and tell him. He has some big deals coming up and doesn't want to interrupt them."

Aunt Mae sighed. "My oh my, we hate to lose you. I know Melvin will be crushed. I don't know how we'll get along without you."

Rose stirred the bowl. "Don't worry. He purchased a place just outside of town and I'll be close. It's on the east side. I saw it last night, although it's not much to see. Just a piece of dirt right now."

Aunt Mae put her arm around Rose. "You're nineteen—almost twenty—and a woman now. It's time you had your own life. Do you still want to help around the store? I'm guessing not since it appears Charles is doing well."

Rose placed the bacon strips on the griddle. "I don't know the answer to that either. Until we're married, nothing will change. I guess I'll find out soon enough."

Aunt Mae gave her a strained smile and turned back to making breakfast.

A few minutes later, Samuel returned. He seemed to sense something was different. Instead of waiting for him to notice her ring, she repeated the news and received a less than joyous response. He didn't ask questions like his wife, but instead took his seat at the table and started reading the *Seminole Sentinel*.

Rose said nothing, letting the matter drop. She already knew it was going to be tough for him to accept. Perhaps later she could talk to her uncle. *Perhaps.*

<hr>

Three days later, a Wednesday, Samuel had still not said a word about Rose's engagement. As far as he was concerned, nothing had changed.

Like usual, he had sent her to the bank to make the deposit. As she was leaving there, she ran into her fiancé, who was meeting with the bank president. Charles's roommate, David Bane, was also with him. Charles excused himself to talk to Rose and explained he would be driving to Lubbock for a day or so but would return Friday evening and wanted to take her out to dinner. Rose said she'd be waiting.

Now it was Friday and past nine o'clock. Obviously, he'd been delayed.

Aunt Mae, who was sitting in the living room with Rose, grew concerned. "I hope everything is okay and that they didn't have a breakdown. Or worse. I'm praying that they weren't involved in an accident."

Samuel, sitting in his favorite chair, lowered his paper, interested in the topic.

Rose wanted to reassure them and herself. "I'm sure he had some business deal and was delayed. He'll be back by tomorrow."

Aunt Mae nodded. "Sure he will, hon."

But he didn't show up the next day. By Sunday, Rose was concerned. She took the car to Charles's house, something a single girl didn't do. There, she found only David Bane, who was packing a suitcase.

"David, where's Charles? Is everything okay?"

He stopped what he was doing and lit a cigarette. "There was a drop in the market on Thursday. We had some margin calls and had to go to Seagraves to deal with it."

Rose shook her head. "What's a margin call?"

David exhaled some smoke. "If the stock price drops below the amount of money you have in your account, the broker can sell the stock to prevent their loss. But that leaves the investor with a loss. Prices rose a bit on Friday, so there's some confusion as to what we own and what we owe."

"Are you two partners?" Rose asked.

David flicked some ashes in an ashtray. "On some things. I'm not in on most of his land deals. But we have deals together on stocks and bonds."

Rose put her hands on her hips. "Okay. So, when will Charles be back?"

"I don't know. Probably next week. It depends on the markets. And we're so far from New York, we don't get the news fast. If he can put up enough collateral and prices stabilize, everything should be fine." He crushed out his cigarette. "Don't worry, when he gets back I'll tell him to see you right away."

"Thanks, David. I'm just worried. We had a date Friday night and he didn't show up."

David smiled. "Oh, he's crazy about you. He wasn't with another girl or anything like that. Speaking of which, I might be interested in a few of your friends. Perhaps when Charles gets back, we could talk about setting me up with one of them?"

For the first time in days, Rose smiled. "Of course. I'm sure my friends would jump at the chance."

"Excellent. Now I need to get back to packing. Until then."

Rose left and returned to her house. She was still concerned, but at least she knew her fiancé hadn't been in an accident. That provided some comfort.

On Monday, she found Samuel alone at the shop and told him what she knew. He explained that the stock market was basically gambling and the men he was friends with stayed away from it. He implied that Charles wasn't doing "honest work" and might not be a good catch. "Rose, that kind of life is much different than what we do here. There will be highs and lows. You're rich one day and broke the next. I can't live like that. Some men like Charles and his friend David can. You see, here in the store we have real goods. It's not fictitious profits like all this stock market magic. Who knows where all that money is going?"

Rose didn't really understand but said nothing more.

It was late Tuesday evening and Rose was about to go to bed when she heard some light tapping at her window. Frightened, she turned to get Samuel, who would come running with a shotgun, but stopped when a familiar voice drifted through the glass.

"Rose, it's me. Charles."

Cautiously, she went to the window and pulled back the drapes. There, she saw the distraught face of her fiancé pressed up against the glass. She was about to undo the latch and open the window when he pointed to the back door. "Come outside for minute. Please."

Rose nodded and closed the blinds. Everyone was in their bedrooms preparing for sleep. This made it easy to slip unseen out the back door. There was Charles, hunched over, his back leaning against a beaten-up Ford with David in the passenger's seat. They both looked terrible.

"What's the matter?" she said, feeling the panic rise in her chest.

He stepped away from the car and moved closer to the house where the light was better. "The stock market dropped twenty-five percent on Monday and Tuesday, not counting the big drop last Thursday. It's bad, Rose. Bad!"

"Where's your Imperial?" she said, trying to make sense of all this.

"Gone. I traded it for this Ford and some cash. We're leaving Gaines County and probably Texas. I don't know where we're going, maybe Mexico."

"I don't understand, Charles. Why are you doing this?"

"Because I owe everyone. Banks. People. Investors. They trusted me with their money and now it's all gone. The checks I've written in the last week will bounce and they'll try to prosecute me. I can't go to prison, Rose. I'm not built for it."

"But I'm sure they'll all understand, won't they? It's not your fault. You can tell them the stock market dropped. They'll forgive you."

He let out a short laugh. "*Forgiveness.* Now that's a concept the banks don't understand, even if I was willing to take that chance. Maybe your Baptist church would forgive me, but not these folks."

Rose placed a hand on his shoulder. "I can't believe this is happening. Please don't go. Let's work this out."

He took her hand off her shoulder and stared at the engagement ring. Before she could say a word, he slid it off her finger. "I'm sorry, but I need this back. It'll get me more cash down the road. I promise I'll be back one day and replace it with a bigger one."

Tears welled up in her eyes as she rubbed her empty finger. This was a calamity. A complete nightmare!

Charles leaned over and kissed her on the lips. "Please don't tell anyone you saw me. I've got to go before they put out warrants and start looking for me. Best of luck, Rose. You'll do fine."

Words stuck in her throat as he hopped in the Ford. She wanted to say something—anything—but nothing came out. She was helpless as he started the engine and drove off. The Ford was a mile down the road before she saw its headlights finally come on.

Suddenly, a harsh wind blew off the Llano Estacado. It was cold and biting, smelling of oil, but she remained in place, hoping—*wishing*—this was a dream. When his headlights disappeared, she turned to go back inside. The door had just closed behind her when a cloud of sand hit the house. It sounded like it wanted to rip their place in two. Yet it was something she was used to, so she put it out of her mind and went to bed, hoping that when she awoke, it would all be better.

The next morning, she got up, dressed, and went to the kitchen to help with breakfast. As she passed the living room, Melvin was there pacing back and forth. This wasn't normal.

"What's bothering him?" her aunt asked. "He just started this pacing."

Rose cleared her mind and went up to the boy. "What's the matter, Melvin?"

He did his usual grunts, saying a few words and gesturing wildly. Rose stepped away from him and grabbed a coat. The temperature had dropped during the night and was quite cold.

"Where are you going?" Aunt Mae asked.

"Outside. He said something is going on in town."

She looked both ways down the street and saw a neighbor rushing out of his house. "What's the matter?" she yelled.

"It's the bank," he yelled back. "There's a panic!"

She rushed back inside and saw Samuel just sitting down to read his morning paper. His eyes caught hers. "What's the matter?"

"The bank. There's a rush on the bank!" Rose said frantically.

He glanced at the *Sentinel*'s headline: *Black Tuesday. Stock Market Collapse!*

The paper floated to the floor as Samuel ran out the door. Her personal nightmare had spread.

Chapter Seven

December 1934
Cuauhtémoc, Mexico – Campo 110

The winter wind whistled around Jacob, whirling up an occasional dust devil. He moved closer to the barn, at times leaning against it to block the wind, all while smoking a cigarette. In warmer weather, he liked to walk to his pile of rubbish at the end of the land where no one could see him. But it was too cold for that and he was in no mood to walk fifteen minutes each way for a single smoke. The only benefit of the cold wind was that his children weren't likely to stumble upon him, especially at six in the morning.

His children!

He had eight of them, but his oldest son worried him the most. Young Jacob was halfway between fourteen and fifteen, and most likely to spread the word about his father's smokes. Helena, the eldest of all his children, usually helped Judith with the household chores. She didn't have much opportunity or reason to come to the back side of the barn. The rest were too young to care.

Jacob tried to put that worry out of his mind and took a long drag from his cigarette. The nicotine helped him get going faster in the morning. If he could sneak one in the afternoon, he could happily make it through the long day of endless labor: slop the hogs, feed the chickens, break out fresh hay for the horses, milk the cows, repair this and that, walk to the general store and buy some dry goods, check on his two cows in the common field, and even stand guard when it was his time. The list went on and on.

His neighbor, Mr. Dueck, also had the same long list, though he no longer joined Jacob for a secret smoke. After a nasty bout of typhoid, he claimed the cigarettes made him sick to his stomach. Jacob recalled the day when Mr. Dueck had given him his pack.

"Take them," he said. "I'm done."

"At least you'll be saving some money," Jacob told him, trying to make him feel better, all while enjoying the windfall.

Unfortunately, this stopped the casual chat sessions between the two men. Unless he sought someone out, Jacob had no one to talk to about the state of his farm and the problems he faced. At least with the never-ending work, he didn't have any time to seek comfort.

Jacob used his shoe to scratch at the ground, kicking some dirt up against his barn. It had been twelve long years since the Mennonites arrived here, with twelve full growing seasons under their belt. Through failure, the colony had learned that planting more than one crop a year was futile. The fierce rains in June and July, and the lack of it during the winter, made a two-crop venture impossible. The only way they could add some extra fruits and vegetables to their pantry was through the large garden behind their house. The women watered it by hand and tended to it if the men didn't have time. It wasn't much, but at least it was something.

Jacob drew in one last deep breath and exhaled the smoke through his nose before dropping the butt into a hole he'd made with the tip of his shoe. The sun was just coming up, casting a red glow across the land. With the colors of summer long gone, all Jacob saw were the browns of the earth and the grays of the structures. Most colonists had no money for paint, so the boards stayed bare.

Pulling the collar of his shirt tighter, he went into the barn and stashed away the evidence of his crime. Nell saw him first, tossing her head back for some attention. He patted her on the head for a few moments and proceeded to set out the morning hay for both her and Jack, their new work horse. Prince had recently died of some disease—no one in the colony knew what it was—leaving Jacob to sell the hide to some Mexicans, since he couldn't bear to use it to cover his buggy seat. He buried the rest of Prince a short distance from the barn.

While the horses ate, he killed some time looking over his rickety tractor. It was a mess, having barely made it through the last harvest. He and

Mr. Dueck shared all the expenses on it and talked about replacing the hunk of metal. They had saved up enough money to purchase another one and were hoping to talk to Mr. Bergen yesterday, but he didn't come by. Mr. Bergen was the colony's buyer, with equipment contacts in El Paso and other places. He had been working on locating the tractor they wanted and finding out the sales price. With today being Sunday, Jacob and Mr. Dueck planned on looking for him in a few hours when everyone showed up for church.

Jacob heard a bellowing behind him. It was the two milk cows, their udders heavy with milk. The cows knew they wouldn't be fed until they were milked, so they urged Jacob to hustle. He turned around, dusted off his hands, and grabbed a pail.

The seat of the well-used wooden stool was cold. Jacob could feel it through his overalls. He thought to himself, *I wonder how many times I have milked a cow.* With at least two cows to milk morning and evening, and starting when he was seven, it had to be over 30,000 times. The only breaks he had were when he was sick or on the train coming down to Mexico with his family. *That was it!*

He milked the cows and let them feed. Pouring the fresh milk into a tall, metal bucket, he sealed it up and then lugged it to the house. Like always, he stamped his feet on the steps to get the dust out, a habit he brought with him from Canada, though with the polished dirt floors inside, it made little sense. But it did keep Judith happy.

The warm air hit him as soon as he opened the front door. The fireplace was roaring. This was the responsibility of his son Jacob, who, as with everything else, took the task seriously. It was also part of his job to bring in all the wood, which he would pile up neatly in a box near the fireplace. Each child had their chores.

Jacob took the milk bucket into the kitchen and set it down. The scene was like every other morning: Judith hovering over the stove, baking pastries and fresh bread while keeping an eye on the bacon and eggs. Helena supervised both the coffee pot and Anna, who was setting up the table. Anna, twelve years old, frowned, putting up with her older sister's orders.

No one said a word to him as he went back into the living room, where he noticed the rest of the children in the hall playing with some toy they had made for themselves. His son Jacob stayed apart from the rest of the family, reading his Bible by the fireplace.

"You're going to have that book memorized," Jacob said to his son.

"I hope so," the boy replied, briefly acknowledging his father before turning his attention back to the Bible.

With nothing to do but wait, Jacob took this brief opportunity to rest, something he rarely got to do, and lowered his thin frame into a wooden rocking chair. Leaning back, he rubbed his eyes. In about an hour, they would hitch up the buggy to their two horses and trot off to church, where they would sit on hard wooden benches for four long hours, listening to a message that was among a hundred or so passed down over the last four centuries. No one ever changed the messages, they simply repeated them. And no one ever questioned why.

After an initial prayer, the first forty-five minutes would be consumed with singing. Then the preacher would stand up and read the prepared message for two and a half hours before sitting down and listening to another forty-five minutes of singing. When that was done, church would be adjourned, and everyone would make their way back to their homes so their wives could prepare yet another meal.

Jacob began calculating how long he could make it in church before he had to take a break. Usually, he cleared the first round of singing and maybe twenty minutes of preaching before he quietly slipped out to join a few other restless men. They would use the latrine or get some water—anything to kill time.

Why?

Because everyone in the colony worked so hard during every hour of every day, they were thoroughly exhausted. Some of them occasionally fell off their benches, either passing out from exhaustion or falling asleep. However, making a noise in church was severely frowned upon, which would most certainly happen when you fell off a bench. It had almost happened to him on several occasions, usually around harvest time. Since the women sat on the left side of the church and the men on the right, Judith wasn't there to elbow him in the ribs to stay awake. But somehow, he'd found a way to endure.

Though this religious marathon was tough on the worshippers, the preacher had it worse. He didn't leave the platform for the entire four hours, sitting in his chair until taking to the pulpit for his sermon, where he stood and talked for hours. On many Sundays, the preacher struggled to finish, his voice giving out from the same exhaustion the others had. It was painful to watch.

"Meal time," Judith said, startling Jacob from his chair. With no radios or artificial sounds allowed, it wasn't much of a problem for her to get everyone's attention.

"Let's go, children," he said, waving his arms in the direction of the kitchen.

All the kids, including the sullen Jacob, scurried to their seats while Judith brought over the last of the dishes before taking her own seat. Jacob bowed his head and silently began his own prayer because it was forbidden to pray out loud. Instead of his usual prayer, he said a prayer from his heart. *Dear heavenly Father, we ask your forgiveness and for your blessings upon our family, our land, and our animals. Please allow this food to nourish our bodies and make us strong. And please grant us favor in your eyes so that we may continue to serve you in all our ways. Amen.*

Everyone sat in complete silence, heads bowed and hands folded, as they prayed to themselves the usual prayer in High German: *Segne Vater diese speise, uns zur kraft und Dir zum Preise, Amen.* Bless Father this meal, for our strength and to your praise. Amen.

This set off the clatter of forks, spoons, and dishes echoing around the room. Jacob munched on some bacon and ate his breakfast in silence, glancing over toward Judith. She was pregnant again—the thirteenth time—and had recently told him she believed it was a boy. "A kicker this one is!" she said.

To date, they had lost three daughters and two sons—Bernhard and Johann. They had reused Bernhard's name and he was now seven. Because she had given birth to Johann last year and he died six months later from the pox, they decided to reuse his name.

"Please pass the cream," Anna said.

Jacob handed it to her.

"Papa, do we have to stay behind when church is over?" she asked.

Jacob tore off a piece of bread and spread some butter on it. "No. I'm sending you all back in the buggy. I'll walk home when the meeting is over."

"Oh good!" Helena said. "I want to look at the material I just got to make my new dress."

She was crafting a dress out of fabric they had purchased a few days earlier. Most of their clothes were homemade with the foot-treadle sewing machine. They also passed down their clothes until there was nothing left of them. It was how they lived.

Judith spent her spare time, when she had any, teaching her three daughters how to sew. Most Mennonite woman could make their own clothes. It was expected. Of course, they also learned to cook. This meal was another example of Judith's supreme talent in that regard. Scrambled eggs from eggs collected thirty minutes earlier. Toast from bread baked yesterday. Thick slices of bacon from the hog he butchered and cured thirty days ago. Plum preserves Judith canned three months earlier. Fifteen-minute-old milk. Cream spun yesterday by Helena. In good times, there would be hunks of ham, winter squash, and beans—the beans being a new addition to their recent crops. But times were tough and the weather solely to blame. The Great Depression was destroying many farmers in the country to the north, yet Jacob and the other colonists had no idea or concept of a depression.

Jacob glanced at his watch. "Children, finish up. We need to leave for church shortly. Jacob, you get dressed and meet me in the barn to hitch up the buggy."

"Yes sir," he replied, sliding back his chair and taking off for his room— one he shared with two-year-old Cornelius and six-year-old Abraham.

Jacob went to his and Judith's room where he put on his black suit. When that was done, he ever-so-gently pulled the bed out from the wall, sliding behind the headboard where a cleverly cut piece of wood allowed itself to pop up. Behind it was a small glass jar filled with rolls of money. Jacob unscrewed the lid and dumped the cash on his bed. Wetting his fingers, he proceeded to count it all out. He needed to know the exact amount so he could tell Mr. Bergen to order the tractor—*if* the price was right. Satisfied with the amount, he put it all back and quietly pushed the bed up against the wall. Since none of the Mennonites in this colony used banks, they hid their money in places like this.

Jacob opened the door and saw Judith, who was coming in to put on her black dress. He walked past her and went out to the barn, where his son was already busy getting the buggy hitched up.

Once everyone was dressed and loaded up, they took off down the main avenue, stopping to let out Cornelius and five-year-old Aganetha. They would stay with a neighbor along with other children in Campo 110, as they weren't yet allowed in church.

With other buggies filling up the road, they fell in place, forming a Mennonite train headed toward salvation.

⋙◆⋘

At 11:30, church was over, and the meeting was called to order. Mr. Peters, the Ältester, was there as was Mr. Klassen, though he was no longer the mayor. Mr. Froese had taken his place and was somewhat stricter than his predecessor.

The new mayor clapped his hands. "Men, we must talk about a serious issue—one we should take control of right now. I'm referring to our children."

Jacob had assumed this was coming. Several children had been hanging around the local Mexicans and another group called the Mestizos. Mestizos were Mexicans of mixed descent—a combination of Spaniards and American Indians—some of whom had been chased south from Texas by the U.S. Cavalry in the 1800s. Recently, these rebellious children had talked of leaving the colony and exploring the surrounding cities. This was a major problem since the Mennonites were a self-contained community, expanding solely through childbirth and refusing to go out into the world to convert new believers.

"I must remind you," the mayor said, his face growing red, "that when we left Canada over ten years ago, our children were having the same problems. They were unrestrained, wild, unruly, and didn't honor their parents, much less listen to them. When the Canadian government offered us a compromise: teaching our normal studies in the Low German language so long as we also taught one full hour of English each day, we said no. Instead, we demanded full control over our children like we had been promised when we moved from Russia. And now, even though the Mexican government is living up to its promises, our children are being corrupted. It's happening all over again."

He went on to list the various offenses: vandalism, lying, theft, and not coming home on time. He avoided mentioning any names, but everyone knew who they were. Jacob was so thankful his children weren't on the list. He hated belting them, and those unruly children had been whipped hard. After this meeting, they might be whipped again. Some men were brutally tough on their offspring.

"If we lose control of our children, they will leave our colony. When that happens, it's the beginning of the end, not to mention the loss of their souls."

Several men chimed in, adding their opinions to the mix. Seeing where this was going, Jacob tuned out the rest of the meeting and waited for it to end so he could meet with the equipment buyer. Finally, it did.

"There you are," Mr. Bergen called out. "I'm sorry I couldn't come by yesterday, but I had problems with one of my animals." He was dressed in the same black suit all of the men wore.

"I understand," Jacob said, shaking his hand as his neighbor Mr. Dueck joined them. "Do you have a price for us?"

"Yes, of course, but with the poor financial state of the Englanders, my usual supplier in El Paso was not able to provide the tractor you seek. Instead, I contacted a source a great distance away, in another part of Texas. They are willing to ship it through El Paso and feel they will have no problem getting you a tractor like the one you desire. However, the model is called a John Deere. It's supposed to be a premium brand of tractor." Mr. Bergen reached inside his jacket, producing a slip of paper and handing it to the men. "Here is their price."

Jacob took the paper and looked at it with his neighbor.

"What does that word mean?" Jacob asked, pointing at the paper.

"Oh, that's nothing. That's just the name of the city where the supplier is located—Seminole."

Jacob turned to his neighbor. "Is this price acceptable?" It was understood that the buyer, acting as a middleman, had added his fee to the number.

Mr. Dueck nodded. "Yes, it is. I have the money. Do you have your half?"

"I do," Jacob replied.

The buyer smiled. "Good. I shall order it tomorrow and come to your house tonight before supper to collect the funds. If everything goes smoothly, you should have the tractor by mid-January, in plenty of time to turn your fields."

The men shook hands and the buyer left.

"That is a good price," Mr. Dueck whispered.

"I agree," Jacob replied, his mood rapidly changing. "The Englanders must be desperate to sell it. Why don't you come over to my house after lunch and we can combine our money while we wait for Mr. Bergen to visit with us."

"Yes, that's good. He will stop at your place first anyway. Now let's get home—I have some work to do after lunch."

The men patted each other on the back and started for home together.

After lunch, a happier Jacob snuck out for his afternoon smoke. When he was done, he went to his bedroom and once again quietly pulled the bed from the wall. Pushing on the special piece of wood, he stared at his glass jar.

An intense panic rose up from his stomach to his chest and settled in his heart. Sitting on the bed, he took a moment to collect himself. Then he pulled out the jar and inspected it. Dropping it on the bed, he flung open the door and raced to the kitchen, not caring if the children saw his secret hiding place.

"Judith, come now!" he ordered, his voice shaking.

Instantly, she knew something was wrong. "What is it, dear?"

He motioned for her to follow him. As soon as she walked into the bedroom and saw the empty container, she knew what it meant.

Jacob held the jar up. "The money—it's all gone!"

Days later, a group of Mennonite children were caught sneaking into another house and, after severe beatings, confessed to several thefts including Jacob's house. Unfortunately, the money was never found, and Jacob had to rent his neighbor's new tractor. It would be many more years before he could own a John Deere.

Chapter Eight

April 1936
Seminole, Texas

A long, sleek automobile pulled to a smooth stop. Its four whitewall tires seemed brand new, untouched by miles and miles of hard, dusty road. Even the spare tire made a scene, sitting smugly on the passenger's running board just behind the engine vents. More than one person turned their head as it passed by.

A man in his forties climbed out of the crimson-colored Auburn Speedster and went around to collect his passenger—a petite, younger woman. She gingerly stepped out of the vehicle, displaying her designer hat and double-strand of pearls. The man was also well dressed, wearing a Park Fifty custom-tailored suit while leaving his Dobbs hat on the dashboard.

"Come on, Birdie," he said, wrapping his arm around the little figure. "I want to get some Wrigley's. If we're going to be walking around talking all day, I'm going to need something to keep my jaw moving besides conversation."

The woman politely laughed as they walked up to a store with a sign that read *C.C. Cothes & Son – The Rexall Store.*

"Are you Mr. and Mrs. Duchene?" a voice called out.

The couple spun their heads to the left.

"That's right," the man said. "Are you Rose Henderson?"

"I am," Rose replied, moving up to the couple and shaking their hands.

"Sonny said you could show us around town, the best places to shop and eat and so forth."

Rose smiled. "Of course. I took Sonny on a tour and we had a great time."

"Well, honey, I just want to show the missus all of Seminole since she'll be the one stuck in town all day. We'll probably be here a good two weeks because I need to check on the drilling and lease up some more land. I want Birdie here to have something to do while I'm gone."

"Absolutely," Rose said. "There's plenty to do in our nice town. I think you both will find the people here very welcoming."

Mr. Duchene laughed heartily. "Darlin', I find that when I spread ten-dollar bills around, people are always welcoming."

Rose laughed nervously, not sure how to take his comment. "Would you like to start here?" she said, pointing to the drug store.

"Here? I was about to get some Wrigley's. Is a drug store part of the tour?"

"It is. Mr. C.C. Cothes bought the City Drug Store in 1917 and changed the name to what you see now. Recently, we incorporated the town and put in a new government—one with a mayor and commissioners—and Mr. Cothes was made the first mayor. Most folks call him Chunk, though. I think your wife will like shopping here. They're very friendly and carry a first-class line of drugs and sundries. It's where I shop."

Mr. Duchene opened the door. "Right now, I need to get some chewing gum. Let me do that before we start."

Rose went in with the Duchenes and escorted them around. After Mr. Duchene had purchased his gum, Rose followed them back outside and pointed down the street to an old structure. "Let's walk to the Austin house. This will give you a little history of the area."

As they got closer, Mr. Duchene noticed a car out front. "Is that an old Hupmobile?"

"It sure is," Rose said. "That's actually part of the museum. Mr. Rollins had the local franchise and sold Hupmobiles for a while. And let me tell you, Mr. Rollins was quite a man. He was a sheriff and later, a county commissioner. He also started the First Baptist Church."

Mr. Duchene chuckled. "Sounds like my kind of fellow—a man who gets things done."

Rose nodded. "He was."

They walked inside the museum.

"And this looks like the house I grew up in," Mr. Duchene remarked.

"Actually, it was built in 1904—over thirty years ago—by Emma and William Austin. They settled south of town and built this—the area's first store. It's two stories and had living quarters, a general store, hotel, and post office—which they named Caput."

"Caput?" he said. "What does that mean?"

"I've been told it's Latin for head or top. I've thought a lot about it and my best guess is it was some kind of joke. You know, they were out here all by themselves. I could just imagine them putting a sign up telling everyone, 'Hey, we're in charge here.' Of course, no one around would've understood Latin."

"You're probably right, but how did they get it to this spot?"

"In 1906, the building was cut in half at the other side of the draw where it was built and dragged by horses across the draw over a mile north to this courthouse square. It reminds us of the beginning of our town."

Birdie finally perked up. "Why did they pick that area to set up? Seems kind of lonely."

Rose acknowledged her question. "It was, I'm sure. You see, we have wells that were dug by Indians down in the draw. There's a bunch of them. They used to feed their horses and such. When the cavalry scouts found them, word got out and this area became a stopping place for folks traveling through. Trading began. To take advantage of it, hardy people like the Austins set up a store and made money."

"Brave people," Birdie added.

"Ain't no braver than people like me who go out and drill a hole deep in the ground looking for oil."

Birdie patted her husband on the shoulder. "Still, Henry, you're not likely to get shot by an Indian and have an arrow sticking out of your chest."

Mr. Duchene laughed. "Maybe not, but going broke or getting blown up don't seem too good either." He turned his attention back to Rose. "So, do you get your water from these wells?"

"No, we don't use them anymore. Instead, we have a tall windmill on the outskirts that pumps underground water into a large tank and feeds our pipes. But there's talk of our new commissioners passing some bonds to pay for a proper water supply, like the big cities have."

Mr. Duchene gave Rose the once-over. "Say, you're a pretty bright gal. Are you married?"

Birdie hit him again in his arm. "Henry, that's a personal question."

"Oh, I don't mind," Rose said. "No, I'm not married."

"I guess she just hasn't found the right one," Birdie said.

Actually, she had. His name was Charles Simpson. Yet he disappeared into a dusty night. She still remembered the moment when he took the ring—*her* ring—and drove off. It was over a year later when the sheriff called her and said there was a man in jail requesting a visit from her. She dressed up, making herself look nice, and took the long walk to jail.

Once there, she was led to a back room where, behind bars, a shirtless man huddled over a sink, washing the shaving cream from his face. When he turned around, Rose recognized his big smile. It was David Bane—Charles's close friend and business partner.

"Rose, you look even better than last time, and certainly better than anything I've seen in quite a while. I'm sorry for you to see me like this."

Rose moved up to the bars. "David, what happened? I've been desperate for any news."

He wiped his face with a rag and started buttoning his shirt. "They caught me in New Mexico, just past Hobbs. I should've gone farther like Charles told me, but I assumed I could blend in, that no one would recognize me. I was wrong."

Rose gripped the bars. "What did you do?"

He released a long sigh. "Charles and I borrowed heavily. That's how we were able to buy and lease everything. We were going so fast that we didn't always make sure of things. We didn't have a good bookkeeper."

"What are you talking about?"

"Sometimes, we accidentally sold more than one hundred percent of a lease, like a hundred twenty percent of something. Believe me, we didn't mean to, but when we found out, instead of paying back the twenty percent and moving on, we did nothing and kept going. When the market crashed, we were wiped out. That prevented us from paying anyone back, including the banks and investors."

Rose shook her head in confusion. "But I thought you were making money."

"We were. Lots of it. And paying our bills, too. Everyone was happy. People love you when you're winning and making them money. But when you start losing, trust me, they want blood—*your* blood. If they're going to lose all their money, it makes them feel good to put people in prison. That's where I'm heading."

"Oh my," Rose said, her mouth hanging open. "For how long?"

"I've worked out a deal with the government. I'll do five years in state prison. They're passing me through here so I can sign the paperwork. Then they'll ship me to Huntsville."

Rose reached through the bars and touched his cheek. "David, I'm so sorry. Have you heard anything from Charles?"

He looked around and lowered his voice. "No, we split up in New Mexico. He might've gone to the west coast, maybe even Alaska. He always talked about that. But Charles is smart. He knew I'd get caught and tell someone that, so he probably went in the opposite direction. I wouldn't be surprised if he went south to Mexico. He always liked it warmer."

"Mexico," Rose said, stepping back. "Huh."

"Why do you say that?"

She pinched her lip. "Because a few months back, we began trading with a religious sect down there, some place near Cuauhtémoc. These people speak Dutch or German. It's a strange language. The puzzle is how they found us. It's not like we have advertisements down there."

David grimaced. "Yeah, I guess it could be that Charles put a word in someone's ear. Or it might simply be happenstance. I don't know."

They stood there, saying nothing, absorbing all this. Finally, David spoke up. "How are things around here?"

It was Rose's turn to let out a long sigh. "Not good. A lot of shops have closed. A few months after the crash, several businesses posted notices in the *Seminole Sentinel* about needing their customers to come in and pay their bills. Samuel didn't want to do it, but finally gave in and posted a notice."

Rose remembered the painful words she'd helped Samuel put together:

Notice to our customers and friends: We have several accounts that are overdue. We need these customers to make payment arrangements immediately as we have been placed on a cash basis with our suppliers and thus will require cash on all purchases from now on. This also means we will be providing cash prices on all of our equipment and supplies. If current economic conditions had not made this necessary, we certainly would not be taking this step. We here at Henderson's Hardware, Implements & Harness hope you continue to stop by and see us."

After that, her aunt and uncle only took cash, although to settle up some of the accounts they agreed to take some cattle, hogs, and other animals they could sell or slaughter for food. Over time, they'd built up a small herd of animals that required tending to. All of them, including Melvin, helped out.

"I'm sorry," David said, gripping the bars. "I hear it's like that all over the country. Are you still single?"

Rose frowned. "Yes. The town gossipers spread my nasty story around, chasing away the eligible bachelors. They seem to like the new teachers who get posted to the local schools. There's been a rash of them getting married." Rose forced a smile. "I caught a few bouquets in the last year, for what good that's worth…" her voice trailing off.

David reached through the bars and grabbed her hand. "I can't tell you how sorry I am. That market collapse was a once-in-a-lifetime event. Unfortunately, it happened in our lifetime."

She hung her head. "Yeah, just my luck."

"Listen, Rose, Charles was in agony when we drove away from your house that night. We were both in a state of panic. We had so much wealth and suddenly, we had nothing. For a man, it's very shocking. Charles told me he was coming back one day to see you. I don't know when or how because with all the warrants out on him, he'll be arrested on the spot. But I truly believe he'll be back one day. Although neither of us expect you'll still be single. What are you now, twenty-one?"

"How old are you, darlin'?" Mr. Duchene said.

Rose snapped back to the present.

"Henry, it's not proper to ask a woman her age," Birdie said, hitting his arm for the third time.

"It's all right, ma'am. I'm just about to turn twenty-eight." *And with no prospects in sight,* she thought.

"Twenty-eight?! Listen here, young lady. This Seminole Pool—as they're calling it—is going to bring plenty of young, single men to this area. They'll have pockets full of cash."

"Henry!" his wife said. "Please, a lady doesn't need to think about those things."

Mr. Duchene grinned, winking at Rose. "You just keep your eyes open, darlin'."

Rose knew he was right. The town had suffered like everyone else until 1935, when oil production ramped up. Almost overnight, the Hendersons began selling John Deere tractors and equipment to the oil drillers who needed to clear roads to their drilling sites. The leaders of Seminole even talked about how the oil business was protecting the city from the worst of the Great Depression. And when drillers hit the Seminole Pool a few months earlier, the floodgates of oilmen opened up. As her aunt told her, "It's just as easy to fall in love with a rich man as it is a poor man."

"Say, honey, do they sell alcohol here?" Mr. Duchene said, licking his dry lips.

"No sir. The commission recently voted on the issue. It failed eighteen to one."

"I'd like to meet the guy who voted yes and buy him a drink!" He placed his hands on his hips. "So, you're saying I'm going to have to drive to Andrews or Lamesa for a little hooch?"

"Well," Rose responded, lowering her voice, "the commission did decide that the local doctors could prescribe whiskey for medicinal purposes." She smiled coyly. "Perhaps you have some condition that requires it."

Mr. Duchene slapped his hands together. "I'm likin' you better and better. No wonder Sonny told me about you. I don't suppose you happen to know a proper doctor who can issue a prescription—for my condition and all." He whispered, "It's to steady my nerves."

"I do. We're headed that way."

104

"Lead on, sweetheart. This tour is getting better and better."

Rose found herself laughing and having a good time with this character. It was a nice diversion.

As they walked, she took them past the North Side Barber Shop, introducing them to Leonard Nolley, the proprietor. Next was the City Cleaners and manager, O.J. Daniell, who waved his cigarette around wildly, proclaiming, "We can press your suits and dresses for only seventy-five cents!"

They continued on to Singleton Dry Goods Company and looked through the rows of products. Next was the New Palace Theatre, where they had the teller list the pictures they were showing. Finally, she took them to Dr. Turner's office, where Mr. Duchene peeled off some bills and picked up two prescriptions for him and Birdie. The doctor even directed him to a local "pharmacy" that would fill it.

"Where are you staying?" Rose asked.

Mr. Duchene pulled out some cash from his pocket. "The Hotel Texas here in town. I'm not driving to Lamesa every day. Say, how much do I owe you for this wonderful tour?"

She used to tell her customers one dollar. But with these oilmen, she'd learned to say, "Pay me whatever you want." Most of the time she received more than a dollar. One time, a man paid her ten dollars.

"Darlin'," he said, peeling off several bills, "you've done such a good job and because I want you to keep an eye on my Birdie, get her involved in some local events and all, here's twenty bucks."

"Wow, Mr. Duchene, thanks! I'll check on your wife and make sure she knows about current events. You can count on me."

"Great. I truly believe that. Now if you'll excuse us, we're going to fill our prescriptions, pick up the car, and check in to the hotel."

Rose thanked them again and watched as they headed down the street. Then she turned toward home and walked past the old First State Bank building. It had survived that terrible day in October of 1929 but couldn't survive what came after it. Finally, it closed. The bank had been such a great partner to the local businesses, providing much needed credit for everyone to grow, that everyone in the town was sad to see them go, though no one was surprised.

"How was your tour?" Aunt Mae asked as Rose came into the business office.

"Great! He paid me twenty dollars."

Aunt Mae's face registered shock. "We're going to have to start charging you rent."

Rose chuckled. "I sure hope not. I guess I need to work for my keep, so what can I do?"

Aunt Mae reached for some keys on her desk. "Can you take Melvin to the pasture and set out the feed? Samuel didn't have time this morning and is making a delivery with the truck."

"Sure," she said, taking the keys from her aunt. "We'll be right back."

Walking through the office, she found Melvin tucked away, sitting on the floor, engrossed in the alignment of dozens of marbles scattered about, like he saw a pattern. She lowered herself to her knees.

"Melvin, we need to feed the cows. Come with me." She made hand gestures as she talked.

He moaned and grunted as he got to his feet and followed her outside to the car. Rose made sure his door was closed tight before starting up the Ford. A few minutes later, they arrived at a pasture they rented from a local rancher.

The two walked to a metal shed where the hay was piled up inside. She undid the lock on the opposite side and swung open the doors. The cows were already there, behind the fence, waiting since dawn.

She handed Melvin a pitchfork and together, they started throwing the hay over the fence, where the hungry cows pounced on it.

Rose thought about all the cows. She knew it was the last thing the Hendersons wanted to own, yet they had no choice. They had made deals with farmers and ranchers to sell their equipment for stock since the tractors just sat around getting rusty. With very few people having cash, it was an arrangement born out of necessity.

The hay they received to feed the cows was yet another arrangement. Samuel had made a deal with a farmer to grow the grass with the Hendersons' tractors and give them enough hay to feed their cows until the natural grass came back in the spring, which was just about now. Samuel had also made a deal with that same farmer to grow a crop of broom corn. Broom corn was used to make brooms, which the farmer traded for anything to eat or wear. This was how difficult life was for everyone.

Rose and Melvin finished tossing the hay and put away their pitchforks. This was a time that Melvin loved. He would stand at the fence and watch the cows eat, finding some joy in seeing which cow moved the others out. To Rose, it looked like he was studying them.

While she killed time with Melvin, she thought back to Charles. Was he in Mexico? Was he spreading their name around to potential buyers? Or was it just a coincidence and he was long gone, never even thinking about her?

She recalled the dust storm that hit the night he left. They had experienced more and more storms like that. Of course, neither Rose nor anyone else at that time knew the cause: that all those plow boys who had rushed to bust up the virgin prairie sod in Kansas, Colorado, Oklahoma, and Texas had actually been responsible for this calamity. It turns out the deep-rooted grass they stripped bare was holding the soil together *and* trapping moisture. With the grass gone, the moisture disappeared. This meant less rainfall, which sent the area into a deep drought. The dirt heated up, sending plumes of thermals skyward, driving fierce winds across the land. This wind, with no grass to stop it, lifted the dirt and carried the fertile soil with it. To where? No one knew.

These "black blizzards," as some folks called them, rolled across the land, sometimes piling up dirt twenty to thirty feet high against any structure standing in its way. This fine silt found its way inside homes, where frantic housewives struggled to clean it off every possession they owned. Just north of Seminole, Texans got used to turning plates and cups over until they needed them. And everyone knew the taste of grit in their mouth. It was a terrible way to live.

Seminole and Gaines County sat on the fringe of the Dust Bowl. They didn't suffer the harshest effects as their neighbors to the north did. Still, they had their share of black blizzards. Rose knew full well that breathing a lungful of sand meant death, either immediately or months later. They called it the brown plague. Infants, children, and elderly people were especially vulnerable.

107

Rose put that out of her mind and let herself drift back to Charles. Which state would he have gone to? She wracked her brain, trying to remember the places he had talked about. Nevada? Arizona? Colorado? Based on what David told her, he probably went far away, maybe to the Northeast. Or maybe, just maybe, he did go to Mexico.

Melvin moved sideways, growing agitated. Rose snapped out of her daydreams and looked around for a calf in distress, which was his usual observation. Seeing none, she held his shoulders square and stared into his eyes. After several grunts and gestures, she took off running for an adjacent barn. Nervously fumbling with a lock, she swung it open and ran to the other side, pulling up the bolt and freeing the large door. Rose pushed hard, opening it to the pasture. This was when she felt the wind on her face, which quickened her pulse. She ran hard, not caring about the three dangerous bulls watching over the herd of females.

"Shoo!" she yelled, waving her arms, desperately trying to get the cows to stop feeding and move toward the barn. "Shoo! Shoo!"

Glancing over her shoulder, she spotted a rolling cloud on the horizon. It was large enough to kill all these cows as soon as it hit—unless she was able to get them in the barn. She had to try. Her family was counting on it because they represented food, currency, objects to be traded. Their survival now fell on her shoulders.

Suddenly, something touched her back. Certain it was a mean old bull, she recoiled in fear.

"Melvin!" she exclaimed, having lost sight of him.

He had two sticks in his hand, hitting them in such a way that the cows took notice. Cocking their heads awkwardly, they started moving. It was a miracle.

Rose stared back at the cloud—the black death—and wondered if they had a chance. Melvin continued hitting the sticks together frantically, moving the cows toward the barn.

Rose tried to guess how much longer they had before it hit. As each cow moved forward, she thought, maybe we can make it. *Maybe...*

Chapter Nine

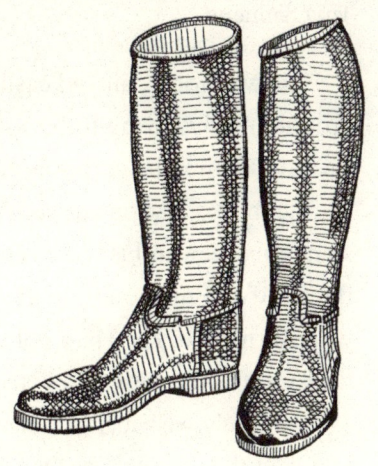

October 1941
Cuauhtémoc, Mexico

The old buggy crawled slowly along the endless flat land, following ruts from previous buggies. There were the occasional tire tracks from trucks that ventured up the mountain. They all led to the sawmill—a place where they could select the exact size and quantity of lumber they needed for a very low price.

The sawmill was run by Mexicans, having been set up two years earlier. Its owners assumed correctly that lumber would be in demand. It made sense too, with blades and belts available from U.S. suppliers at very low prices due to the staggering economic depression. Once the Mexicans ran a single line up the mountain for electricity, they could hire other Mexicans to fell and strip clean nearby trees. In no time, they spit out straight lumber and erected two buildings—one where lumber would be cut and another to store it.

To kindle the Mennonites' desire, the entrepreneurs loaded up some of their product on wagons and circulated through the campos, selling directly to the colonists. As soon as the picky Mennonites examined their product, word spread, and they started making regular trips up the mountain. By all accounts, the mill was successful.

Jacob Rempel was happy they were there. He had spent many hours planning and sanding the rough-cut lumber sold from other suppliers. It was time consuming and frustrating. But the lumber from this sawmill was well cut and square. And it was cheaper than the locals' rough product—so long as you were willing to make the journey, as Jacob was today.

His two horses moved easily, pulling the empty buggy across the level ground, rarely having to be corrected. Even though they had never made this trip before, the path was clear enough for them to follow.

Jacob was anxious to see the two-year-old mill, if only to experience something new in his increasingly tedious and tiresome life. He stared at the approaching mountain and hoped the horses would have no problem with the incline. They had not worked together, so this could be an adventure. Or it could be a simple trip.

He sorely wished Nell, his favorite horse, was in the harness, but she had died the year before. One morning, he went to the barn and Nell was sprawled out on her side. He knew something wasn't right because the horse in the adjacent stall, Jack, was highly agitated.

Jacob had flung open the stall door, fallen to his knees, and felt Nell's chest. She was gone. He remembered lying there next to her for a long while, not willing to let his precious horse go. She had survived the long train ride from Canada to this rough place and put in seventeen hard years helping him and his family survive. Nell was his best animal companion. With her gone, it was like the last piece of Canada went with her.

His eyes still watered as he remembered finally getting to his feet and dusting off the fresh hay he had put in her stall the night before. He felt for the apple in his pocket, the one he was going to give her half of. Instead, he gave it to Jack, who chewed it up quickly. Then he fetched his two oldest sons, Jacob and Bernhard, who helped him load Nell into the wagon and hitch Jack to it so he could sell the hide to the Mexicans. He would need every dollar to buy another one, which turned out to be Queen, one of the horses now hitched to his buggy. The other horse belonged to his neighbor, Mr. Dueck, who also needed some lumber from the mill. Two other neighbors had put in orders and given Jacob money, which he hoped to use to bargain a better price. Even with a good part of the return journey being downhill, both horses were needed for such a large load.

The thought of Nell swelled his eyes, but so did a lot of things lately— like his son Franz. He was born six months ago and lived less than four months. Jacob and Judith buried him in a simple pine box, made of lumber from the Mexicans' new mill. He cried at that funeral too, even though his heart had long ago prepared for such pain. After all, Judith, now forty-five, had given birth to eighteen babies, of which they had buried seven—so far. Sadly, other Mennonites had similar experiences. That's why the Mennonite coffin maker was always prosperous.

Jacob's thoughts shifted to his living children. His two oldest daughters, Helena and Anna, had married Mennonite boys and lived in different campos. His oldest son, Jacob, was dating a girl and would likely get married soon. Part of the lumber he was buying was destined for a house in Campo 105 that his son was purchasing. The house was only available because the family occupying it had loaded up a rickety truck and taken off for Canada. This was common. Relatives in the northern country wrote back telling them about another starving, desperate family from Mexico who had appeared at the Canadian border showing passports belonging to the two adults and perhaps one or two children. The rest were considered Mexican citizens, which caused headaches with the border guards. It usually took the existing Canadian Mennonites traveling a few miles to the border and putting up money or guarantees to free the frail travelers and take them to a colony for help. When the other Canadian Mennonites saw them straggle in, they lost whatever desire they may have had to go to Mexico. They also spread the news to their brothers and sisters, giving it a life of its own: "The Old Colony Mennonites in Mexico are poor and starving." That was their firm belief.

Jacob knew it was mostly true. The overwhelming majority were barely getting by. Yet it wasn't for lack of trying. There were some changes they had made that did help. One of them was growing sorghum and mixing it with the normal feed. This boosted milk quality and production. In fact, the milk was so excellent, they hauled the excess to a cheese factory he'd started at Campo 110, where it was turned into a soft white cheese known as *queso menonita* or *queso Chihuahua*. Unfortunately, the factory turned into a financial burden, so he sold half of the stock to Mr. Peters, and later all of it.

Another ray of light was apple crops. It had taken all this time for the trees to be planted and bear significant fruit, but it looked like it would soon be another Mennonite signature crop. And after delaying for several years, they had finally planted beans and corn, like the Mexican farmers did. To no surprise, the crops did well in this climate. The problem came when they tried to sell the surplus to the Mexicans. Since the Mennonites were a self-contained society, they didn't have any contacts or middlemen to help move the product. This led to heavy discounts to locals who were willing to forgo the Mexican suppliers and do business with the Mennonites. Having no bank accounts or the ability to accept drafts delayed payment, causing not only headaches, but financial losses. In time, though, they were able to find outlets for their crops and receive the going rate in cash.

Lack of water was another constant problem. At first, everyone used the community well. Once a family had some extra money, they drilled their own well. Then they discovered another problem: the depth of the water.

Jacob's neighbor just six houses away had had to drill three hundred feet down to find water. He was forced to erect a tall windmill to pump it up to the surface. Now, windmills dotted the area.

A few venturous farmers saved up their money and purchased iron pipe, which they ran to their fields. They desperately wanted to grow more than one crop per year, and water was the key. However, they were only able to irrigate a small part of their land since the volume of water was not constant and the pipe too expensive to run across their entire property. As for Jacob, he couldn't even afford one extra piece of pipe since most of his money went to funerals and weddings. It never stopped.

The path ahead began to rise, making the horses work a little harder. Still, it wasn't much work for them. Jacob weighed less than 150 pounds and the buggy wasn't much more. He clicked his cheeks to let them know he was still back there and in charge, not that they misbehaved. He could see ahead and was about to start tugging on the reins, steering them away from any danger. The last thing he needed was for one of them to take a bad step.

With an occasional tugging, it took another thirty minutes for Jacob to arrive safely at the sawmill. The loud whine from the blades pricked up the ears of his horses; a noise they had never heard before. For that matter, neither had he. In Canada and Mexico, he had always purchased lumber from a middleman, paying more for the privilege of having it dumped at his doorstep. Hopefully, this trip would be worth it.

The office was easy to spot. It was in the front of the warehouse, its entrance signified by an unpainted door propped open. Jacob guided his horses over to the hitching posts and pulled back on the reins. When the buggy stopped, he set the brake and climbed down, unhitching one horse at a time and leading it to a trough where it could drink some cool mountain water. As soon as they were satisfied, he spread some oats on the ground and set a loose rope so they could eat and move around. With his animals taken care of, he proceeded to the small office to conduct his transaction.

The Mexican inside sat at a desk and stood to greet him. "Welcome, sir," he said in rough German. "How can I be of assistance to you?"

Jacob pulled the list from his pocket. By now, he spoke decent Spanish and was able to communicate. "I'm in need of a variety of lumber. You can see the sizes here. I'm hoping with such a large order, the price will be favorable."

"Of course," the Mexican said, switching to Spanish. "We don't want you traveling all this way, only to return empty-handed. It would send a bad message to others, who might never make the trip."

This man was an excellent salesman. In one breath, he had both assured Jacob he would get a good deal while letting Jacob know that if he didn't like it, he could travel back with nothing, making this trip a complete waste. In the latter case, they'd both lose.

Jacob nodded. "I'll wait here while you see what you can do for me."

"Certainly," the Mexican said, before taking off to the back of the warehouse.

This gave Jacob a chance to walk around. Outside, he found a pipe with a lever and turned it. Water flowed out, cool and fresh, better tasting than the water from the Bustillos Valley where he lived.

He removed some kringle and a roll from his overalls, examining it. Slices of ham and onion hung over the sides of the roll. He bit into the sandwich and munched quietly, breathing in the clean mountain air. It had a touch of coolness which reminded him of Canada. Seeing all the trees around also brought back memories. Many times in the last eighteen years he had thought about loading up Judith in the buggy, and whoever else wanted to join him, and taking off for his home country like so many other Mennonites. But then he came back to reality and knew his wife would be a hard sell, along with his older children. The whole scheme was a dream, something that would never come true, especially since the pressure from the other colonists to stay was immense.

The Mexican soon returned with another piece of paper. "Mr. Rempel, we have everything you are looking for. We can load up your buggy and you can be on your way in fifteen minutes. Here is our fee for everything."

He handed the paper to Jacob, who stared at it with excitement. The price was less than half of what they paid down in the valley.

"Yes, this is excellent. Let me count out the money and you can proceed."

Sure enough, fifteen minutes later, Jacob and his happy horses were heading down the mountain with a full load. The trip home was pleasant, although he had to ride the brake at times to ensure the buggy didn't push the horses from behind. When he reached the valley, the view gave him a different perspective of their settlement. The windmills were the first thing he spotted. The trees came next, followed by the houses.

He eased the horses along the well-traveled roads near the colony until he reached Campo 101, his first customer.

Mr. Peters came out and unloaded his share of the lumber. When Jacob handed him some change, the man smiled and returned a little money. It was common to pay a small fee for a delivery like this. And with the price so low, Mr. Peters had more than enough left to pay it.

The next stop was another house in the same campo. There he met Mr. Friesen and repeated the process. This wood was destined for something joyous: a new baby cradle. His daughter Anna would rest in it until she grew older. Then, to everyone's surprise, she would catch the eye of Jacob's future grandson. But right now, Mr. Friesen just wanted his wood at a good price, and Jacob was providing that service.

The buggy made its way to Campo 105.

"Hello, son," he said, hopping down to help his son Jacob unload the lumber.

"Hello, Father. Did you get a good price?"

"Very good," he replied, handing him the extra money. It was also understood that family didn't pay a delivery fee, not that Jacob would've taken any money from his own son. "Did you talk to the Ältester?"

"Yes. He said he will put my name down. Do you think I have a chance?"

"Son, I think you do. Everyone knows your grandpa and great-grandpa were chosen as Ältesters. If they study your lineage and your interest in it, they will know you qualify. And they all realize it takes stamina to stand up there for two and a half hours reading the sermons. Really, it's a job for a young person."

His son smiled. "Let's get this wood inside. I need to make some repairs."

"Of course," Jacob replied. "I will help you."

⋙◆⋘

It was Sunday and the colonists filed into the church. The men, having removed their homemade overalls and boots, wore good quality black suits and took their places on the right side of the church. The women assumed their places on the left, with everyone sitting on hard wooden benches. Above them hung a rack with long pegs protruding outward. This gave the men a place to store their straw cowboy hats, ensuring they didn't disappear.

Seated on the pulpit was the Ältester. Before the service began, he approached the podium and raised his hands. "Brethren, the results of the election are in. You have elected one among you to be your preacher. He shall faithfully carry out his duties under the watchful eye of God. He shall have all of the responsibilities of a preacher and shall attend the weekly meetings alongside myself and the other preachers. And now, to announce your new preacher."

The worshippers fell silent, waiting for the Ältester to speak. Slowly, he removed a slip of paper from his jacket pocket and unfolded it. After clearing his throat, he spoke. "The man who has been selected is Jacob Wiebe Rempel."

Jacob watched as his son stood and received congratulations from the men around him. The Wellington boots that every preacher wore—the

115

armor of God—would soon be covering his son's legs. He knew it was something his son wanted. The boots alone commanded respect.

After Jacob made his way to the pulpit, the Ältester shook his hand and congratulated him before turning back to the congregation. "We must say a prayer to bless him and his time as preacher. Please kneel."

They dropped to their knees.

"Please repeat after me—Heavenly Father, we ask for Your blessings, Your wisdom, and Your protection for our brother Jacob Wiebe Rempel. Please guide him and keep him strong. Do through him what You wish for us. Amen."

He again shook Jacob's hand and let him take his seat before the singing began.

The next week, Jacob would take his place at the pulpit and read one of the many recycled sermons that dealt with subjects like suffering or perseverance or obedience. But for now, he basked in the warm glow of admiration, looking out to the congregation and seeing his male friends smiling and nodding their heads. What the new preacher didn't realize was that they weren't so much smiling because they were happy for him, but because they were thankful it wasn't them.

Chapter Ten

February 1943
Seminole, Texas

Twenty men stood around in loose groups, talking and smoking cigarettes. Most all of them had on winter coats with the collars turned up. The frigid wind carried the smoke from their cigarettes and the vapor from their breath toward the approaching bus. This was the bus that would take them away, away from their friends and family, away from Seminole, away from their home.

A young man moved to the curb and clapped his hands. He was Pastor Curtis at the First Baptist Church.

"May I have your attention please!" he yelled, his hands raised high in the air.

It was a large group he was shouting to, and included parents, siblings, and even girlfriends. Several others were townspeople who had shown up to wish the boys well. Rose Henderson was among them.

It was nine a.m. and the bus was almost there. They could see the driver's face.

Pastor Curtis continued. "I want to say a prayer before you get on the bus. So please, may I have your attention."

This last plea did the trick and the crowd was silenced.

"Dear Heavenly Father, we ask for Your blessings and protection for our boys from Gaines County. Please guide them and keep them strong. Please help them to lead good Christian lives and bring them back home to us. Amen."

The twenty men turned to their mothers, fathers, and girlfriends to say goodbye. Kisses were plentiful with more than a few teary eyes, for these men were draft inductees and about to board a bus headed for the Fort Sill Induction Center.

These gatherings took place each month, with this being the fourteenth one since Japan bombed Pearl Harbor. There would be many more—too many.

Rose mingled with several families, hugging the boys and consoling their loved ones. When the bus finally stopped, she and another woman handed each man a care package from the Women for Victory group. Each package contained paper, envelopes, and stamps, along with homemade food and other local items. It was a little something to remind them of home.

Once the men were on the bus, she stood with the others waving goodbye. All these men would eventually return home on this same bus, with at least two of them stowed below in caskets. Every Texas county experienced this.

Rose pulled her coat tighter and walked with Mrs. Floyd Stark to their next appointment. The same women's group responsible for the care packages was meeting at Mrs. Singleton's house to work on their knitting quota. The Red Cross, in conjunction with the War Production Board, had issued a quota for each county. The local women were heavily encouraged to knit the items needed: gloves, mufflers, and turtleneck sweaters. Mrs. Stark headed up the effort, rotating get-togethers three to four times a week at different places. The idea was that each woman in Seminole—and the rest of Gaines County—would come to at least one meeting each week and help knit. It was also an excellent time for local gossip to be served, along with tea, coffee, and whatever snacks they could make from the rationed goods.

"How did it go?" one of the ladies asked.

"Like always," Mrs. Stark said. "Brave faces with tears."

Rose held up two packages. "We had these left over since two of the boys were picked up in Lubbock. Where should I put them?"

"Just set them on the cabinet over there," Mrs. Singleton said. "We'll take out the food and ready them for next month's induction. Now sit down and start knitting. We can use your help."

Rose took the long needles from her purse and joined seven other women, all weaving together strings from olive-colored balls of yarn. It was the color the military specified.

"Rose, are you dating one of those boys that just left?" Mrs. Temrill asked.

"No. I'm afraid they're all too young for me."

Mrs. Temrill lowered her spectacles and stared at Rose. "Too young? You can't be over twenty-five, dear."

Rose knew she looked young, having spent most of her time indoors, unlike many of these women who were older and more weathered from the outdoor manual labor they had to endure in the 1920s and '30s.

"I'm thirty-three."

Though everyone else knew, Mrs. Temrill didn't. She was almost seventy and could barely see, so everyone else looked young to her.

Mrs. Clark changed the subject. "Did you read in the *Sentinel* that our last corn crop was the biggest in county history?"

"Yes, I saw that," Mrs. Stark said. "It also claimed the temperature dropped to one degree above zero several nights ago. I sure remember that. I went to check on the chickens and they were all huddled together instead of sitting on their own roost. I've never seen that before."

Mrs. Higbie nodded. "Yes, animals will continually surprise you. When I was growing up, I had a favorite pig named Henry. He would take his right hoof and scratch out a line whenever he wanted something. One was for food. Two was for water. Three lines meant he wanted me to scratch him all over. It was the darndest thing. He was really smart."

"What happened to him?" Mrs. Temrill asked.

"One day my dad said he had to shoot Henry. It was time, he said. I grabbed his leg begging him not to do it, but he dragged me all the way outside. When he finally shook me off, he had the rifle in his hand and before I could catch him, I heard the gunshot. By the time I got there, I knew Henry was gone. But then I saw seven or eight scratches all perfectly in row. He had never done so many. To this day I believe he knew he was going to get shot. Maybe he was begging me to save him or just saying goodbye. I don't know which it was. I cried for days. Eventually, though,

I got used to death. All the chickens, pigs, hogs, and cows. You can't be a farmer without death."

"I've only killed chickens," Rose said. "But when we took cattle for trade, one time a black blizzard came up fast and Melvin and I had to get the cows into the metal shed before it hit. We thought they all made it in as we waited out the storm with the cows, praying they wouldn't crush us against the railing. When it finally passed, we opened the doors and let them back out. That's when I heard some moaning.

"In the confusion, one of the baby cows had crashed into the fence and was cut up bad, almost dead. There was no way to save it. I had to run and get a knife from the truck and cut its throat to stop the suffering. I stood there and cried like a baby until a cow came up and licked the dead calf. That was her baby. I just put my arm around her and we stood there together mourning for a while. Then Uncle Samuel showed up and helped me load the calf into his truck. We took him to our house and slaughtered it. Back then nothing was wasted."

"And nothing's going to be wasted today," Mrs. Stark said. "Not during this war effort. Which reminds me, ladies, we are about to get our second set of rationing books. This one covers canned, bottled, and frozen fruits, vegetables, and juices along with dried soups and fruits. So be prepared. Each housewife will have to list out what foods she has on hand and swear to it before she gets her books. They want us using up what we have before we buy more. They really need all the food they can get. After all, those boys can really eat."

Several women chuckled as a few took the opportunity to pour a cup of hot tea or coffee.

Mrs. Singleton put down her needles for a moment. "Say, did you hear about those gypsies that came through last week? They were reading everyone's palms and charging a dollar for it. 'Tell you your future,' they said. Such a nasty paganistic ritual if I ever saw one."

Another lady agreed. "Yes, one night I saw a line out the door. They were set up at the Richards-Mitchell building. It was something else!"

"That's right," Mrs. Singleton went on. "But after they left town, all sorts of things were missing from the building. Sheriff Trimble tracked them down and arrested five of them. They had gasoline rationing books, duplicate license tags and plates, things they could sell on the black market. The *Seminole Sentinel* listed it all out. We're just lucky they didn't get away with it."

Rose added her thoughts. "Must be crummy fortune tellers if they couldn't even predict they'd be caught."

The women howled with laughter.

Mrs. Temrill bit into a sweet. "Say, these butter cookies are good, Fay. You always make the best."

"Thank you. I can give you the recipe, but since the rationing is tightening up, you may have a hard time getting the sugar."

"Oh, an old lady like me can always get a little extra sugar."

The women grinned as they drank their coffee and tea and knitted. Before long, talk drifted back to the war.

"Did you hear about those Belew boys?" Mrs. Singleton said.

"No, what happened?" Rose asked.

"They have three boys in the service, and one of them wrote back to say he was fighting on Guadalcanal. Their camp was bombed by the Japs, but they decided to leave up the tents and other structures and move a half mile away. Now the Japs keep bombing the same camp twice a day, thinking they are still there. That's real smart."

"Yes, I heard about that," Mrs. Stark added. "He also said eight hundred natives approached them and wanted to join the Marines." She glanced at Rose. "Weren't you dating one of those Belew boys?"

"No. I was teaching him to dance so he could ask out another girl. That's the story of my life."

"Pretty girl like you? Why, you're going to catch the eye of one of those rich oilmen."

"The teachers always beat me to them," she said.

"When this war's over, you'll have your pick of the litter. Just you wait and see."

Rose stopped knitting. "I'm afraid this war could go on for a long time."

The women frowned and shook their heads, for they all knew what that meant.

"Rose, I need your help." It was her uncle, who had just come from the shop.

"Sure, what can I do?" she replied.

"We received another order from those Mennonites down in Mexico. I need you to go over this order and draft a telegram replying to them. Then I want you to take it to the telegraph office and send it."

"Of course. I'll do it right now."

He handed the order to her. "As you know from the past orders, they don't use the rubber tires even though we send the tractors with them. But this time, because the tractor is not being used in food production for the war effort, I can't send it with the tires. Instead, I'm wrapping the rims with wood to protect them during shipping. When they receive it, they'll install some metal fins, but the rims must be in good shape for them to do so. I want you to explain why there are no rubber tires. Also, explain how the price will be reduced to compensate for that. Tell them how we are rationing everything, including rubber and metal. I have a lot of spare parts but may run out of them at some point, depending on the government. I just want them to be aware of what we are up against."

"Okay," Rose said, "I know what to do. How did your meeting go?"

"Great. I think these politicians understand that our business must be exempt from all the rationing rules. They need us to keep the farmers in business."

"Do we have enough tractors to sell?"

"With the tractors on hand and the ones that have already been produced before they turned the factories over to the War Production Board, I think we have enough to get us by for a few years. But if the war lasts longer than that, we may have to go back to a horse-drawn plow. I sure hope not."

Rose had read that all the automobile and tractor factories were now manufacturing jeeps, tanks, and transport vehicles. Government officials were overseeing all aspects of manufacturing, ensuring that everything was used for the war effort.

"I hope not, too. I'll get started on this right now and run it over to the telegraph office. I'll take Melvin, if that's okay."

"Sure," Samuel said. "And that reminds me, I gave one of those war bond pins to him and I've lost mine. I have a speech tonight and would like to wear it. Can you track that down for me?"

"I'll try. Are you selling some bonds?"

Samuel explained that Gaines County was selling more than expected. "With the crops being good and oil production bringing in all that extra money, people understand the need to buy them. If we lose the war, our money will be no good anyway. So, we might as well lend it to the government."

Rose had heard this speech countless times before. Once he got started, it was hard to stop him. When he paused to take a breath, she slipped past him to a desk just off the dining room, sitting down to compose the telegram.

Once that was done, she went to round up Melvin, but ran into her aunt.

"Where are you going?" Aunt Mae asked.

"I'm heading to the telegraph office," Rose told her. "Do you need anything in town?"

"No, but I just made some muffins. Can you drop them off for Fanny Bingham? It's her birthday today."

"Of course. I'm taking Melvin. He enjoys the telegraph office, and it's rare that I go there."

"That's fine, dear. He's in his room last time I checked. How was the sendoff?"

Rose slumped her shoulders. "Like all the others. Nervous and sad all mixed into one."

"Did you knit with the ladies?"

"Yes, I did. I heard that one of the Belew boys wrote back and is fighting in the Pacific. He's okay, but it sounds like there's lots of killing and bombs."

Aunt Mae lowered her voice to a whisper. "I never thought I'd see the day when I'd be grateful for Melvin's condition. Yet here we are, with all these boys going off to fight and God knows how many won't come back alive. At least I know Melvin won't be going."

Rose nodded. "You're right. I never thought about it like that."

Aunt Mae handed her the muffins. "Give these to Fanny with my love and best wishes. She has two boys in the war and with her husband in

Washington drawing up plans for more attack planes, she's lonely. Please invite her to your knitting sessions, even if she just sits there. She can make conversation, at least."

"I'll do that," she said, leaving her aunt to find Melvin.

A short time later, they both arrived at the telegraph office, hustling in to avoid the cold, biting wind. Even though the sun was out, it felt colder than earlier, when she had wished good luck to the boys leaving for Fort Sill.

Ed Lamont ran the telegraph office and greeted her. "Hello, Rose. You're sure a nice sight to brighten my day. What can I do for you?"

"Thank you, Mr. Lamont," she said, blushing. He was at least fifteen years older, but he was single. "I have a telegram to send to the Mennonites down in Mexico again. Here it is."

He studied the message and turned around. "Alfred, send this out."

"Yes sir," the young man said, taking the paper to a back office.

"He'll count the words and bring back an invoice. Say, are those muffins for me?"

"No, they're for Mrs. Bingham. It's her birthday today."

He slapped the counter. "Well, just my luck! I was going to take a telegram to her from Mr. Bingham wishing her happy birthday. Can you do that for me?"

"Of course," Rose replied. "We need to save gas whenever we can."

"Actually, I was going to send poor Alfred by foot, so we just saved him the trip and possibly some frostbite. How's Melvin doing?"

Melvin stood in the corner staring at the poster of Morse code. He was mesmerized by patterns and lists. Next to the poster were sheets of photos and sketches of wanted criminals, just like at the post office. A few years earlier, they had taken down Charles's picture. Although she said nothing about it, Rose had been very relieved.

"He just takes each day for what it's worth. You know how it is."

Mr. Lamont moved down the counter, closer to Melvin. "How old is he?"

"He's thirty."

"Barely looks a day over twenty. Just like you."

Rose turned her head and blushed again. That's when Melvin began getting agitated.

"Did I say something?" Mr. Lamont asked.

"No. Sometimes he senses events that are happening—things we can't see."

She grabbed Melvin's shoulders and turned him to face her, staring into his eyes. "What is it?"

He made signals with his hands, grunting and moaning.

Rose turned back to Mr. Lamont. "I'm afraid it's bad news."

Mr. Lamont looked confused until Alfred appeared from the back office and handed a telegram to his boss. As Mr. Lamont read it, a deep frown appeared.

"Oh no. Today of all days."

"What is it?" Rose asked. "Can you tell me?"

He let the message drop to the counter. "The military chaplain is away at Lubbock for some kind of meeting. He won't be back for two days and I can't hold it until then."

Rose covered her mouth. "Is it someone I know?"

He sighed heavily. "Mrs. Bingham. They've lost their oldest boy, Clarence. Somewhere in New Guinea. His platoon was attacked, and he was killed in action. Oh my, this is terrible. Just last week I got one that said Rufus Teague was being held prisoner by the Japs. His anti-aircraft regiment on Corregidor was captured. You know the Teagues. They live on a farm northwest of here. Rufus has a cousin here in town, Mrs. W. H. Burns. And he joins Buford Cooksey, a corporal from Seagraves who was already captured. At least their boys are still alive."

"This is terrible!" Rose said. "What do we do?"

"We need to fetch one of the reverends from the Baptist or Methodist church."

Rose held her hand out. "I'll go and get him. Then I'll pick up Mrs. Stark, too. She knows what to say in times like this. And if it's okay, I'll let Melvin stay here and pick him up on the way back."

"Sure, that'll be fine. But please give Mrs. Bingham my condolences. Twice a week I deliver telegrams from her husband. I have to think he knows by now."

Rose spent some time explaining to Melvin what was going on. Assured that he understood, she buttoned her coat and put on her gloves.

"Thank you for doing this, Rose. Really, I can't tell you how much I appreciate it."

"Mr. Lamont, my grandpa told me stories of the Indian wars and how they settled the west. If this war is anything like his stories, it's going to be a long one, and we'll lose a lot of boys."

"You may be right. But we can always pray you're wrong."

Chapter Eleven

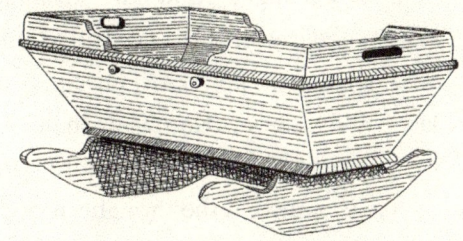

May 1946
Cuauhtémoc, Mexico

Jacob guided his horse through the main avenue of Campo 105, surveying the houses. The morning air was warm and dry, though later, it would be hotter. He was grateful for the cool shade cast by tall trees on either side of the road, their large canopies reaching far into the street. The decent weather and shade made his ride enjoyable, even if each leaf was covered with a fine layer of dust.

Jacob remembered twenty-four years ago when this entire plain had been flat as a griddlecake. They had planned to plant trees along each side of this very road so one day, it would look just like this. In fact, every campo had large trees lining its main street, with only a few gaps here and there where lightning or disease had claimed the unlucky tree. With the weathered facades on every house and the rows of trees, it looked as if the land had been like this forever.

Jacob counted the houses. He was looking for the seventh one on the right—his son's house. Now that they went to separate churches, he didn't see him as much. He made this trip every month to remedy that.

As Jacob neared the place, it seemed like yesterday that he and Judith were attending his son's wedding. The girl he was dating when he bought his house went back to Canada with her family, so he took an interest in Katharina Giesbrecht. She was staying with a family, helping out with their daily chores because they had a young child to care for. A few months later, Jacob and Katharina were engaged, and then married.

To Jacob, they seemed like a good match. For Mennonites, marriage was like a partnership. Submission was the key. It was what God wanted. Still, his son appeared to have strong feelings for his new wife, which was always preferable. Birth control was not allowed so they could have as many children as possible. Thus far, two daughters had been born to young Jacob and his bride: Katharina (named after her mother) and Maria. Now, she was very pregnant with a third. Hopefully, it would be a boy.

Jacob smiled at the thought of a grandson as he eased Queen over to the railing and tied her up. No sooner had his foot hit the ground than he heard loud moaning from inside his son's house. He quickened his step and knocked on the door. A woman ran to the door and opened it. "Mr. Rempel, please come in." It was a neighbor.

"Is my son here?"

"No, I'm sorry, he's not. He's attending a meeting with the other preachers."

"How is my daughter-in-law?"

The lady rubbed her hands nervously. "She just went into labor and is struggling. This is a difficult pregnancy. I'm afraid I must attend to her. Could you keep an eye on the children?"

"Certainly," Jacob said as she took off for the bedroom.

He went to one of the bedrooms, where three-year-old Katharina sat playing with a toy. Her little sister, Maria, was crawling around in a crib, trying to get out.

Jacob patted Katharina on the head. "And how are you doing this bright morning?"

"Papa!" she managed, since her vocabulary had not fully developed.

He bent down and kissed her several times. "Are you playing with your toys?"

"*Jo*," she responded, showing him her doll.

"That's very nice. And how's your sister?"

Katharina ignored his comment, so Jacob reached into the crib and lifted the little girl up. She smiled and pinched his clean-shaven skin.

"How are you, Maria?"

The fifteen-month-old giggled and slobbered while he kissed her several times. He had just set her down when the neighbor appeared, out of breath.

"Mr. Rempel! I need you to get the midwife. The bleeding is too much."

"Has her water broke?" he asked.

"Not yet."

"I'll go immediately."

He sprinted as fast as his fifty-one-year-old body would go. Undoing the rope, he placed his foot in the saddle and lifted himself up.

"Let's git!" he commanded as he pulled the reins to the side. Queen twisted around and pointed in the direction of the road. That's when Jacob shook the reins several times and kicked her ribs, setting her into a trot, followed by a gallop. The horse was rarely asked to run, so Queen instinctively knew it was urgent.

Jacob was halfway to his destination when a light sandstorm came up out of nowhere. This happened several times a month, especially in May and June. He pulled out a bandana and covered his mouth and nose with it. The horse, tossing her head from side to side, was having a harder time.

During a particularly strong gust, Jacob pulled into a stranger's yard and took shelter behind the barn. This allowed him a chance to get down and wipe away some of the sand that had accumulated in Queen's lower eyelids. He checked the horse's nostrils and cleared some sand from them. Once the wind died down, he hopped back up and continued on.

Ten minutes later, he arrived at the midwife's house. Jacob tied up Queen and ran to the front door. After pounding on it several times and receiving no answer, Jacob turned the knob and found the door unlocked. He stepped inside and yelled, "Hello! Is anyone here?"

There was no reply.

Jacob stood on the front porch and looked around. The house to the east appeared busy with activity so he hustled over and knocked on that door. A red-faced woman wearing an apron answered. "Can I help you?"

"My name is Jacob Rempel. I need the midwife but she's not home. Do you know where she is?"

"I do. Their son was held up last night by robbers and Mr. and Mrs. Bartch went over there to console them."

Jacob clenched his fists. Robbers, either Mexicans or Mennonites, had been bursting into homes wearing sheets and bandanas to disguise their faces. Their usual procedure was to beat a few of them before pulling out a gun and forcing one of the adults to show them where the money was hidden. Some Mennonites held out while others gave in rather quickly. Since they didn't use banks, it was a continuing problem.

"I understand," he said, frustrated. "May I have a piece of paper and a pencil? I need to leave a note."

"Yes, of course. Please come in."

Jacob removed his cap and followed her to the kitchen.

"Here you are, Mr. Rempel," she said, handing him the items.

He scrawled out a quick note. "Here's your pencil back and thank you for your hospitality." Without waiting for a reply, he rushed outside and over to the midwife's house, where he shoved the note between the door and the jamb. Then he climbed aboard Queen and left as fast as he could.

Jacob had the horse in a trot as he pondered what to do next. Without warning, the previous sandstorm revived. Caught between traveling to another midwife much farther away or heading to his son's meeting, he decided to do neither. Queen couldn't hold up in this weather with sand blowing straight at her. Instead, he wheeled the horse around and put the wind at her back. If the wind direction held, he would head to his son's house and hope for the best.

The horse had galloped a good distance before the wind's intensity increased, stinging Jacob and his horse from behind. When the wind shifted directions, Queen slowed, not wanting to go on. Feeling the sand pelting his left side, Jacob knew he was beat.

He reined the horse over to another stranger's house and made for the barn, which had some activity inside.

"Hello!" Jacob yelled out. "May I shelter my animal in your barn?" He was already off his horse and leading it through the opening.

"Certainly," the farmer said, dropping a pitchfork. "Bring her over here." He pointed to a water trough.

Queen shook her head several times as she drank from the trough. Without asking, the farmer dipped a rag in the water and wiped Queen's eyes, letting some of the moisture rinse them out. Gobs of sand and mucus appeared, which he gently wiped away.

"There. She should be fine in a few minutes as she clears the rest of the sand."

"Thank you, sir," Jacob said, moving toward the man. "My name is Jacob Rempel."

The farmer shook his hand. "Nice to meet you. My name is Mr. Schmitt. Where are you heading?"

Jacob dusted the sand off his clothes. "I was fetching the midwife, but she was gone and not likely to come back in time."

"Where is she?" Mr. Schmitt asked.

Jacob explained.

"Ah, yes," Mr. Schmitt said. "It's terrible. If dealing with the harsh conditions isn't enough, now we have these robbers. I hear some Mennonites are hiding a small sum of money in one spot that they can give to these criminals while their other money is put away somewhere else."

"Yes," Jacob said, "and one of my neighbors won't even tell his wife where it is. He's prepared to hold out through the beatings."

"He might die then. It hasn't happened yet, but I fear it's only a matter of time."

Jacob shook his head in disgust. "I've heard that some of them are colonists, though it's hard to believe."

"I'm afraid sin is among all of us, brother."

The wind's howling forced the farmer to close and lock his barn door.

"I guess we're stuck in here. I'm sorry you can't help your daughter-in-law, but it's all in God's hands."

"Yes, of course," Jacob said, hanging his head. "If He wanted me there He would stop the storm."

They stood in place for a while, saying nothing until the farmer pulled out a long bench. "Please take a seat," he said to his guest.

The two men sat there listening for the wind to die down, but it was relentless. It might be minutes or hours before he could travel again.

The farmer spoke first. "You know, the cattle rustling is still bad around here, despite all the precautions we have taken."

"Yes, that's true. I'm thankful I haven't lost a cow yet. It would be devastating if I did."

"I don't know how it is at your campo, but here, many families have left. It's not just the robbers and theft that's chasing them away. There's no more land for their children to buy. And the land we have can't support two and three generations. There are just too many mouths to feed."

Jacob nodded. His son had told him the population of Mennonites had swelled to 12,000. This was up from the original 7,000 that had come down to Mexico, including both the Swift Current and Manitoba colonies. And it accounted for all the deaths and families going back to Canada. But putting aside this land shortage, there was still pressure from the Mexicans to leave. "They don't pay taxes," said the Mexicans. Now that he understood Spanish, Jacob had heard this complaint and many more.

Jacob finally stood and went to the barn door. Opening it up a crack, he saw the storm was still blowing hard. He closed it and paced around the barn. A large pile of potatoes drew his attention. "It looks like your potato crop did well."

"Yes, they seem to take to this soil."

Jacob inspected a few of them. "I'm going to plant some next year, I believe."

"You won't be disappointed."

Jacob moved to a new John Deere tractor. "How is this holding up?"

"I've been happy with it—so far. And it takes only seven days to get parts from the dealer in Texas. Now that their war is over, they have enough metal to make them."

"Where in Texas is the dealer located?"

"A town called Seminole. They also started shipping the rubber tires again, though none of us can use them."

"Maybe the tires can be sold to the Mexicans..." Jacob said but his words trailed off as the farmer surprised Jacob by jumping up and running to the barn door. Opening it slightly, he peered outside before flinging it wide.

"This is your chance!" the farmer yelled. "The wind has died down."

Jacob was way ahead of him. His feet slid into the stirrups as he kicked Queen. "Let's git!" he commanded as the horse responded. "Thanks for the hospitality," he yelled as they galloped by.

Once he was on the main avenue, he pushed the horse to its limits. There was an occasional gust of sand-filled wind, but nothing they couldn't handle. Queen, sensing the importance of the mission, worked hard to deliver her passenger to the proper destination.

It took a good ten minutes to arrive, but when he did, he slowed Queen to an easy gait and hopped down, leading her to the barn where his son had an extra stall. Once a sweating Queen was secured, Jacob ran to the house.

He rushed up the steps inside and heard nothing. The silence caused his heart to drop. He had lost so many children it was a pain he was almost used to. But his son hadn't lost anyone—yet. This would be his first.

"Hello?" Jacob said softly. "Is anyone here?"

Footsteps from his son's bedroom sounded, followed by the neighbor he had seen earlier.

"Mr. Rempel! Is the midwife with you?"

"No, she was consoling her daughter. She won't be coming. Am I too late?"

"No, you'll be happy to know the baby came right after you left. And it's a healthy boy!"

"What? Really?" Jacob stepped back to make sure he was hearing her words properly.

"Yes. Would you like to see him?"

"Of course."

She led him into the bedroom where his daughter-in-law rested, her head propped up with a pillow and her rosy cheeks next to a tiny baby.

"Katharina, are you okay?"

"Yes," she replied. "We thought there might be a problem, but there wasn't. Would you like to hold him?"

"Absolutely!" Jacob said, inspecting his shirt sleeves and overalls. He had dusted himself off in the barn and was about as clean as he was going to get. He had held eighteen babies from his wife and the first two from his daughter-in-law. He felt confident he could handle it.

"Here you go. Meet your grandson—David Giesbrecht Rempel."

"David. That's a wonderful name."

Jacob picked up the baby and brought him close to his chest. His tiny fingers moved all around, trying to grab at anything he could find. A smile

133

stretched from ear to ear on Jacob's weathered face. He rocked little David for a few minutes until the neighbor spoke up.

"Mr. Rempel, would you step out for just a moment? I must clean Katharina up and make sure she is well."

"Of course."

He took his grandson out in the hall and let the neighbor close the door behind him. Jacob was pleased with how happy the baby acted. He seemed content.

Jacob glanced both ways down the hall to make sure he was alone with his grandson. Then he brought little David right up to his lips and whispered, "I'm going to make you this promise: You will have a better life than me. I'm going to find a way to get you out of this place. I promise you that! But first, you need to grow up big and strong."

He kissed the child on the forehead and, with a gentle rocking motion, put him to sleep.

Chapter Twelve

July 1949
Seminole, Texas

Rose placed the wet cloth on Velma's forehead as her good friend wailed. Her screams were ear-piercing. At the foot of the bed was a midwife, solemnly waiting in silence for the baby to crown. Velma gripped the sheets and screamed again. "Aaaaaaiiiiiiii!!"

"That's it, dear," Rose said. "Let it out. Just let it all out."

She took the cloth off, dipped it in a bowl of cool water, and wrung it out before returning it to Velma's forehead. This brought a new round of screaming.

"I see the head," the midwife said. "Keep pushing, Velma! Keep pushing!"

Rose stood back as her friend arched her body and screamed. This cycle went on for another fifteen minutes until there was one final blood-curdling shriek. When it stopped, her friend fell back, crushing the pillow with her head as she took in huge gulps of air.

"I've got it," the midwife yelled. "And it's a boy!"

Rose touched her friend's shoulder and smiled. "Congratulations, Velma. You have a boy."

Velma gave her a quick smile before closing her eyes in exhaustion.

The midwife cut the umbilical cord and tied a knot while the baby boy made soft noises. But he wasn't crying. Not yet.

When he was cleaned up, the midwife wrapped a small blanket around him and brought the baby to Velma's chest. By now she had recovered enough to hold him and kiss his warm cheek.

"Our first boy," she said in one breath. "Wait until Dan finds out."

"Do you want me to go tell him?" Rose asked. "He's pacing around outside."

"Yes, that would be nice."

"But don't let him come in," the midwife added. "I have to clean her up. It will take some time."

Rose stopped at the bedroom door and gazed back at the scene. There was Velma, holding a little boy, his arms waving and fingers clenching. It was a perfect picture of life's beginning.

Quietly, she closed the door, passing by the room of their two-year-old daughter, who was being watched by a neighbor. This girl and the new boy were part of the emerging baby boomer generation—children born to families when the war was over and the soldiers returned. This classification fit Velma and her husband, Dan.

Dan Shuler had served proudly in the United States Air Force, dropping bombs on European factories and troops until they surrendered on May 7, 1945. When the wave of men returned, a tidal wave of children ensued. Any business dealing with baby products was doing extremely well.

Rose opened the front door and saw Dan pacing back and forth, smoking another cigarette. She remembered him as a young boy, calling on Velma before he left Seminole. Rose, whose house was next to Velma's, used to talk to Dan a lot. But that was before the war and before the newlyweds purchased a house two streets over. Now, he was a chiseled man. The war had that effect on every boy who left and returned.

Dan had his back to the house but turned around when he heard the door close. "Any progress?" he asked nervously.

Rose nodded as she made her way down the steps. Once she was standing in front of him, she gave him the news. "Dan, you have a healthy baby boy."

He grabbed her shoulders. "A boy?! Are you sure?"

"Yes," she said, smiling. "I saw him myself. The midwife is cleaning her up now. They'll tell you when you can come in and see him. It won't be long."

He released her and stepped back, staring at the orange morning sky. "A boy! I'll be able to play catch with him. Take him to his first baseball game. Teach him how to fish. I can't believe it. I'm so happy."

"Do you have a name picked out?"

"I wanted David, but Velma wants Paul. Since she's the one doing the heavy lifting, I'll go with Paul."

"Paul's a nice name," Rose said. "Very biblical. Of course, so is David."

Before he could reply, the midwife stuck her head out the door. "Rose, I need you to run to the drugstore and pick up a list of items I have for you. Dan, you can see your new boy after you give Rose ten dollars—Velma's orders."

They all chuckled as he pulled out his wallet and gave her the money.

"I'll bring you back the change," she told him.

"Sounds like my daughter fifteen years from now," as he let the screen door slam behind him.

Rose laughed to herself and decided to make the walk to Cothes Drug Store, as their name had been shortened to. Reeves Cothes, the pharmacist, had also fought in the war. He was unlikely to be working on the Fourth of July and thankfully, her list didn't include any prescription drugs.

As she reached the end of a long block, she spotted the new Seminole High School building in the distance. It was a massive structure that was ready for the fall class of 1949. She had heard that some folks passing through town thought it was a college campus. When they were told it was just a high school, they couldn't believe it.

The high school also reminded her of Grandpa because they had an Indian for a mascot. Rose laughed to herself. If Grandpa could only see that, he'd give back his Indian Wars medal. Or maybe not.

As she neared the courthouse, she observed two boys trying to remove the gas cap from a truck. They were young, perhaps six and eight. She passed by them and found what she needed in Cothes Drug Store. On the way back, the kids were still there, but now they had a tube stuck down the tank. She shook her head. There was always something going on in Seminole.

Rose had made it a short distance away when a blast knocked her flat on her stomach. With dirt in her face and ears pounding, it was hard to clear her mind. She struggled to her feet and turned around to see what had caused the blast. That's when she saw the two boys on their backs, their clothes smoking. She picked up her bag and ran to them.

It was bad. Most of their clothes were completely burned. The exposed skin was either a deep red or charred black. She knelt next to the oldest boy. He was moaning, too stunned to cry.

"Can you hear me?" she said several times.

He was nonresponsive, his eyes rolling around.

She moved over to the other boy and he was the same way. That's when she noticed a small flame coming from the truck's gas pipe. Jumping to her feet, she dragged each boy another fifty feet away, then knelt back down to tend to them. Rose did what she could to comfort the boys, but it was clear they were seriously injured.

By now, several bystanders were there, including her uncle.

"What happened?" he asked Rose. She told him what she knew. "You go on," he said. "I'll take it from here."

Finding it hard to speak, she nodded and backed away as a siren screamed several streets away. A minute later, a fire truck roared up spraying water everywhere. This was followed by an ambulance. Rose watched all this for a few minutes more before leaving the scene and letting the professionals do their work.

She staggered back to the Shulers' and dropped off the package. They had all heard the explosion and wondered what had happened. After she told them, they looked sick, the same way she felt.

Twenty minutes later, Rose was in her room cleaning up. She shakily splashed cold water on her face to remove the nightmarish images burned into her mind. The explosion had been a disturbing sight, not just for her but for the bystanders who came to help.

Aunt Mae was sitting in the living room with Melvin when Rose arrived home. She wanted to know all about the explosion and once again, Rose told the story. Of course, her aunt was shocked.

"I thank God Melvin was never fascinated with matches or fire," Aunt Mae said. "It could've been real bad."

"Yes. He's always been a deep thinker about objects and patterns. He stays away from dangerous things. I know there's a genius in there that we can't fully understand."

"I thought you were going to some ball game this morning."

Rose had been invited by a girlfriend to attend a baseball game between the Phillips 66 camp and the Texaco camp. Because of the Gaines County oil boom, petroleum companies had set up groups of houses for their workers and naturally, competition arose between the camps. Baseball games were the logical outlet.

"I am, but it doesn't start until eleven. I planned on having more time to get ready, but with Velma's baby and the explosion, it looks like I'll be a little late. I was going to take the Ford. Is that okay?"

"Sure. I'm going to relax here until Samuel comes back. He was at the office adding up the receipts for the first six months. I guess he'll be delayed now that he's helping out with the boys."

"Will you be here when I get back?" Rose asked.

"We may go to the Tower Theater to see a matinee. Now I don't know. He still has to check the books and that's a lot of work. On a positive note, I think it's going to be a good year so far. The economy is really booming."

"I thought so. I've been filling out orders every day. And we're selling tractors at least once a week. These new John Deere models are a gold mine. We're truly blessed."

"Yes, we are. But enough of me jabbering away. I'll let you get ready."

Rose closed her bedroom door and changed her outfit. She could tell it would take a great deal of washing to clean her dirty clothes. As she dressed, she thought of little Paul and the injured boys. Life was so incredibly fragile. One minute a new being entered this world and the next, two little boys faced death. (Two weeks later, the boys would leave the hospital, their burns classified as serious. Thankfully, they would go on to lead normal lives.)

Rose slid a new dress over her thin frame and fixed her hair, picking out pieces of dirt and debris. Then she rifled through her drawers looking for a visor. In the bottom drawer, she found it, but not before she spotted an old piece of paper. Carefully pulling it out, she unfolded the document and discovered a long-forgotten memory.

It was the Gaines County map Charles had given her twenty years ago. The land he controlled was shaded along with various notes like "Leased Minerals" or "Option to Buy." She sat on the edge of her bed, studying it, thinking back to the good times they had. She wondered where he was and what he was doing. Did he think about her? Was he even alive?

This trip down memory lane lasted a few minutes longer before she carefully folded the paper back up and returned it to the bottom drawer. She sighed a few times, stared at herself in the mirror, and thought about her age—thirty-nine. Her child-bearing days were withering away.

Patting her knees, she decided to stop this. After all, she had a ballgame to attend.

⋘⋅⋙

There weren't many bleachers to choose from, so it was easy to spot her friend two rows up.

"I'm sorry I'm late, but there was an explosion in town."

Becky slid over to make room. "We heard about it. Here, I saved you a seat."

She had to scoot past two children and their mother to get to her friend. "I was there. The blast knocked me down."

"Oh my, are you okay?" she asked, looking Rose up and down.

"Yes, but it could've been worse. The boys didn't look good, though."

"They actually belong to a driller in another camp. Word spreads fast around here."

"Oh no! I hope they're all right." Rose settled in and straightened her visor. "Did I miss much?"

"It's the third inning and Ted's team is ahead by one run. That's Ted there, playing shortstop."

"He's a nice-looking man. How long have you been dating?"

"About two weeks. He's does something on the rig, I'm not sure exactly what. But he's nice and sweet to me. Thinks I hung the moon for some reason."

"Well, didn't you?" The girls laughed.

The game progressed as Ted's team retired the other team and came up to bat. Ted was up first. He worked the count full and fouled off two more balls before lining a single into the left field. When he saw the left fielder juggle the ball, he tried to stretch it to a double, taking off for second. It was going to be a close play, so he slid hard.

"Safe!" the umpire yelled.

Rose, Becky, and several fans clapped along with Ted's teammates. Then Ted started limping. The manager ran out to check on him. A few minutes later, Ted removed something from his back pocket and gave it to the manager, who patted him on the shoulder. Apparently, he was okay and would stay in the game.

The manager bypassed the dugout and came running to the bleachers. "Becky, Ted said for you to hold his wallet. He forgot he had it in his back pocket." The manager stepped up two rows and handed the wallet to Rose, who was closer.

"Say, you're not Becky," he said teasingly.

"This is Rose," Becky said. "She's my good friend. My good *single* friend. Rose, this is Eddie Fulghum. Ted works for him."

Eddie tipped his cap. "Hello, Rose. It's nice to see a beautiful flower like you out here."

Rose grinned. "You must be in sales."

Eddie laughed. "No. Geology actually. You'll have to excuse me since I've got to get back to the game. You know, I'm the manager. It's kind of important."

The two smiled at each other as he walked away.

Becky elbowed her friend. "Maybe he'll invite you to the fireworks tonight. They're setting up a big shindig. It'll be fun."

Rose rolled her eyes. "Why do I feel like this was a set-up?"

"Maybe some of it was, but not Ted getting injured and forgetting his wallet."

"Okay, I just wondered. Still, he seems nice. And he looks close to my age. He is single?"

"Of course. He's never been married either. These men move around a lot and it's hard to have long-lasting relationships."

"It looks like you and Ted are managing," Rose said.

"For two long weeks."

The girls shared a good laugh and watched the rest of the game. When it was over, Eddie caught up with Rose and pulled her aside. "What did you think of our big win?"

"You guys were great. I guess that all-important manager had something to do with it. Have you won a lot of games?"

"A few, if our pitching's good."

"Well, it was today." Rose wasn't sure what else to say, so she went silent.

They stood there for a moment, until Eddie spoke up. "Say, our camp is putting on some fireworks tonight. There'll be some snacks, some beer, and some music. Would you like to come?"

"Sure, that sounds fun."

Eddie frowned. "The only problem is that you'll have to drive yourself to our camp since I'm involved in putting it together. I'll be tied up for a bit. Do you mind?"

"Of course not. I drove here."

"Great. I'm looking forward to it."

They talked for a while longer before Rose said goodbye to Eddie and her friend and drove home.

When she arrived, Melvin was the only one there. She acknowledged him, making sure he was doing well before fixing herself a glass of tea and settling in to her comfortable rocking chair in the den. As she rocked back and forth, she thought about her full day. A baby born. Two boys seriously injured. Finding her old boyfriend's map. A possible new boyfriend. For what was normally a dull, slow life, things had certainly picked up.

She started thinking more about Eddie and what he was like. Then she came back to Charles and what kind of life she would've had with him. Her mind spun with all sorts of daydreams until she closed her eyes and drifted off to sleep.

The sound of the front door opening woke her up.

"How are you doing?" her uncle asked. "You weren't hurt, were you?"

"No. I'm fine. I went to a ballgame and it took my mind off the incident."

"That's good to hear. After you left, the ambulance hauled those boys away fast, but it doesn't look good. They were burned all over."

"That's too bad. I've tried to put it out of mind but haven't been too successful. Did you finish with the books?"

"Yep. We had a record-breaking six months. With the new line of tools we put on, and all the farming and ranching exploding, it's no wonder.

The soldiers are back and working hard to make up for lost time. We just happen to be selling what everyone needs."

"That's great news," Rose said. "With all the orders I've been handling, I figured that was the case."

Samuel set some files on the table. "Listen, we're going to watch some fireworks tonight. Would you like to come with us?"

"No, I can't. I met a man at the ballgame and I'm going with him to see some fireworks at their camp. My friend Becky is going too. Can you take Melvin with you? You know how he loves the fireworks, the patterns and the noise."

"Sure. I understand Velma and Dan had a boy. That gives them one of each."

"They named him Paul. Dan was beyond excited."

"That's great. I'm happy for them." He kicked off his shoes. "I'm going to relax on the couch for a while and take a nap. It looks like you've had a head start."

Rose chuckled. "Just resting my eyes."

"That's what I'm going to do."

He stretched out on the leather couch. Melvin, who had been over in the corner, got up and stood in front of Rose.

"What is it, Melvin?" she asked.

He ignored her, calmly walked over to his father, and touched him.

"What's the matter?" Samuel said.

"It's something having to do with you," Rose said. "Do you owe him something?"

"No. Not that I know of. Maybe he wants a coin." Samuel shifted to an upright position and reached into his pocket for a dime. "Here you go, son."

Melvin took the dime and dropped it.

Samuel shrugged his shoulders. "If you don't want it, I'll take it back."

Melvin started shaking as Samuel bent over to pick up the coin. By now, Rose was out of her rocking chair, unsure of what was going on. Just as Samuel touched the dime, he grunted hard, clutched his chest, and fell to the side, his head slamming into the wooden floor.

Rose was there, trying to get him stretched out as her aunt came running from their bedroom.

"Samuel!" Mae Beth screamed. "Samuel!"

Rose shook him several times but saw his eyes glaze over. She knew even before Aunt Mae was down on her knees holding his head up what had happened. Uncle Samuel, at age fifty-six, had joined Grandpa.

Chapter Thirteen

December 1956
Cuauhtémoc, Mexico

David Rempel, ten, opened his eyes and stared at the ceiling, listening intently for a sound that his parents were up and moving. After a few seconds of silence, he pulled the covers closer to his face and took a deep breath to relax, allowing a grin to spread across his face.

It wasn't time yet.

This was his favorite moment of the day. He was rested and refreshed—a feeling that would disappear as soon as he hopped out of bed. Right now, though, he had no responsibilities or demands. It was his time, to use as he chose.

One bed over was his brother Jacob, who was four and a half years old. They had the whole room to themselves while four of his sisters crammed into a space the same size as theirs. Margaretha, his three-year-old sister, still slept in a crib in his parents' room. None of the seven children who'd been born to his mother had died. But with his friends constantly losing siblings, how long could his family's good fortune last?

David's tummy rumbled, and he wondered what Mother would cook up for breakfast. Usually, it was a bowl of oatmeal and homemade bread. Whatever it was, he decided to load up his bowl as much as his mother would let him. He was hungry.

His mind drifted to the few toys he owned. One was a wooden wagon he'd made from his father's carpenter's tools. His dad rarely touched them or performed any manual labor for that matter, hiring in Mexicans to do the field work he should've been doing. Instead, he liked to give sermons and perform his preaching duties, standing tall in his long overcoat and knee-high boots.

David was very unlike his father. He had not only an interest but also an aptitude for working with all types of materials such as steel and wood. He had learned to weld, solder, plumb, and woodwork. With money tight, he had made most of his toys using scrap materials lying around.

Bikes were rare in the colony, with only a few Mexican kids from the surrounding areas having them. David could race other boys on horseback and rope calves for sport. He even got into an occasional fight, rolling around with some boy and getting after it. Other than that, he worked during every spare moment of the day. Since most every colonist needed money for the bare essentials, toys were an unnecessary extravagance.

One thing his dad did buy for him was a black-and-white sheepdog. David named him Fiex. The two were inseparable. Fiex even wanted to follow David to school until he trained him to stay home. After a few days of watching his master leave and come back, Fiex settled in and understood the routine, waiting patiently by the fence line for David's small figure to appear down the main avenue. Of course, David discovered that a sheepdog made rounding up the cows for their morning milking easier—a gift that helped with the chores. His dad was smart.

A noise from the other room filtered through the thin walls. His mother was up lighting the wood stove. His precious moment was over.

David swung his feet to the cold dirt floor and went to wake Jacob, but his younger brother was already climbing out of bed and headed to the outhouse. David took the opportunity to slide into a fresh shirt before reaching down and pulling up his blue jean overalls. With the light from a hall lantern, he laced up his cheap shoes—his only pair—thankful to be wearing them. If it was summer, he wouldn't be allowed to wear any shoes because it would wear them out. During the winter, though, when the ground was cold and hard, he could put them on. The only other amenity he had was a thin jacket that barely protected him from the wind. The cold always seeped through.

The girls in the adjacent room were making noise like they always did. He thought about telling them to keep it down but remembered what had happened a few days ago when they were carrying on at bedtime. He had gone in there and told them to quiet down, teasing them, when his father appeared, belt in hand, and whipped him good. It wasn't fair since he was trying to get to sleep, but many things in his life weren't fair. Because he was a preacher's kid, his father was stricter than other parents. People in the colony were quick and willing to tell his father anything he or his siblings did wrong. At least Dad was strict with his sisters, too. They saw the belt more than once.

David moved to the kitchen, where the stove's warmth enveloped him. During winter, the house was perpetually cold—not freezing, just cold. Sometimes he wore his jacket inside the house, as did the others. Today, though, it wasn't necessary. His mother had the furnace stoked up and the fireplace back to life from the glowing embers of the deep night.

Spying a glass of yesterday's milk sitting on the counter, he dodged his two older sisters and promptly tossed it back before filling up the same glass with some well water. That too went down easily. Now he was ready.

Without any instructions from his parents, he located his old thin jacket on the coat rack. Next to it hung his new coat—a thick one, with a nice fur collar. It was a rarity that he could wear anything new during the week since it was worn only on Sunday. He wished he could wear it now to stay warm but that was impossible. His sisters didn't get a new jacket because the family couldn't afford to clothe everyone. Children were supposed to suffer the hardships of life. And they could never say anything about it because Mennonite children were not supposed to speak much or ask questions. Instead, they were taught to keep their head down and work every minute of the day.

David zipped up his old jacket and walked outside, where his best friend, Fiex, waited for him. On cold nights, Fiex could sleep near the fireplace—which he had done last night. When his mother awoke, she opened the door to let him out so he could take care of his business. Now, Fiex was ready to work.

David patted him several times. "Good boy. Let's go."

The two made their way to the barn. Going to the back side, he opened the door to the pasture and sent Fiex out to round up their six milk cows.

As always, the cows were ready to get inside the barn because they wanted to be fed. It took a few minutes for David and Fiex to get them in their stalls and the feed set out. Soon enough, his sisters came in with buckets to begin milking the cows. This was their responsibility. His job was to clean out the stalls of old hay and droppings and put fresh hay down. He also had to feed their two horses, which were always high-stepping with excitement when they saw him coming. They were hungry, too.

When he was done with all that, he cleaned up the barn, which was a perpetual mess. During the end of this chore, he went to a corner of the barn and picked up some toys he had been playing with. He should've put them away last night, but he hadn't. He was thankful his father hadn't seen them lying around or he would have seen the belt again.

Pulling the wagon to its designated spot, David remembered an incident several years earlier when he noticed several litters of kittens in the barn, the product of four or five cats that kept the rodent population in check. For some reason, his young brain thought it was necessary for him to round up the kittens and take them to a spot for their own protection. He circled around the barn, locating each litter and transferring it to his wagon. By the time he was done, dozens of kittens crawled around in the bed, confused and crying. Trailing behind the wagon were four momma cats also crying. That's when he realized he'd made a big mistake.

He stopped the wagon and stared at the cats, who seemed to be pleading with him to set their kittens free. He decided that he had to give them back, but he faced a dilemma. Which kitten belonged with which cat? How was he going to get them back to the right mother?

After pondering all this, he tilted the wagon over, setting the kittens free. Upon seeing their babies, each cat grabbed up a kitten and carried it back to the nest. David smiled. Even though he didn't know which kitten belonged to which cat, the mommas knew. A few minutes later, the problem was resolved and everyone was happy again. From then on, he left the kittens alone, mainly because the cats hid them so well he couldn't find them. *Animals are smart*, he thought to himself.

It was almost seven-thirty. He had been working for an hour and a half and it was time for breakfast.

David sat down at the table with five siblings on either side of him. Only Margaretha was too young to participate, remaining in a small homemade carriage in the corner. Mother carried over a large dish of porridge and they all said prayers silently. When they were finished, the table became a frenzy of spoons and bowls, while cups were filled with fresh milk. Besides porridge, fresh bread and jam were served. Breakfast was usually this sparse, with supper being the biggest meal each day.

Fifteen minutes later and a trip to the outhouse, David was headed toward the schoolhouse, dressed in a pair of fresh overalls and a nice shirt. Next to him were Katharina, Maria, and Helena. His other siblings were too young to attend, with six being the proper age for first grade.

They had barely made it to the main avenue when the street was flooded with children from the other houses. By the time they reached the end of their thirty-home colony, the group had swelled.

The one-room schoolhouse was nearby. Being in third grade, David joined his class and found his usual seat. The younger grades occupied the back benches while the higher grades sat closer to the front. Like church, the girls sat on one side and boys on the other—eighty students in all, with each grade represented. In most schools, this would be a problem. However, schooling for the Mennonites was much different. Lack of individual attention would not affect their education, at least the "education" they were given.

As he sat there waiting for the teacher to begin, he remembered how easy the first grade was, studying only the ABC book—or *Fiebel*, as it was called in German. This simple primer helped them understand the letters and how to pronounce them. That was it.

In second grade, he had been given the Catechism. This booklet had been used by Mennonite congregations and schools for decades. Since Menno Simons was a Catholic priest for many years, the tradition of reciting from it was kept. The teacher would ask a question to the verse and they would have to memorize it, such as: How do you get eternal life? David would write the Bible verse and a short description of it, which the teacher reviewed.

Once they had mastered that, they moved on to the New Testament (in its own book) and the Bible. So far, the class had gone through the New

Testament verse by verse. They weren't reading the New Testament to discover the true meaning of the parables and Jesus' teachings but simply to learn to read better. Neither history, science, art, nor literature were taught. Math consisted of a few problems on the chalkboard with no books to study or learn from. The teacher would put a math problem on the chalkboard and the students would copy it down on small slate boards. They would work it and see if they could come up with the correct answer. If they didn't understand something, they soon found out that their teacher was more of an announcer than an instructor. The truth was that none of the teachers had ever had any outside education other than the same primitive learnings they were now passing on. The Mennonite educational system was simply a closed loop—regurgitating the same lessons year after year, never asking themselves if things had changed and there was new information out there.

Biology was another subject off limits. If the students came to passages in the Bible dealing with sex or nudity, the teacher would say, "You don't have to read this one. Just skip it." Of course, David and his friends would read it after school and try to figure out what it meant. The forbidden text was like a magnet for young boys. That's what they wanted to read. Even though they never had homework, the boys brought their Bible home so they could read those passages. Several times, David asked his parents about the prohibited text, but they weren't any help. "We're not teachers!" they responded harshly. It seemed no one understood much of anything, other than farming or ranching or the trade they had learned.

Occasionally, when a farm animal was being born, David and his siblings were chased away, banned from witnessing something like that. If an animal was mating, they were told to shut up and move on. Fortunately, kids like David didn't know there was anything else out there. They were blissfully ignorant.

A noise from behind brought David back. He stared at the vacant desk to his left, the one belonging to Johan. Johan was home tending to the farm since his father was injured and bedridden. It had happened last Sunday, four days earlier. With a light snow and cold wind, the stoves in the church had been stoked up. Johan's father was sitting near one when, two hours into the service, he passed out and fell backward, splitting his head open on the bench behind him. The embarrassed family claimed he was ill, though most parishioners suspected it was the usual culprit—physical exhaustion combined with a mind-numbing four-hour service and a nice warm stove. Many of them had fought fatigue and feared passing out.

They had rushed him into a little building in the colony where a Mexican doctor occasionally appeared. He wasn't in that day, so a fellow Mennonite with some basic medical knowledge examined him. This layman dispensed powders and pills and occasionally injected the patient with penicillin. He could perform some minor stitching, but Johan's father needed more, so he was taken to the nearby Mexican village in hopes of locating the doctor. Hopefully, he'd be all right.

With the teacher babbling on, David took a deep breath and settled in, hoping to endure the next four hours until noon arrived. At that point, he and his siblings would walk home for lunch to find Mother had fresh bread and slices of meat. This would be washed down by more milk. After lunch, David would play with Fiex for a few minutes until he joined the moving mob of students traveling back to school for another three hours of nothing.

Finally, at four, David's school day was over. He came home and changed out of his nice clothes and back into the chore overalls he'd worn that morning. It was his job to feed the horses and cows again. He also cleaned out the barn—*again*. This time, he brushed down the horses. When that was done, he set up the hammer mill, which was operated from a belt running to the tractor. This turned the wheat into a fine powder. Sometimes, he had to operate a threshing machine to separate the wheat from the chaff. Then he could grind the wheat kernels into whole wheat flour.

When he was done with all that, David carried a sack of flour into the kitchen, a place his mother never seemed to leave. With his three sisters helping, the room was crowded.

David took in the familiar aroma of freshly baked bread and said, "Here it is, Mother."

"Lean it against that wall over there," she said, pointing. "Before you disappear, I need you to take something to Grandma Rempel. Your father won't be back in time from his Thursday meeting, so you'll have to do it. Get your jacket on while I put it together." David nodded and did as he was told.

Ten minutes later, he was on Doell, the horse in a trot, with the night descending fast. The trip to Campo 110 was uneventful—an easy ride—since the winds were mostly gone. He passed the rows of houses with their oil lamps burning through the windows. Occasionally, a dog sauntered over, eventually turning around and leaving them alone.

As he eased Doell into his grandparents' yard, he noticed the open barn door. Instead of taking his horse to one of the hitching posts in front of the house, he sauntered over to the barn to see who was there.

"Hello, young man," his grandfather said, moving closer to help with Doell. "What brings you here?"

"Mother told me to deliver this to Grandma." He showed Jacob the package.

"What is it?"

"I don't know. She wrapped it up, and I didn't look inside."

"I guess we don't need to know, do we?"

"No, sir," David replied.

Jacob led the horse to a stall. "We'll put Doell in here, and you can stay for supper. It's almost ready. And since your momma serves supper later than we do, you might be able to eat twice. Now get over there and fetch those oats. Let's feed this old girl."

"Yes, sir," David said, grabbing a bucket. While he fed the horse, his grandfather peppered him with questions. "So, how is school going? Are you learning something?"

David hesitated, unsure of what he should say. "Umm, I-I don't know."

Jacob chuckled. "You mean you know but you're not sure you can trust me, right?"

A grin creased David's face. "Yes, sir."

Jacob sat down on an old tree stump he used for a workbench. "Why don't you trust old grandpa. I might surprise you."

David pushed some hay with his foot. "Well, it's just that I go to school expecting a meal and I'm never fed. I don't learn anything except how to read big words and do a few math problems."

"I see," Jacob said, leaning back against a post. "So when did you first realize that school wasn't what you'd thought it would be?"

David paused, thinking about his last two years. "I guess it was when they told us if we did good and read the lesson well, a red rooster would sneak in at night and lay a peso on our book. A few weeks later, I found one. So did most of my classmates. That's when the teacher had a rooster in the room to show us how it was laying pesos."

"Did you take your peso?"

"No. When I started questioning the teacher, he said, 'Look at his wings. It comes from right under there.' I said to him, 'You are a liar!'"

Jacob leaned away from the post, his brow furrowed. "In front of the class?"

"Yes, sir. I talked with some older kids and they said our father was the one who put it there. Sure enough, the only time it happened was the day after his weekly meeting with the teacher."

"What do you think about that?"

David set the bucket of oats down. "More lies. That's all school is. And the other day, I asked Uncle Johann what was beyond our colony. He told me there was a clothesline hung with sheets of dough, like a wall. If I went past that, I'd fall off the earth."

"Do you believe him?"

"I'm not sure. I don't know who to believe anymore."

Unexpectedly, his grandpa pulled him close and hugged him. "Listen to me. After supper, you and I will take a walk. We'll talk some more. But in the meantime, don't say a word to anyone about what we discuss, understand?"

"Yes, sir."

David collected his package and followed Grandpa inside. There, waiting for him, were Cornelius, Susana, and Johann, three of Jacob's children who were still teenagers and living at home. Incredibly, Susana was just eight years older than David.

Judith took the package from David and told him to take a seat for supper. This meal consisted of cabbage soup, meat-cheese, and bread. Like David's house, very little discussion occurred as everyone ate what they could. When David finished, he noticed his grandfather watching him and set his fork down.

"David, thank you for coming by," Jacob said. "I'll help you with your horse so you can be on the road before it gets too late."

Johann jumped up from the table to help, but Jacob waved him back down. "No need, son. I'll take care of it. You finish your meal."

Jacob grabbed his jacket and handed David his. The two walked in silence to the barn, where Jacob proceeded to a stall and tapped on a piece of wood. David couldn't see what he was doing but noticed that he wasn't getting Doell ready.

"Come on," Jacob said. "Follow me."

A half-moon lit up the barren field, showing them a well-worn path. They trudged along until they reached the end of the long field, stationing themselves behind a large pile of rubble. Jacob reached in his pocket and produced a cigarette and a lighter. Once the glowing ember had smoke spewing from it, Jacob took a long drag and turned to David.

"The reason I'm letting you see me smoke is because I know you won't tell anyone. Right?"

"I won't tell anyone, Grandpa. I promise."

"Good. Now I'm going to tell you a few things. First, you won't be learning anything more in school. You'll suffer through the next seven years like we all did. The second thing you need to know is that the world doesn't end at the edge of our colony. It goes on forever. I know. I've lived in Canada and came through the United States. There's a whole 'nother world out there. I promise you that."

"Okay," David said, not sure what else to say.

His grandfather scratched a tooth with a dirty thumbnail. "Here's why I brought you out here. I want to start you thinking about leaving this place. It's no good here. You can't hardly make a living. When you grow up, you go back to Canada. Do something different. You hear?"

"Yes, sir. But why don't you leave?"

Jacob exhaled a cloud of smoke. "Believe me, I would if I could. Your grandma's family has a strong hold on her. She wouldn't stand for it. But that shouldn't stop you. You start learning all the trades you can so you can work in Canada and make good money. This life is no good. I'm giving you the greatest gift of all—permission to leave."

David stood in the deserted field, watching his grandpa finish his cigarette. When he finally dropped the butt and crushed it out, he reached over and patted David on the shoulder. "Someone in our family has to be the first to leave this place, and I think that person is you. Don't let me down."

"I won't, sir."

"Let's get back and get you off before we're caught."

David closed his family's barn door, satisfied that Doell was taken care of for the night. He went inside the house and heard his parents arguing, a rarity.

"We have no choice!" his father said. "It's been decided and that's that."

His mother held David's new jacket. "But it's just animal fur. It's not extravagant or prideful."

His father refused to make eye contact. "Nevertheless, the Ältester made it clear that it was a sin and needs to be returned."

Hearing this, David realized that his new fur-collar coat was prohibited, and his family would be in trouble if they didn't get rid of it. Once his father's anger subsided, his mother stopped arguing and folded the coat up, placing it on a cabinet so she could return it the next day.

David fumed as he turned around and walked outside, ignored by everyone except Fiex. David sat on the top step and petted his best friend, staring through the bare trees at the half-moon. He wondered what it was like in Canada, or anywhere else for that matter. Then his mind drifted to the rubber tires. Why did they have to get rid of them and use those wheels with the stupid metal paddles? It was hard to understand how God wanted them to suffer when He had created such an array of fruits and vegetables to be enjoyed. And what about the beautiful flowers? Were they off limits, too? And the fur on his new jacket—was it not created to give some warmth? It didn't make any sense.

He was contemplating other aspects of Mennonite life when a gunshot sounded. Gunshots weren't unexpected, but they usually happened in the morning or early afternoon when the animal could be properly butchered. Sometimes a horse had to be put down and that could happen at any time.

A second shot echoed off the walls of their house and barn, causing Fiex to stiffen. Even the dog knew something wasn't right.

Two more shots rang out in rapid succession. This time, David stood up and looked in the direction of the sound. The door behind him opened and out walked his father.

"Did you hear that?" Jacob asked.

"Yes, sir," David replied. "Four shots,"

Jacob rubbed his hands together. "That's never happened before. Something's not right. Do you know where it came from?"

"I think the west, maybe Campo 115."

"Get the horses ready," his father commanded.

David ran to the barn with Fiex racing behind. Minutes later, father and son were mounted on their only two horses and headed off, an increasing noise drawing them closer.

Soon, they pulled up in front of a house with neighbors running everywhere.

"What has happened?" Jacob called out to one of them.

"Poor Cornelius," a man said. "He had a dispute with a Mexican and the Mexican broke into his house and shot him. He's dead!"

David watched as the words registered with his father, causing his head to drop in despair. If David was unsure before, now he knew for certain: No matter what, he had to leave this place.

Chapter Fourteen

July 1961
Cuauhtémoc, Mexico

David stood at the rear of the barn, his back against its gray planks. A few butterflies danced among the fresh vegetation bursting through the ground. This was always a unique time of year. The rains brought life from the dead soil, at the same time marking the beginning of a four-month period of backbreaking work. It seemed everything good produced something bad.

A cloud of smoke chased a horsefly away as the nicotine dissolved in David's blood, giving him an edge and setting his heart pumping. It was the only real pleasure he enjoyed—never mind that it was strictly forbidden. Each Sunday, he listened to his father rail on and on about the evils of tobacco, while outside, dozens of men hid behind buildings and got their fix just like him. It was so hypocritical.

Alcohol was another good example. His mother had grapes and made red wine for the church to use during communion. She kept it in a special jug in the back of his parents' closet. David knew this, because several years back, he had snuck in with a glass jar and poured out a good measure. After slipping past his brother and sisters, he'd gone to the far end of the field and drank it all. Young, small, and inexperienced, he sat in the sunshine, fascinated by the rays of light bouncing in different directions while his vision blurred and his limbs grew numb. Before long, he felt sick. He tried to get up but couldn't walk. With nothing else to do, he sat there for several hours until his feet stayed under him.

The next day, he rationalized his bad behavior, telling himself that no one had ever said he couldn't drink it. He'd even seen his father sample it from time to time. One day, he overheard his dad telling his mother that there were men who had problems drinking and their wives were at a loss of how to stop them. David had already recognized this, because he'd seen them staggering around. Whenever his father received word that one of them was at it again, he added parts of old sermons to the scheduled one, perpetually hammering on the inherent dangers from "the fruit of the vine."

A few weeks after David's secret experiment, he'd asked his dad if he could drink some of the wine, just a little. "Oh, no," his father replied. "Absolutely not. The wine is for communion and at least ten years old. It has too much alcohol in it. More than a tiny bit will kill you."

He knew the death part was a lie, but he had to admit it had been quite a ride.

David adjusted his straw cowboy hat and blew out another cloud of smoke. This was one of the rare moments of the day he had alone. His dad was going over church business, while his brother and sisters had scattered themselves inside the house. The eldest son at fifteen, it was David's job to handle most of the chores, since his dad rarely did manual labor. He didn't have to because his children did everything.

Like normal, his sisters had rolled out of bed and milked the cows. Then they'd helped his mom fix breakfast while David had cleaned out the barn. After eating breakfast, he and Fiex had started toward the common field to cut out the cows for weighing. His dad wanted to know the total weight so he could sell one for much-needed cash.

David gazed down at the black and white pile at his feet—his best friend, Fiex. The sheepdog followed him everywhere, helping him with any chore. He even protected him from angry cows and hogs, chasing them away if they got too close. David couldn't imagine having a better dog. Sometimes he found himself confessing his problems to Fiex. Maybe he was hoping for some kind of answer, or at least inspiration to carry on. But Fiex's dark eyes would just gaze up at him with unconditional love, waiting for his master's command.

He took one final drag, enjoying as much of it as possible. With a sigh, he dug his toe into the dirt below and dropped the cigarette into a hole, covering the evidence up. It was his last cigarette. He'd have to buy more.

He reached into his overalls pocket and counted out his change. Just short. The money he usually carried was from picking up extra beans at harvest time and trading them at the general store. He was only supposed to buy drinks and candy there, and he had for many years. But one day, he'd broached the forbidden subject with Mr. Dyck. "Which kind do you want, son?" the man had said curtly, showing him two brands.

"What's the cheapest?"

A few minutes later, with his heart slamming in his chest and the forbidden tobacco in his pocket, he'd walked down the main avenue as if he'd just gotten away with murder. In a way, he had.

Stuffing the change back into his pocket, he thought for a moment. He could usually finagle a dime or two from Grandpa Rempel, but the old man hadn't been around for several weeks, so that option was out. Maybe he could get Mr. Dyck to sell to him on credit. It was only a nickel.

David jogged back to the house and opened the front door, yelling inside. "Mom, I'm going to walk to Peter's house to borrow the post-hole digger. Do I have permission?"

She stepped out of the kitchen, peering at him. "Okay, but you get it and come straight back. You understand?"

"Yes, ma'am," he replied, turning to leave. But his mother was still talking.

"I'm not going to have a son like the Blatz boys. They're lucky to be alive."

"Yes, ma'am," he said again, shutting the door as Fiex jumped up to follow him.

Walking down the main avenue, he shook his head. The Blatz boys were real trouble, always getting into something. When anything turned up missing, most of the neighbors considered the Blatz boys the likely suspects. They had taken whippings for most of the high crimes and misdemeanors in the Swift Current colony, even though they couldn't possibly have committed them all. After the previous Halloween, though, no one put anything past them.

It was a long October night and the colonists had wakened to find a nasty surprise. Starting at their back door, each house had a narrow, well-beaten path leading to the outhouse. Most of them didn't notice their outhouse had been moved a few feet closer. It was only when they took care of business that they realized something was wrong. There was no hole below them. For the rare few, their outhouse was moved a few feet away from the house, thus exposing the hole along the path. In the early light, sleep still caked in their eyes and attention waning, the owners of those faced a different type of calamity—certainly an eye-opening experience.

For the neighbors who were fortunate not to have their outhouses moved, they found pieces of equipment resting on their fences. David remembered finding several empty milk containers sticking on the posts of his. Since his sisters didn't have the strength to remove them, he and his father had to do it before the milking could begin. This upset everyone's morning routine and added to the anger building against the perpetrators.

Because this was such a large prank, the Blatz boys couldn't hold it in. They told everyone. This was a flaw in their personalities, one which ensured the leathery hide that had formed on their butts would remain there until adulthood.

By now, the boys had been whipped in public in just about every campo. It was part of the Blatz boys' daily routine. They never seemed to mind or get the message. David did—*mostly*. He avoided getting into trouble but was willing to lean over the edge at times. With encouragement from his grandfather, he kept pushing the boundaries ever so gently. He could hardly wait until he was an adult and didn't have to take endless orders to be quiet and not speak. It was so depressing.

He passed Peter's house and continued toward the general store. Once there, he found the store empty except for Mr. Dyck. He was standing behind the counter tallying up cans of fruit. David approached him, nervously clearing his throat. "Sir," he said, digging into his pocket and spilling his change on the counter. "I'd like to purchase a pack of cigarettes, and I'm a nickel short. Would you please let me owe it to you?"

Mr. Dyck's eyes flicked down to the change on the counter before he glared at David. "I can't do that, son. You have no means of income and will have me sitting here for a year, keeping track of that one nickel you owe me."

David stared down at Fiex, who was busy sniffing the floor. "Umm, I could probably get a nickel in a week or so," he said, meekly. "It wouldn't be that long."

Mr. Dyck shook his head. "I just can't do it. I just can't." David turned to go, then paused when Mr. Dyck's smooth voice sliced through the air. "But, if you come across some fresh eggs—I'm always willing to trade with you." He gave David a wry smile. "I can sell *those* fast."

David nodded and left the store with Fiex in tow. He'd understood the implication and wasn't about to steal anything.

Peter was working in his barn when David arrived. "Where's your father?" David asked.

"Went to town to pick up some cement tile. He took Benjamin."

Benjamin was Peter's older brother. "What's he going to do with the tile?"

Peter leaned his rake against a post. "He's putting them down in the kitchen. Someone in campo 104 did it and they don't have water slopping all over the floor. It just drains on through somehow."

To David, that sounded like something his family should have, especially since his mother was always slipping on the polished dirt floor. The smooth surface was almost like the frozen ponds back in Canada he had heard everyone talk about.

"How did you get permission to leave?" Peter asked.

"I told Mom I needed to borrow your post-hole digger. But I went to the general store first to buy cigarettes. I couldn't because I'm a nickel short."

"If you got time for a smoke, I'll lend you one," Peter said with a shrug.

David raised his eyebrows, mouth already watering. "Sure."

He followed Peter to the corner of the barn, hidden from view of the main entrance. Peter slid his hand behind a piece of wood, pulling out his secret stash. Within moments they were puffing away.

"You know," Peter said, "I tried to get a hold of some wine but couldn't. They have it hidden real good, if they even have it. You sure I couldn't get some of yours?"

"Nah," David replied. "They're watching it close, especially after I took a good part of it. I think they have a line marking the level."

Peter thought for a moment. "You could pour water in it and they'd never know."

"I can't do it." As much as he hated to admit it, he felt just like Mr. Dyck. "I would get a whipping for sure. Besides, we'll be old enough soon. Then we'll get our own from the Mexican vendors who come around. I wouldn't be surprised if Mr. Dyck sold some. He seems to have everything."

Peter blew smoke at the wall, abandoning the subject. "Aren't your parents going to be wondering where you are?"

"Probably. I'm going to tell them you needed help with your new tractor. Okay?"

They glanced at the John Deere sitting in the middle of the barn, its clean metal paddles sticking up from the rims. David went to inspect it, impressed. A tag hanging off its seat caught his eye. *Seminole, Texas.*

He studied the unused rubber tires piled on top of each other next to the tractor. The requirement to burn tractor tires had been eliminated, so they could be sold for cash instead. David assumed Peter's dad was waiting to sell them when either planting or harvesting was in full swing—when the local Mexicans needed them badly. They'd pay more when they were desperate.

Seeing David eyeing them, Peter said, "Do you think we'll ever be allowed to use our rubber tires and stop using these paddle wheels? Your dad could do something. Does he ever talk about it?"

"No," David replied emphatically. "I can't talk to him about anything."

"Same with me and my dad," Peter said, sighing. His mouth twitched a little before he took another drag of his cigarette. "Will anything ever change?"

"No." The word was disappointing, but it was the truth. There was no point in pretending otherwise. "All they say is, 'That's the way it's always been done,' or 'I don't know.' At least I have my grandpa. He's taught me a lot of trades, and I can really talk to him. Still, he doesn't know much. He says everyone here is kept ignorant on purpose. It's just the way it is." David crushed out his cigarette, handing the butt to Peter. "Here. I need to go before they come looking for me."

"Okay," Peter said. He stuck the two butts into a glass jar, sealing and returning it to his secret cache.

David started his walk home, depressed. Talking with Peter had only reminded him how boring farm life was. Without the ability to really talk with his parents, combined with the rule against visiting the other kids, information of any kind was slow and uneventful. So was the opportunity for mischief, the Blatz boys notwithstanding. Somehow, there had to be a better life out there. Surely, this wasn't it.

For five more hours, David worked at his chores, sweating in the blazing July sun. After a noon meal, Fiex followed him out to the common area. The dog ran in circles until David cut out and weighed their four cows. Feeling as exhausted as Fiex looked, David cupped some water from the trough into his hands, watching Fiex's pink tongue lapping it up. He tucked the piece of paper with the cows' weight into his pocket, then wiped his forehead and considered starting for home. Out of the corner of his eye, he spotted a Mexican fruit truck just rolling up under the large oak tree. The prospect of meeting a Mexican and maybe getting some information or cigarettes definitely outweighed his return home. He made the quick decision to check it out.

David spoke a little Spanish, and the vendor spoke some Low German. Together, they communicated nicely.

When David raised the subject, the vendor was more than happy to sell him a pack of cigarettes for a nickel less than the general store. The cigarettes were cheaper and shorter than the ones Mr. Dyck sold, but David wasn't choosy.

A young boy with the vendor approached and asked him why he wasn't in school. David explained how all boys stopped at thirteen, while the girls went until they were twelve. "Besides," David said, "school's out. It doesn't start back until September."

"Do you ever leave the village?" the boy asked innocently.

David shook his head. It was mostly true, though he had left the village once. When he was ten, his father had taken him to a smaller village close by to get fuel for their tractor. It'd taken an hour on the buggy to reach the tiny Mexican shack, where a large tank sat. He had helped his dad pump the gas, exhausting himself. Once they'd screwed the cap back on and exchanged some money, they headed home. Hardly any conversation passed between them.

Parental silence and growing curiosity were why the boys in each campo questioned the Mexicans every chance they got. The boys would ask them about life outside the settlement, trying to pick up information about all sorts of subjects. Even though the language barrier was significant at times, they plowed ahead anyway. If one boy learned something, he'd spread it to his friend, who no doubt embellished it. By the time it reached the fourth or fifth friend, who knew how much was accurate? Regardless, every scrap of information David picked up continued feeding his restlessness, making him want to leave more and more.

With the fresh pack of cigarettes in his pocket, he found a secluded spot behind the truck and lit one up. He was halfway through it when the vendor decided to move to another spot. As the truck's engine revved up, David noticed a black and white tail sticking out from under the car. In seconds, he jumped up and banged on the vendor's door, yelling at him to stop. The Mexican had just put the truck into gear when he pressed his foot on the brake.

"Fiex!" David yelled, relief washing over him as the dog sprung up from under the truck, no worse for wear. A second longer, and he would've been run over.

David waved off the Mexican, signaling him to drive on. Giving Fiex a scratch behind the ears, he watched as the truck took off, leaving a dust cloud in its wake.

That was close.

———⟫⟫◆⟪⟪———

It was a week later when David's father, Jacob, told him they were going into town. Jacob had seen the cement tile in Peter's kitchen and wanted some for his kitchen. At least, that was the story. In reality, David's mother had come back from Peter's house excited about something, and the next thing he knew, his dad wanted the tile. David could barely contain his excitement. He was finally going to town, a mysterious place that held so much promise.

The big morning arrived, and David hurried to hitch up both horses to the wagon. Suddenly, a gunshot echoed in the distance. Each time David heard that sound, he remembered the night Cornelius had been killed by an angry Mexican. The Mexican was eventually arrested and went to jail. Before the year was out, though, he was free. That's how it was in Mexico.

The trip into Cuauhtémoc took five long hours. Starting at six in the morning, they arrived at eleven. Outside of town, David's father pulled the buggy over and handed David some food his mother had packed. They ate in silence, the same silence David had been brought up with. It never changed or ceased to frustrate him. Once the meal was over, his dad picked up the reins and set the horses to moving.

In minutes, David's eyes grew wide. Cars and trucks flew by. He'd never seen so many. Everything seemed new—not like all the tired, worn-out equipment he saw in the campos. His amazement only deepened as they approached the cement factory.

David and Jacob toured the plant and watched a massive machine with large wheels lower itself, putting pressure on the tiles. Next to it, several Mexicans held a flat piece of metal, pushing the cement into the form before they placed a woodgrain finish on it. David was so fascinated he didn't—*couldn't*—move. He just stood there, watching the men do the same task over and over again, with each tile looking exactly like a piece of wood. It was hard to understand.

Prying himself away, David followed his father into town while the men loaded up their wagon. Each step he took brought a new face, each different and exciting. There were young Mexican girls staring at him. He smiled back, knowing it was strictly forbidden to date a Hispanic—or a Mexa, as they were called. Back at the campos, they couldn't even kiss a Mennonite girl or hold hands. Passing notes was about it.

He felt his dad tugging on his shirt. "In here," he ordered.

David stepped inside a small store and saw candy everywhere. The upper shelves were lined with colorful hard candy with chocolates peppering the lower levels. His dad pointed at some dark treats, placing several coins on the counter. The woman quickly produced two pieces of chocolate and handed them to his father, who turned and gave David one. Before anyone could stop him, David tossed it into his mouth and chomped fast. Whatever it was, it was both magical and succulent—far superior to anything back home.

The taste lingered in his mouth as he followed his father around town, inspecting cloth in one store and saddles in another. When Jacob glanced at a clock in a third store, he grabbed David and hustled outside, walking briskly back to the plant, where they found the buggy fully loaded and ready to go. Jacob ran his eyes over the tile and shook hands with the manager. With one last look at this brave new world, David reluctantly found himself back where he started, next to his father as they traveled the dusty road home.

Because of the great distance and the fact that the horses couldn't make the round trip in one day, they detoured to his maternal grandmother's house close to town. She welcomed them with a nice meal and a comfortable bed, giving them each their own room since all her children had left and gotten married.

While the adults talked, David sat silently in the corner, listening to his father and grandmother carry on about all the colonists going back to Canada. David didn't dare tell them that his grandfather had said Mexico was the poorest land the Mennonites had ever encountered. He wondered what they would think if they knew Grandpa was saying such dangerous things.

As the night dragged on, David's mind drifted back to Cuauhtémoc and all the things he'd seen. He wondered if the place on the tag of Peter's new John Deere tractor offered a similar life. *Seminole, Texas*. He turned the words over and over in his mind, until he felt himself falling asleep. There was so much to process, he'd be turning it all over for weeks.

Shortly after his visit to town, David and his friends found themselves with a few extra hours of free time. They swam and goofed around in the river that ran through the colony. With the recent rains and the runoff from the nearby mountains, the river was near flood stage. One of his friends, Franz, stayed close to shore. He'd almost drowned the previous year. If it hadn't been for David diving in and pulling him up from the bottom, he would've died.

Franz's mother had baked a nice dessert for David and made a big show of bringing it to him several days later. For a glorious moment in time, David was a big hero. Now, all of that was forgotten as the boys splashed around, enjoying some rare leisure time.

David told them about his visit to Cuauhtémoc and all the things he'd seen. A loud honk interrupted his stories, sending everyone sprinting from the water toward another Mexican vendor truck. It pulled under the same oak tree, offering an assortment of fruits and candy. The boys slipped on their shirts as they ran, crushing their cowboy hats down around their ears and digging for a few coins to buy some candy. Fiex ran behind them all, barking loudly, trying to herd them.

The boys inspected the vendor's goods, lingering over their selection. Once they made their purchases, they sat under the tree's large umbrella, enjoying their sweets. Soon, more boys arrived, turning the place into a small city. It wasn't much like Cuauhtémoc, but even David couldn't help but feel the same buzz of excitement.

With the goods flowing out of the truck, the Mexican had to shift around some boxes in the back. When he did, the truck rolled forward slightly. A short, sharp bark caught everyone's attention.

"What was that?" Franz asked, sitting upright.

With his heart in his stomach, David was already up. He ran to the front of the truck, pushing it backward with all his strength. Tears had already made their way to his eyes as Fiex pulled himself from under the vehicle, limping away slowly. David followed after him, desperately trying to talk to his friend, but Fiex wasn't paying attention. Instead, he stopped to lie down in the fresh green grass, panting hard.

David's fingers preened through the black and white fur, words tumbling out of his mouth before he could even think about them. It only took a minute or so for Fiex's labored breathing to stop completely. David hugged the little body close, tears sliding down his cheeks and chin, landing silently in the grass.

At that moment, he was absolutely sure he would never stop crying.

Chapter Fifteen

November 1, 1964
Cuauhtémoc, Mexico

David sat at the kitchen table, sharpening his pocketknife on a whetstone. It was already honed to a razor's edge and didn't need more work, but David didn't care. He needed something to do until his parents passed out from exhaustion.

A few hours earlier, his father, Jacob, had spent two and a half hours standing and reading a two-hundred-year-old sermon. While his father was only in his mid-forties, the years of harsh farm life and preaching had taken its toll. By noon on Sunday, he was completely wiped out. But not until after lunch.

David's mother, Katharina, on the other hand, never seemed to stop. She was always cooking, serving, and cleaning—an endless loop interrupted only by church or sleep. Her Sunday feast was always the best meal of the week. That was where she tried out new dishes or served big favorites, ones that required a certain meat or special vegetable. As usual, David had stuffed himself. Now, he sat at the table in his Sunday best, waiting for the snoring to begin.

He passed his knife over the stone a few more times and stopped, glancing down the empty hallway. Twenty minutes earlier, his mother had shuffled down the same hall to her bedroom where she went to "rest my eyes," as she called it. For her, napping seemed like a sin, especially when there was always more work to do.

He listened carefully for his dad on the couch and was rewarded with the sounds of heavy breathing. It was time to put his plan into action.

With his eight siblings scattered around the house in various states of rest, he grabbed his hat and went back to the kitchen, slipping out the door and closing it as quietly as possible. It took him less than five minutes to fasten a saddle to Doell and ride out of the barn, heading toward Peter's house.

Along the short trip, David brushed away some straw that had attached to his outfit. The clean material of his shirt and jacket felt smooth and foreign against his scrubbed skin. The night before, he'd taken a bath in a real cast iron bathtub. The contraption worked by building a fire underneath it and heating the water inside the tub. It was primitive, but it worked. Each family member took a bath and had continuous hot water, although not necessarily fresh. Still, they had something that was a rarity in the colonies; "a forbidden luxury," as some complained.

Before the new bathtub, they had all bathed in the barn by kneeling in a galvanized oval tub, taking turns with a steady supply of hot water and bucketfuls of cold to rinse off with. The water was never quite hot enough, especially considering the lower November temperatures. During the summer months, they didn't need hot water, and simply enjoyed splashing around in the cool well water.

It felt strange to look down at his hands and find the dirt gone from beneath his nails. He tried to enjoy it while it lasted, knowing full well that this was the cleanest he'd be all week.

He reached Peter's house, finding a saddled horse hitched to a rail by the road. He pulled Doell up just as Peter jogged out from the barn, giving him a little wave. He, too, was dressed in his finest clothes, a jacket pulled around his thin frame.

Peter untied his horse's reins and mounted up. "Did anyone see you leave?" he asked.

"Nah," David replied. "They're all napping in the house. Besides, I told them earlier I might ride over to your house."

"Will they be mad if they find out where we're going?"

"Of course," David said, looking down the road as Peter pulled his horse alongside Doell. "They want me to stay with them forever and do all the work for free. I'm tired of it! I'm eighteen, after all."

Peter nodded with understanding. "I'm glad that at least my older brother and sister are gone. My parents are already used to the idea that I'm going to leave one day."

They rode at a comfortable pace, passing by a few houses. No one was out and about today. Suddenly, a grin creased on Peter's face. "I hope we see some cute girls."

"Me too," David laughed, pulling his jacket tighter. "I need to find a wife and get out of here."

During their five-mile trip to Neustadt Campo 101, the two boys talked mostly about girls. The sun was bright but low in the sky, failing to provide much warmth. The trees, barren and leafless, rattled in the wind. David could feel his cheeks getting a little colder, wiggling his fingers to keep the blood flowing.

"Do you know which street it is?" Peter asked as they got closer.

"Yes, I think so." In all honesty, he hoped his information was correct. Another boy had told him where all the young people met, and he'd taken his word for it. He pushed himself up in his stirrups. "It can't be too hard to find, especially if everyone is there."

As they rounded the corner, David's words rang true. At least sixty boys and girls milled around the general store for the campo. Next to it sat a closed carpenter's shop, where even more lingered. The area was more of a business district than a residential area—a private place, where the prying eyes of adults didn't intrude.

They rode down the middle of the street, checking out the scene, a moving wave of large straw hats and colorful bows. Groups of girls were clustered together, with an occasional boy talking to one or two of them. A few clusters of boys stood at a distance, deciding how best to approach their desired target.

A dark-skinned girl with a bright purple ribbon hanging off her hat sat on the wooden steps of the store catching David's eye. She smiled at him. He smiled back, already feeling his cheeks warm a little. He and Peter rode a short distance, checking out all of the prospects before dismounting and tying up their horses.

"What do you want to do?" Peter asked.

"I spotted a girl down there, the one who has that fitted plaid dress on. I'm going to talk to her."

Peter pushed his hat back. "Okay," he said reluctantly. "I guess I'm on my own, then."

David could hardly focus on Peter's words, giving him an apologetic glance before turning around, eyes locked on his destination. A few acquaintances called out to him as he continued toward the girl. He nodded and moved on, biting the inside of his cheek as he got closer and closer.

She brushed herself off as she stood. A small, secret smile tugged at her lips as he approached.

"Hello," he said at last. "I'm David Rempel."

Her smile grew a little. She was oddly calm, not at all showing the nervousness that David felt. "I'm Anna Friesen."

David shifted his cap, blinking in surprise. "I know your name."

She raised her eyebrows. "You do?"

"I've seen you in church. I remember that day—the one when you were standing in the baptism line."

She laughed, her amusement reaching her eyes, making them sparkle a little as she met his gaze. "That was so long ago."

A silence grew between them, and David tried not to fidget. Around them, snippets of conversation made their way through the breeze, reaching their ears.

"Would you like to sit down?" she asked.

"Sure," he managed, tilting his hat back.

They brushed off the steps and positioned themselves close to each other, but not too close. He could feel her warmth in the air, making its way through his jacket and sending shivers down his spine.

"That's a nice saddle you have," Anna offered.

He leaned back on the stairs, giving her a grin. "Thank you. I got it after working last year. It's my first one." David's father had helped pay for it, since he'd been sending him all over the place to deliver this and pick up that. Like bathtubs, most colonists didn't have saddles.

The small talk began to come more easily. Anna always had a witty comment or question to ask, and David didn't have trouble providing the

171

answers. She fascinated him—her words smooth and collected, and she knew exactly what to do to fill the silence. He could hardly remember what they talked about, only that one topic ran into the next, that talking to her was easy and wonderful and new all at once.

He learned that she was called the "little Mexican child" due to her naturally dark complexion, which was tanned because she refused to wear a hat outside when she worked. This was contrary to the fair, white skin of the rest of the colony's women, a look most men desired.

They sat and talked until a cool wind snuck up David's jacket and slipped inside his shirt. Anna wrapped her arms around herself, rubbing them for some warmth. David didn't say anything as he took off his jacket, putting it around her shoulders. This drew stares all around, including from Peter. It was a signal to everyone that she was his—at least for this temporary visit.

Anna looked at the jacket and grinned, pulling it around her thin frame. She scooted a little closer to him, launching back into their conversation. This was her acceptance.

For the next ten weeks, David made the trip to Neustadt Campo 101 to visit Anna. He brought her little candies and other inexpensive gifts, listening as she discussed the events of the past week, asking him about his life. Gradually, he found himself learning more about her.

Anna was the last of eleven children. Her father, Jacob Friesen, had died two years earlier. David liked the fact that both her brother and father shared the name Jacob, just like his father and grandfather. It was a nice connection.

Whenever he came to visit, she would wear this small, secret smile. This enamored him, along with the way her eyes lit up when she spoke. All of it made his heart pound in his ears. Her intelligent conversation and quips only gave him more reasons to like her.

With each visit, he felt more and more that she was the girl for him. And he was certain she felt the same way.

Every moment he was away from her gnawed at him. He could think of nothing else but her, finding it hard to get through some of his chores.

Then he would remind himself he needed money to have her, and refocused his efforts. The thought of money pushed him through the week until Sunday, when he could sneak out and see his girl again.

Peter continued to ride with him. He, too, had found a girl he was interested in. Doing this together, David thought he was safe. But in January, word leaked out.

"You've been sneaking away and riding to Campo 101," his father said, pointing his finger at David's chest. "Haven't you?"

Unafraid, David pushed back. "Yes, sir. I'd like to find a wife."

Jacob's neck turned red. "You're too young! Too young to be seeing girls."

David suppressed a smirk. *Sure, I just need to stay here another ten years and run the farm for free.*

"Who are you seeing?" his father demanded.

"Anna Friesen." David's voice was firm and unwavering. Even Jacob couldn't hide the surprise that touched his eyes at David's newfound confidence.

Jacob regained his composure. "I know the girl. She's too old for you. You're just eighteen. And what is she? Twenty-three? Twenty-four? Twenty-five?"

Wisely, David held his tongue.

"No!" Jacob ordered. The word cracked at him like a whip, but David didn't flinch. "This will not do. I don't want you to go over there again. Do you understand?"

David said nothing. He could tell he was getting under his father's skin, making Jacob wonder if he could still control his son. David knew that if he said no, his father would be in trouble. *I could leave, stop working. Not listen to him again*, David thought, suddenly realizing how much power he had.

Jacob sensed it, too. He rubbed his jaw and decided not to pursue an answer to his question. Instead, he turned away, fuming.

"You need to find a girl your age," his mother chimed in. Her voice was calm, but held little more reason than his father's. "Younger, perhaps.

173

That's what you need to do." It was as if the decision had already been made. She was simply telling him what it was.

David maintained his silence, his face stone. It was his best move. When they had exhausted themselves, David lowered his head and shuffled out, trying to hide the hurt in his eyes, showing them that they had won.

The next Sunday, his parents watched as he slipped out of his Sunday best, certain he was giving up on Anna. As they fell deep into their naps, David eased his clothes back on and snuck out the back. Nothing was going to stop him from seeing Anna. *Nothing.*

On the ride over, he thought about telling his new love about the problems he was having. He gritted his teeth, deciding against it. If he was going to be a man, he needed to protect his woman from the harshness of the world. And that started now. Unfortunately, his father had connections. Being high up in the clergy had its advantages.

As expected, Jacob again broached the subject at supper one night. David had no doubt that one of his father's many spies had told him about the secret meetings. He could sense his anger beneath his nonchalant expression. Not only was his oldest son defying him, but he was seeing a girl who was considered an old maid. This would not stand!

The table fell silent as Jacob spoke, his voice uncharacteristically calm. "Son, I understand you're still seeing Anna Friesen."

All eyes fell on David, waiting for a showdown. David wouldn't give in. He called up Anna's face to his mind, using the image to give him strength.

"Yes, sir."

"She's too old for you," Jacob said forcefully. "I told you that before. Don't you remember?"

"Yes, sir."

His brothers and sisters stared at their plates, listening to every word, yet careful to avoid their father's anger.

"You're barely old enough to start a tractor," Jacob said, pounding the butt of his knife into the table. "I don't want to discuss this again."

David hung his head. "Yes, sir."

David glanced at his mother, who, like his siblings, had her eyes trained on her food. Nothing more was said about the matter.

The rest of the week crawled by as David raced through his chores, thoughts consumed by his father's words. When Sunday arrived, he knew what he had to do.

Several months later, after the torrential July rains had passed and the seed was firmly in the ground, David announced to everyone that he was getting engaged to Anna Friesen. By now, his father had given up. It was that or lose his son, something he wasn't willing to do. Besides, he knew that when a boy's heart was in a girl's hand, nothing would get it back. Still, he wasn't happy about it.

The date was set: Sunday, August 15, 1965. By tradition, Jacob sat down more than a full week before the ceremony and wrote out an invitation, listing the names of each person he and his wife, Katharina, wanted to attend. When he was done, he called his son to his desk. "David, I want you to add the names of any friends you want attending your wedding." He handed him the letter. "When you're done, give it back to me."

David looked it over and added several names. When he gave it back to his father, Jacob took it to the campo teacher, who rewrote it. Once the announcement was made public, the teacher would start the circulation.

Anna's family created their own letter, with the names of their relatives and friends they wanted to attend. Then Anna was given the opportunity to add her friends. Their letter was taken to their campo's school teacher, who made two handwritten copies.

The actual announcement was made in church on Sunday, one week before the wedding. The next day, two copies of the letter circulated on the bride's side and one on the groom's. As each person received the letter, they crossed their name out and forwarded it to someone else on the list. The last person who crossed their name out delivered it to the bride or groom. It was in this manner that the parties knew everyone had received notice—not that the gossip hadn't long preceded the letters.

On the day the proposed marriage was announced—Sunday—David's parents rode over after church to have lunch with Anna's mother and siblings. There was cabbage soup, cold fruit, *Moos*, and *Rinsbruden*—stew meat cooked with raisins and served with potatoes. It was a nice, polite affair, after which the parties wished each other the best, knowing they would see them in a few days. Now, the real work began.

Over the next six days, David and Anna visited friends and relatives under the pretense of making sure they had received the invitation letter. Of course, the couples they saw knew they were coming and the visits were designed to arrive just before supper. There would be small gifts, such as cups and saucers, forks, knives, and spoons. One of David's uncles gave him five silver pesos wrapped very tightly in brown paper. On Anna's side, a friend of her mother's who happened to be David's first cousin, baked a small round cake for their table. This was highly unusual. Between the food and conversation, David and Anna barely knew what time it was.

Prior to the actual ceremony, any kissing or close contact was strictly forbidden. Holding hands was the only act allowed—and later, perhaps an arm around a shoulder. That was it. Anyone violating these rules was dealt with sharply.

For the wedding, they needed an Ältester. They chose Mr. Franz Dyck. He was the uncle of David's good friend Peter. It just felt right.

David pulled his Sunday best suit from the closet and took it to the living room to brush off. His father was sitting at the kitchen table reviewing some paperwork when he noticed David carrying his suit.

"What are you doing?" Jacob asked, coming into the living room.

"Preparing my suit for the wedding," David replied.

"Oh no. You can't wear black to a wedding. It must be brown or dark blue. I'll take care of it."

A few days later, a vendor came through the campos, selling fine cloth from Mexico City. Jacob carefully inspected his material and purchased enough yardage to make a dark blue suit with pin stripes. He was determined that his son would be the best-looking groom around.

The next day, Jacob handed the material to David and gave him directions to a proper tailor in Cuauhtémoc—thirty miles away. David wrapped it up and made his way to Highway 33, catching a bus headed south into the big city. He had rarely been to Cuauhtémoc and never alone. It was both exciting and scary.

When the suit was ready, David made the return trip and picked it up. The morning of his wedding day, he put the suit on (having failed to try it on at the tailor's shop) and discovered one pant leg was severely twisted. He couldn't imagine how a tailor had missed that. As there was nothing he could do, David did the best he could and endured the occasional stare.

At the church, David and Anna arrived and placed their dining room chairs, ones they'd brought from home, directly in front of the pulpit. Anna, her dress all black, sat next to David as they endured another two-and-a-half-hour message.

When Ältester Dyck was done, he asked the couple to stand. David and Anna nervously got to their feet, sneaking a glance at each other. The vows were administered in Low German, the same words used for centuries in the United States and in Canada.

After that was accomplished, a song was started up by the Vorsanger—a row of men sitting at the front of the church along with the Ältester. With the entire congregation still seated, David took this opportunity to grab his new bride and walk outside, where his horse and buggy were hitched to the Ältester's post—something a groom was allowed to do on his wedding day. David gently lifted his wife up to the buckboard of his father's buggy and made a fast getaway, steering the horse to his parents' home, and beating everyone by thirty minutes.

Killing time, they sat on the porch waiting until everyone arrived and the questions began. One of the first ones was from his father, Jacob.

"Do you still have your teeth?" he said to Anna.

David reeled at the incredible insult to his wife, unsure how to handle it.

"Of course I do," Anna said, laughing it off. "And they'll come in handy when we sit down to eat. What are they cooking?" Deftly, she redirected the conversation to something less offensive.

David, still upset from the insult, meandered through the crowd of visitors with his new wife, before finally sitting down and eating a hearty meal. After lunch, David received the wedding gifts. First was from his parents, Jacob and Katharina: two piglets and fifteen chickens. Giving a cow was traditional but Jacob was not feeling happy about his son's selection of women and his cows were from good stock, so he asked David if he would take an old hay binder instead.

"Sure," David said, surprised at the slight. He would use that machine the first year to bind his bales of hay before his brother-in law, Dietrich, said he wanted it badly. David took a cow in trade. It was in this manner that David finally received his traditional cow, although one year late.

David's paternal grandparents gave the couple four china cups and saucers. But not before Jacob pulled his grandson aside for some private conversation.

"Have you thought more about leaving this place?" Jacob asked the new groom.

"Yes," he replied, looking around to make sure no one was listening. "I'm going to work hard and put away as much money as I can as fast as I can. One day, I'll come and tell you the time has finally arrived." David lowered his voice to a whisper. "But make no mistake, I'll find a way out of here."

Jacob nodded. "Good boy. Now let's get back to the party."

Chapter Sixteen

The morning after the wedding, a strange rooster crowed, waking an exhausted David. He stared at an unfamiliar ceiling and breathed hard, eyes searching frantically for something he recognized until he realized where he was. There was a woman beside him. It was real. Now.

Draped over the chair were his new blue slacks, the ones with a twisted leg. David shook his head. Either the tailor was a criminal or the vendor's material was worthless. Regardless, weeks later David would give the pants to one of Anna's nephews, who wore them to work in the fields, certainly being one of the best dressed farmers around. But before long, it rained and the nephew found himself in distress, for the cloth had shrunk and wrapped around his legs like an anaconda. It took a sharp pair of scissors to free him from the beast. When David saw this, he laughed so hard Anna thought he'd need to see the medicine man.

The new couple had made an arrangement to live with Anna's family. Since her father had died two years earlier, Anna's mother needed help. To sweeten the offer, a small outbuilding behind Anna's house would be their newlywed quarters. A little privacy was a good thing. Yet this arrangement meant he was working for his mother-in-law now. But it wasn't all bad. By tradition, if a girl was unmarried and still at home, she received her first cow when she was twenty-one. It was like a payment for all the years of work, and allowed her to earn her own money. Since her cow produced a calf each year, Anna owned four cows, plus the traditional one she received as a wedding present. When she pressed several hundred pesos into David's hands—her life savings—David felt rich. He'd never seen so much money. It was almost scary.

At the Friesen's, though, his day was different. He did the barn cleaning like always, but now he had to milk Anna's cows as well as his in-laws'. And, he had to haul the milk inside or to the nearby cheese factory, where it was purchased. It was hard work.

After a few weeks of settling in, he started making money by building or fixing things for their neighbors. Soon, he had a good reputation of doing quality work. Once he had some extra money in his pocket, he purchased a wagon and two horses. The wagon was in poor shape, but David bought a car frame and built a box on it, along with a bigger hayrack to hold the grain. This allowed him to make even more money during harvest time.

Ever the industrious man, he purchased a car battery and ran some wires into their house for a little electricity. With his shiplap and floor tile skills, and Anna brushing the boards with a mixture of white calcium powder tinted with ashes from the stove to make a grayish color of milk paint, the place was downright cozy.

After a full month of living at the Friesen's, he had life down. Each day he woke up and did his chores, while Anna made breakfast in the main house. After he had eaten, he kissed his wife on the lips, grabbed a cowboy hat and a jug of water, and headed to their fields two miles away. If he didn't bring lunch with him, Anna would carry over a fresh jug of water and a basket of food for him to eat. At sundown, he made the long walk home to find his lovely bride waiting for him, along with a hearty supper. And when the lights went out, well… that was their time.

Like all Mennonites, the babies came fast. A few months into married life, Anna announced that she was pregnant. Almost ten months from their wedding night, Elizabeth was born. Thirteen months later, little David arrived. By now, the couple had moved from the Friesen's farm to some new land—200 acres—David's father had purchased. There was a small house on it, larger than their cramped outbuilding—a welcome relief to their expanding family.

At twenty-one years old, David made a deal with his father to work the crops on a four-to-one basis: Jacob paid for the seed, fuel, and tractor, and kept three-fourths of the crop. David kept the remaining fourth to live on. The year after that, the deal changed to 50-50. This gave him a chance to make some real money.

Not all the land was planted, allowing David to put his cattle in the fields of wild grass. He worked hard to help them reproduce, which brought in even more money. He had to admit that life was much better here than under his dad's thumb. Still, he was stuck riding around on steel paddle wheels instead of rubber tires, which translated into constant maintenance on the tractor's engine.

Even though this land was rocky, David brought in a good crop of oats and sold it to the Cuauhtémoc locals as well as an oatmeal company. He continued this arrangement until his father sold the farm, needing the money for some reason. This required David and his family to move back to his mother-in-law's place, where David farmed part of her land while one of Anna's brothers farmed the rest. It was a good arrangement.

When David turned twenty-four, he bought his own fifty acres, paying 500 pesos per acre, or a total of $25,000. Because he didn't have that much money, he made a down payment and agreed to yearly installments.

David's family lived in a house on that land, while also renting some acreage from his mother-in-law. The two places were within a mile of each other, so he could walk or ride horseback between them. He made some money by milking cows and raising hogs for sale, and the small crop he produced added a few more pesos to the glass jar hidden in their wall. Life was going well for David and Anna. Their two children—Elizabeth and David—were both healthy and growing. That's when David found himself being pulled aside by his wife.

"I have some news to tell you," Anna said.

David had learned from past events what this meant. "Are you pregnant again?" he said.

"Yes," Anna replied, smiling and nodding her head. "God willing, this will be a healthy baby like Elizabeth and David."

It wasn't.

When Anna was pregnant with Elizabeth, she had seizures. Many times, she had worried she'd lose the child. It was a difficult pregnancy.

Her second child, David, was easy. He came out like he belonged in the world, which of course, he did. Now, Anna looked for any sign of the seizures, but none appeared. However, at eight months, a new problem had developed. With a little extra money available, they decided to see a doctor in the campo.

David took his wife in a buggy after dropping his two children at a neighbor's house. He wanted to make sure she experienced a smooth ride, one he and his horse Gray John could provide.

They arrived at the small wood structure, where David ever so carefully helped his wife down and escorted her inside.

"Good morning, Dr. Enns," David said. "I have a patient for you."

Dr. Enns slid his feet off the desk and stood. "Well, bring her over here. Let's see what's going on." He wasn't a licensed doctor but a man who had picked up the Indian medicinal remedies using local plants, and of course, a man who had been given an interest from God in helping people.

Anna moved to an examining table and sat on the edge. "Do you want me to lie back?"

"Let's get some information first," he said. "How far along are you?"

"About eight months," Anna replied.

"Any problems so far?" Dr. Enns asked, touching her forehead.

"The baby was moving all the time but has stopped in the last few days. It's been very quiet. I think something's wrong."

"You're so far along, I can't believe the baby's not moving. I think you're mistaken," Dr. Enns said. "Let's have you lie down."

Anna stretched out as David helped her back, pulling her dress across her stomach since Mennonites were not accustomed to having a physical examination. Any examination would have to take place through the fabric.

Dr. Enns poked and prodded for a few minutes before rolling up a thick piece of paper. "I haven't done this before; it's not something I do because I don't have a stethoscope. However, I'll see if I can listen for a heartbeat." He placed one end of the tube on Anna's stomach and the other up to his ear.

"Hmm," he said, shifting to another spot. This went on for several minutes as the doctor squinted and concentrated. Finally, he pulled the tube off and put it away.

"What is it, Doctor?" Anna asked, fearful of the answer.

His solemn face told the whole story. "I'm afraid you're right. I can't hear the baby's heartbeat. You're going to have a stillborn."

Anna felt tears welling up. "Oh no!" she cried.

"I'm sorry," he said coldly. "However, you need to take these vitamins to gain some strength. You'll be stronger when the delivery comes." He handed her a bottle.

Anna wiped away her tears and moved off the table. "I understand, Doctor. Thank you for your time."

The doctor nodded as David handed him the money for his services. David could tell he'd delivered that news before, perhaps hundreds of times. Since a Mennonite woman's main purpose in life was to have as many children as possible, a stillborn meant there was a good chance this would be her last. It was sad for everyone.

Back home, Anna took the pills, resigning herself to going into labor at any time. Hers would be yet another lost child in the long legacy of the colony.

Barely two weeks since receiving the bad news, Anna was in the kitchen cleaning a pot and felt something. Putting the pot down, she felt it again. Quickly, she got to a chair and prepared herself for the labor that would expel the stillborn. Then it happened again. Something was moving inside. Anna placed her hand over the womb and waited. And waited.

There it was. Yes, a kick! It had to be.

For the next hour, she sat still, afraid to move, waiting until David strolled in from the barn.

"What's happening?" he said, alarmed to see her sitting there with a puzzled look.

"I think the baby is moving again," she said calmly.

"What?! Let's get you back to the doctor."

David wasted no time escorting her to a surprised Dr. Enns.

"It can't be," he said. "Lie down and I'll examine you."

A few minutes later, an astonished doctor unrolled his paper and stepped back. "I can't believe it," he said. "It's a miracle!"

David and Anna smiled. It absolutely was.

When it was time to give birth, David paid someone to take them to a hospital in Chihuahua, where they knew Miss Fehr, a German nurse, worked. She had come down from Kansas to help translate for the doctors.

Anna's contractions started, but the doctor wanted to slow them down. "Give her a shot of sedation," he ordered Miss Fehr.

Ten minutes later, the doctor checked back. "Anna, can you hear me?"

Anna was out of it. "How much did you give her?" he asked the nurse, pulling her outside so they could discuss it in private.

David was sitting in the waiting room when Miss Fehr burst in. "I've made a mistake and given Anna too much sedative. I need you to pray very hard. She's in labor and the baby is not coming out."

With Anna unable to push, the outcome appeared grim. Panicked, Miss Fehr climbed on top of Anna and began pushing herself. Each time she felt a contraction, the nurse pushed hard. It was a valiant effort.

At eleven a.m., the doctor found David and delivered the news. "Mr. Rempel, your wife had a baby girl. I'm pleased to say she's alive and healthy. However, this will be her last child. Please make sure she has no more children."

David ran to Anna's room and saw her holding a yawning Katharina Rempel, her mop of dark hair everywhere. He bent down, studying his new child, and the little girl stretched, as if she'd been bored, waiting for such a moment. David kissed his wife, but she was too tired and sedated to say much. After making sure his daughter was in good hands, he went outside to get some fresh air. To his surprise, there was Peter, who had married Anna's sister.

"I just had a daughter," he told Peter. "Make sure to tell your wife."

Peter chuckled. "I sure will. And you tell your wife we had a baby boy yesterday."

"Isn't that something!" David said, shaking Peter's hand. "Two sisters having a baby one day apart."

Forty-eight hours later, David was back home, with Anna resting and tiny Katharina sleeping peacefully in her crib. He wanted to stand there and watch her forever, yet the work didn't stop. Cows had to be milked. Animals fed. In no time, he was back to his routine with his family growing before his very eyes.

One day, as David toiled in the fields with a wobbly tractor, fighting both the rocks and the metal paddles, he yelled to the heavens, "That's it! I'm not doing this anymore."

Guiding the Model A John Deere tractor to a small shed, he removed the metal wheels and installed the original rubber tires. Instantly, the tractor transformed into a fast-moving machine. David had never felt the control and speed of operating his machine the way it had been designed. In less than half the time, his work was done. He was beyond excited.

Over the next several weeks, David carefully picked the days (and sometimes nights) he used rubber tires—times when others weren't watching. He confided in a few friends and discovered two other men had been breaking the rule for months. This information gave him confidence to keep going.

David realized his rubber tires were only needed during planting and harvesting. This lessened the chance of getting caught. And, he could change the tires out in ten minutes. It saved him four hours a day. He knew his wife had seen him with rubber tractor tires and said nothing. He also knew she listened to a forbidden radio, one he'd secretly purchased—and raised no objections. They both violated the rules separately, never bringing it up. Hopefully, it stayed that way.

In May of 1972, David turned twenty-six. He got to thinking about how to make extra money. His growing family needed more. He talked with Wilhelm Burg, who had made the trip to Canada to work as a seasonal harvester. Mr. Burg also had a forbidden vehicle in El Paso. It was an old brown Buick, one that he assured David would travel well. After talking several times, the two came up with an idea to leave the colony during early summer before the rains. They would drive from the heart of Mexico all the way to Canada, with Mr. Burg as their guide. He was a rare Mennonite who understood a little English and could read the road signs. With Mr. Burg having made the trip before, David felt like it was a good move.

The two men kept the plan to themselves, not broadcasting it around for fear someone would tell them not to go. However, word did leak out, and by the time they were leaving, the group wanting to travel had grown to six people: Wilhelm and his wife, David, and Cornelius and Abraham—sons of Anna's brother Abraham. There was also a Mexican friend named Carlos.

Early one morning, after kissing Anna goodbye, David, along with the rest of the group, slipped away and caught a ride into El Paso, where Wilhelm's car awaited. With ready transportation, they headed to the immigration office and took out a forty-five-day visa to pass through the U.S. on the way to Canada. On a bright afternoon in May, they exited customs and David found himself in America—a place he'd heard so much about.

The anxious group drove half a day before stopping in El Paso, where David had a new experience: He ate in a restaurant for the first time. David ordered a hamburger with French fries. It was quite the treat.

Once they had downed their food, they traveled to Santa Fe, just north of Albuquerque. There, they stopped for the night, checking into a small motel. It was here that David caught a glimpse of a television for the first time. It sat behind the clerk at the front desk, chattering away to anyone who would listen. The clerk handed David a key to his room, but he could hardly pull himself away from the moving pictures, all bright and new. When he did, he was in for another treat. The motel's bed was extremely comfortable. He had never slept so well, except perhaps on his wedding night.

For the next two days, the group saw wondrous sites—the mountains of Colorado, the fields of Nebraska and Iowa, and the forests of Minnesota. Each large city they passed through fascinated them as much as that TV. For the first time in years, David's grandfather's words came back to him, watering the seeds he'd planted in David's mind about leaving. Going back to the only life he'd known seemed impossible, with all the sights and sounds he'd experienced.

After crossing into Ontario, Canada, they found a place they had heard of that needed workers. The rich tobacco fields of St. Thomas were being harvested, and they found work the very first day on an Englander's farm. At $25 a day for doing the same brutal work he'd done in Mexico, David could hardly believe it. In no time, he felt rich. Life was cooler here too as they were barely ten miles north of Lake Erie, its breeze removing much of the sun's heat. Yes, life in Canada was as sweet as the tobacco leaves he picked.

At night, they stayed in a house the tobacco farmer had for his workers. Then, each Friday, Anna's brother Henry traveled the ten miles west and picked up David, Cornelius, and Abraham, taking them back to Aylmer where they stayed for the weekend. Henry and his wife, Elizabeth, took the boys to a German Church of God, which was much different than the colony's church. This church had a piano to accompany the singing, and the Word was preached as an encouragement instead of "Thou art doomed" for everything. It also had a Sunday school for the children since it was never too early to be teaching them about God. David was amazed at how friendly everyone was. For the first time ever, church was a pleasant experience.

When Sunday evening arrived, Henry took the boys back to St. Thomas, and the week started all over again.

Each day, David headed to the fields while picking up a little English. By the second week, he had cut his hair short and ditched his overalls for a pair of comfortable jeans. He felt free.

When they had put in forty days of backbreaking work, David shook the hand of his boss and piled into Wilhelm's car with the rest of the group for the journey south. They made it back just in time, pockets bursting with cash.

David's mind spun as he walked toward his house, craving more of the world. How could he ever return to this way of life?

His brother gave him a wave as he approached, accepting money from David for milking and tending to the cows while he'd been away. He could see his brother eyeing him strangely, like he'd just arrived from a different world. In a way, he had.

David climbed the porch steps with a bag of gifts and found Anna alone in the kitchen. Her eyes grew wide as she gazed at him, up and down.

"You look so different," she said, circling her husband, careful not to get too close. "What's all that?"

Laughing, he set the bag down and grabbed her gently, pressing his lips to hers. "I come bearing gifts for you and the children. And yes, I missed you. Anna—I have something to tell you."

He pulled her out behind the house, before his children noticed he was home and smothered him with demands for attention.

"What's the matter?" she asked, a look of concern spreading on her face.

"Nothing's the matter," he whispered. "After seeing Canada, I've made a decision and want to tell you what it is…" He paused, unsure of how to tell her. Anna was very close to her family, and he doubted that she'd want to leave. To this point in their marriage, he'd never discussed his thoughts of leaving the colony with her. Not even a hint.

But it was time. He couldn't hold it in any longer. "I know this may be hard on you, but we're leaving this place. As soon as I can sell everything, we're going to Canada. What do you think?"

Anna recoiled from him, covering her mouth, her eyes filling with tears. The glassy look she gave him tugged at his heart, nearly splitting it in two. It was a mix of denial and fear, and he hated seeing it on her.

David swallowed hard. She might say no. If so, this might be a lot tougher than he thought.

Chapter Seventeen

Rose Henderson

May 1972
Seminole, Texas

Rose dipped the cloth into a basin of water and wrung it out. A slight breeze drifted in through the window screen as she placed the damp rag on her aunt's forehead, soothing her.

"Does that feel good?" Rose asked.

Aunt Mae blinked twice, voice raspy and exhausted. "It does. It surely does."

Rose tried smiling. "When this fever breaks, you can get back on your feet and make some of your famous banana cream pie."

"I don't think so, dear," Aunt Mae replied, drawing in a deep breath. "I'm tired. It's time for me to go home."

Rose jerked back, feeling the shock of those words. "Oh, don't say that. You have plenty of time left. You'll see." She dabbed the cloth across her aunt's forehead, working the moisture into her red, cracked skin. "Let me run to Lowery Pharmacy and pick something up. I'm sure they can help."

Aunt Mae shook her head, forcing Rose to readjust the towel. "I doubt it. Besides, I want you to save the money. You'll need it to take care of Melvin." She paused to catch her breath. "I'm afraid I've taken up all of your good years—tending to us, helping run the business."

Again, Aunt Mae paused, eyes closing as her voice retreated to a whisper. "It's time for you to have the rest of your life. That's the least I can do for you. Let me sleep, dear."

Rose sat down, fidgeting as she stared at the older woman, a lump growing in her throat. Aunt Mae had been sick for more than a year, and the doctors said there was nothing they could do. Even surgery couldn't remove all the cancer.

They'd suggested a new facility that had been built in Lubbock. The doctor had called it a hospice. But after checking on the cost, it wasn't possible. Besides, the distance would have taken her aunt too far away. When Aunt Mae said she wanted to die at home, Rose had steeled herself to caring for her as best she could.

It was a labor of love, harsh and unrewarding.

Rose finally got up and went to the kitchen, determined to keep her hands busy. She put on a kettle of water, waiting for it to whistle. Once her cup of orange pekoe had steeped properly, she returned to the living room and sat in Aunt Mae's favorite chair. This gave her a view of both her patient and Melvin, who was organizing his marbles in the corner of the room.

It was hot outside, and she knew she should be running the window unit—but it was on its last legs. They wanted to save it for extremely hot days, and today wasn't the blazing kind. With a nice cross breeze blowing through the house, it was somewhat tolerable.

Rose sipped her tea and looked out the window, watching the cars driving past. It seemed like everyone else's life was in one of those cars, racing to an appointment or perhaps a date. Meanwhile, here she was, watching her life pass by. Still, she was grateful her aunt and uncle had taken her in. If not, she'd probably have been in some orphanage—and who knows where that would have put her.

After her uncle had died in 1949, they had worked hard at the business, keeping it running and making money for ten years. Then more competition had appeared, with men running the new stores, and a few selling John Deere tractors. Since most of their buyers were men, the buyers gravitated to those. Soon, they had found themselves with fewer sales. Without money to upgrade or buy the latest John Deere tractors, they'd made the painful decision to close the business at the end of 1960.

An auctioneer had come in and sold the remaining equipment and fixtures. With an empty building, they'd hired a real estate agent, who'd gotten a good price for it. This set them up for more than six years, allowing them to live comfortably.

In 1967, her aunt's house needed repairs. With money running low, Rose had had no choice but to sell. They had been living on the proceeds of that for the last five years, scrimping and saving at every turn. Aunt Mae received a social security check, which covered the utilities and food but not much more.

Rose knew that they were almost out of money; a few months earlier, she had moved all her aunt's money into her bank account. Mixed with her savings, the total came to just under $1,000.

Rose took another sip of her drink as Aunt Mae's words ran through her mind. *I've taken up all of your good years.* She wondered if that was true. Through some cruel twist of fate, she'd never married. First, there'd been the tragedy with Charles Simpson. If the stock market hadn't crashed, they would have been married and living in a large house, with kids running around everywhere. Instead, she'd been left with the image of him pulling off her engagement ring and fleeing from the police.

The next serious prospect had been Eddie Fulghum, the engineer for Texaco and baseball manager for their team. They were dating until he'd been transferred to Oklahoma, where he'd written her diligently. Then, one day, the letters had simply stopped. She'd assumed he had found someone else until a year later, when a relative wrote to her and said he'd been killed in a car accident.

She'd dated others. There was Billy Stansil, the local butcher. He moved from one woman to another, never serious about settling down. Then there was Michael Mullee, a traveling salesman for a dry goods jobber in Dallas. He'd selected a girl in Abilene and gotten married.

By the time she turned forty-five, the only men who showed any interest were either married or unstable. As such, she'd stopped dating and focused her attention on running the store with her aunt and caring for Melvin, who was basically a man-child. He never got violent, but if he didn't want to do something, she was powerless to make him.

She set her cup down at the sound of Melvin choking, springing to her feet. He was in distress, having trouble breathing. Her first thought was that he was choking on a marble. He rarely put them in his mouth, but he must have done it this time.

She ran to him, pushing a chair out of the way and kneeling beside his retching body. She started to slap his back with the flat of her hand, feeling beads of sweat form between her shoulder blades.

"We need to get it out!" she yelled. "Let me help you."

He pushed her away as he bent over, tears coming from his eyes. Rose quickly inspected his hands and mouth and found nothing wrong. Then it hit her. She leaned back and felt her eyes filling up.

For at least a minute, she stayed next to Melvin. Sadness gnawed at the edges of her mind, forcing more tears from her eyes. When his coughing fit stopped, Rose wiped the tears from her cheeks and slowly got to her feet, working some feeling back into them as she made her way to the couch.

It seemed to take an eternity to make the journey to Aunt Mae, because she knew what she would find. Leaning down, she kissed her aunt on the cheek and removed the damp cloth. Then she pulled a thin blanket over her aunt's body and prepared herself for the even longer journey to the justice of the peace's office. Without a phone or car, her only option was to walk.

A labor of love, she thought. It was yet another tragedy she'd have to endure.

The funeral director of Singleton Funeral Home closed the door and took his place behind the desk. Rose smoothed out the cloth of her dark dress beneath her fingers, waiting for him to begin.

"As you have explained, your funds are quite low," he said politely. "I've spoken with Pastor Lewis at First Baptist, and he's agreed to have the memorial there. We will transport your aunt to the church and then to the gravesite. This will save you money on our facility. Is that acceptable?"

Rose nodded. "Yes, that's fine. What about the casket?"

"I've spoken with my employee, and we have a nice, comfortable model that will fit your needs. We'll be able to use some fabric to dress it up for the memorial service. Believe me, no one will know the difference."

Relief washed through her like a cool wind. "Thank you, sir. I can't tell you how much I appreciate it."

He waved his hand. "No need to thank me. Your aunt was a longtime fixture of Seminole, and we wouldn't think of not taking care of her." He slid a paper across the desk toward her. "Here is the total for everything. Are you able to manage this?"

Rose glanced at the paper and sighed. "Yes, sir. Just please make her as comfortable as possible."

"We certainly will. Don't you worry about it."

Rose left the funeral home and walked down to the Seminole State Bank. Earl Raffton was standing near a desk and recognized her. "Rose. I'm so sorry to hear about Mae Beth. How are you holding up?"

Rose's eyes felt dry. She hadn't gotten much sleep the night before, or the night before that. She couldn't actually remember the last time she'd slept well—or at all.

"I'm fine," she told him. "But every now and then it's hard."

"I can imagine. Come on over to my desk and tell me what I can do for you."

Rose followed the banker and allowed him to pull out a chair for her. When he asked again what he could do, she handed the funeral home's invoice to him and requested a draft to pay it.

"This will leave you with a little over four hundred dollars. Is that okay?"

It wasn't. They'd have to scrimp and save to make it last, and she'd have to get a job. At sixty-two, that wasn't what she had envisioned. She bit her tongue as the word "yes" left her lips.

The banker filled out a form and had her sign it, then left to have the draft drawn up. When he returned, she decided to broach the subject of work. Her back already ached with the thought of it, and her eyes began stinging again. "Do you have any openings here?"

He frowned. "I'm afraid not. But I hear Forrest Lumber is looking for a cashier. And I'd check with the Henny-Penny Grocery Store, too. They're always needing people."

Rose stood slowly, willing herself not to stoop with weariness. She gave the banker a nod, turning to leave.

His voice stopped her. "I'm sure the Howard Gault Potato Company could add another person—it's just that the work there is quite physical. A lot of stretching and lifting."

"I appreciate it," Rose said, with a sad smile. "If you know of a cheap place to rent, too, I think I'll move Melvin and me soon. We don't need all that space."

"I'll keep my ears open, Rose," the banker said. "If there's anything else I can do for you, I certainly will. You know that."

She extended her hand to shake his, feeling his strong grip against hers. With the draft in her purse, she took her time in the midday heat, avoiding the blazing sun where she could. She kept her eyes trained on the ground, hoping that would make the walk back to the funeral home seem a little faster. Death was so inconvenient.

The funeral was a nice affair, with many of Aunt Mae's old friends turning out to pay their respects. That evening, Rose leaned back in her aunt's chair and sighed. "Well, Melvin, it's just you and me now. I guess I start looking for a job tomorrow."

He sat in his corner spot, not acknowledging her statement, as usual.

"Oh, I forgot the mail!" Rose said, getting up to check the mailbox.

She returned with a few envelopes, eyes trained on an especially crisp one. It was from a local lawyer.

"I wonder what this is about," she said, to no one. "There's no property Aunt Mae owned for us to deal with—I think."

She slid her finger under the flap and ripped it open. The letter was short, not at all filled with the lengthy legal jargon she'd been expecting. It simply requested her to visit the lawyer's office to find out more.

The next day, she sat facing a man who appeared to be too young to be a lawyer. He had a small office on the outskirts of town, which probably meant he was just starting his practice. Rose handed him the letter and asked what it was about.

He opened a file and handed her another letter, mouth set in an unrevealing line. "My client wants you to read this first. Then we'll discuss a few matters."

Rose scrunched her face and took the letter, squinting a little to read the handwritten scribbles.

My Dearest Rose,

Words can't express the pain I've endured since the last time we saw each other. I've thought about this moment for a very long time, and how I'd like to tell you what happened when we drove off into the cold night, leaving you all alone. It's taken me a long time to grasp everything— my actions and inactions—and I finally feel like I can talk to you.

After we left, we headed to New Mexico and split up in Hobbs. David wanted to go to California, and I wanted to go in another direction. The next day, I learned he'd been captured so I changed my plans. Where I ended up, I can't tell you. But I changed my name and built a new life, with one eye always looking over my shoulder. It was not a pleasant experience—although much better, I suppose, than David's.

As you know, when the world collapsed in 1930, work was hard to find. I tried several jobs, mostly working with my back and hands. You know that's not me. It was both physically hard and humbling.

One day, I was hungry with no place to live. I stumbled into a business, looking for work. The man there took pity on me as his Christian beliefs required it, or so he told me. I worked hard for him, and with my business sense, I helped him grow his company into something much bigger. When he died suddenly, his oldest daughter returned to help with the estate and the business. She was a few years older than me, and over time, we grew close. Eventually, we married. Soon, children followed. Never did she know about my past.

After the war, our business took off again. We were building a mansion when a beam fell and killed my wife. In a split second, I was left to finish raising the children, a task I was not well-suited for.

In 1949, being a widower, I hired a private detective to check on you in Seminole and see if you were married. He reported back that you were married and running your family's business. It was a depressing report to read. Still, I tried to move on, though I thought about you all the time. Believe it or not, at times, I even considered the risks of returning to you in Gaines County to see if a warrant was still out on me—but I decided against it. Instead, I threw myself into my work and made the business grow even bigger.

I remarried in 1953, and soon found out it was a terrible mistake. She drank constantly, and drove two of my children away. The other one, a boy, helped me with the business. But everyone seemed to hate me.

A few years later, I sent another private detective to Gaines County to check on my warrants. I discovered that after the war, a new district clerk had come in and purged hundreds of old warrants. Mine was one of them. It was a huge relief!

The detective also reported that you were single, having never married. The first detective I'd hired mistook your aunt for you. I slammed my fist through a window when I read the report since I'd missed my chance with you... again!

In 1965, a large firm bought the company and I retired at the age of 60. Two of my three children were estranged due to my wife, and the son was without a job. I soon found myself doling out money to three ungrateful children, who looked at me as a necessary evil. They smiled long enough to get the cash, but whined behind my back for more. One of my daughters used the money to buy a fast new car and lost control, killing herself. I was heartbroken.

My son soon became addicted to alcohol, sobering up only for visits with me to get more money. My wife lives in our house and I've stopped asking what she's doing or who comes over. We never see each other.

My other child carries hate with her, all of it stemming from an incident when I told her she couldn't marry a boy she was dating. She has hated me ever since. I look back on that, and for the life of me, I can't understand why I told her that.

So here I am, a 67-year-old, in a wheelchair in a nursing facility. A surgery to remove a growth proved unsuccessful and I lost the use of one of my legs. The other leg is not doing too well either. Yet I'm still here... barely.

The doctors think I may have a year or two left, but it will be painful and lonely. Perhaps it's what I deserve—misery.

Recently, I've learned that your aunt passed away. I am very sorry for your loss and wish I could be there to comfort you. I know your uncle died in 1949, a few months after I checked up on you. If I had hired a different detective or waited, my life would have been a happy one. Oh, the cruelty of it all!

I want to close this letter by telling you how much shame I have felt, snatching that ring from your finger like a petty thief and running like a coward—it was so shameful and embarrassing. My fear of what would happen to me was too great to stay with you and face the music. I could've had you and been poor, but I chose to run. My reward is wealth and hatred from those close to me. Quite ironic, wouldn't you say? Certainly poetic justice.

I must tell you I loved you then and I love you now. You're the only true love I've ever known, yet the one I've never been allowed to have. I don't know what you feel about me, but whatever it is, I hope you can forgive me.

I also want to tell you I invested the proceeds from your ring into my business. It did quite nicely, especially when the company sold. You and Melvin should be just fine now. When you hand the letter back to the lawyer, he'll tell you all about it.

I love you. I miss you. And I wish you a better life than mine. Perhaps you can bless someone else one day. Goodbye, Rose.

Rose dabbed at her eyes with a tissue and gave the letter to the lawyer. She tried to keep a straight face, waiting for him to speak.

"Miss Henderson, my client has set up a bank account. Whenever you need money, please let me know why you need it and I'll make a draft for you or give you the cash. I will decide which. How are you fixed now?"

Rose blinked several times, as if that would help her process everything. She thought about pinching herself, to see if all this was real. "We have less than four hundred dollars in our account. I'll have to get a job to make ends meet."

He reached into his drawer and pulled out a leather bag. "No, you won't. Instead, you should be looking for a modest home and I'll buy it for you. I understand you have no car. I suggest you begin looking for a practical model and let me know which color you prefer. I'll make the arrangements and have it delivered to you." He unzipped the bag and dug into it. "Here's five hundred dollars to make sure you have plenty of food and your bills are paid."

Rose took the money, fingers trembling. She looked down at the bills. They stared up at her, fresh and new.

"We'll be seeing a lot of each other, ma'am, so I hope you're pleased with my service."

Rose stood, too stunned to talk. When she recovered, she said, "Yes. I am indeed." They shook hands and she left his office, then stopped. Turning around, she went back inside, opening his door in time to see him burning the letter she'd just read.

"Yes?" he said, eyebrows rising ever so slightly under her gaze. "Did you need something more?"

"Can you get a message back to him?"

"Of course. What is it?"

"Tell him I forgive him and thank you." Rose hesitated, her voice cracking. "And tell Charles I've always loved him too."

"I'll send it out today."

With that, Rose walked out and headed home to tell Melvin the incredible news.

Chapter Eighteen

January 1974
Cuauhtémoc, Mexico

David set the heavy stainless steel can down on the kitchen floor, his sleeve catching on an old piece of tape hanging from it. Running his fingers across the worn material, he smiled. It reminded him of the time his third child, Katharina—or Tina, as they called her—had been colicky, refusing most milk offered to her. Anna had asked him to separate the milk from the various cows and label the containers, so she could try the different liquids until she found one her daughter would take. Since breastfeeding was not common among Mennonites, cow's milk was their only option.

After much experimentation, Rose, a sturdy milk cow Anna's mother had given them, was the winner. David had written the cow's name on the tape, marking his daughter's special milk can.

His smile faded as he pulled some papers from the drawer, sitting down at the kitchen table to look them over. He pushed his fingers through his hair as he scanned over the figures, bringing a pencil to his tongue to make the lead darker to correct things here and there. The papers told a story, twelve years in the making.

A noise outside distracted him. He quickly jammed the papers into his front pocket, walking to the porch to find his grandfather on horse and buggy. The old man stared down at him expectantly. Without saying a word, David grabbed the reins and held the horse steady. Jacob's bones creaked as he got down, taking his time.

The old man had just turned seventy-nine and was still riding a horse and buggy, though shaky at times. He'd seen a lot of life and done a lot of living. At twenty-eight, David could only hope he'd have Jacob's stamina by the time he got to be his age.

"Help me into the barn," Jacob said, holding out an arm for David. "I forgot my cane."

The two men made it to the barn, ducking from the winter wind, finding two stumps to rest on.

Jacob said nothing as he lit a cigarette, no longer worried about what anyone thought. After a long drag, he exhaled a cloud of smoke and took in a deep breath. "I guess you're getting close, huh?"

David nodded. "Yes. I just went over the numbers again. With what I made on the harvest and have put away, I think I can make it. And I know I'll be able to sell the land and animals for even more."

Jacob grinned. "Good. That's real good. Are you still going to Paraguay instead of Canada?"

"Yeah," David replied, rubbing his hands together. "I'm getting some of the land Dad owns down there. He bought it from a Mennonite family who left. He wants me to plant crops on the rest of his land and work it in exchange for what he's giving me. It's a good deal."

Jacob rubbed his nail on the cigarette, tapping the ashes off. "When are you leaving?"

"In a few weeks. Tomorrow, I'm going to put the word out that I'm selling everything. Even the Volkswagen."

"Volkswagen!" the old man said, coughing as he chuckled.

David understood his reaction. Never in his life had his grandfather imagined getting away with owning a car. But David had—only after old man Hiebert had purchased one first. That had been two years ago, and he hadn't gotten excommunicated. So far, no one had said anything about it.

"Well, David, it looks like you'll be the first of our family to leave. If I can just see that, I'll die a happy man."

"I'm sure you'll make it," David said, giving him a grin. "You've got a few years left in you."

"Maybe," Jacob mused, staring at the rafters. "Maybe. How's Anna taking it?"

"Not very good. She's close to her mother and doesn't want to leave. But I've told her there's no way to make a good living here. The colony is out of land, and the Mexicans won't sell to us anymore. The government is talking taxes, too. I don't want to be around for it. I don't have a choice. There's no more land." He paused, looking over at his grandfather. "A lot of men feel that way. We're all looking for a place to go."

Jacob nodded, his mouth set in a tight, grim line. "I figured this would happen. When I got here all those years ago, I could see this was a tough place to survive. I can't believe I've made it to this ripe old age. So many others haven't."

"I guess some people never give up. You're one of them."

"And you are too," Jacob replied, an affectionate smile tugging at the corners of his mouth.

The two men stayed in the barn for a while, watching the smoke from Jacob's cigarette drift up into the rafters. David enjoyed the older man's company while he could, trying not to think about it all coming to an end. He'd miss his grandfather's advice and support.

A week later, David climbed into his Volkswagen and started up the four-stroke engine, listening to it sputter and belch smoke as he engaged the clutch. With a lurch, he was off.

David was traveling to Campo 109—a ten-minute ride—to sell his car. He hoped everything would go smoothly, and he'd come home with some cash in his pocket.

A few miles down the road, a tractor bounced toward him, its paddle wheels digging into the road's surface and damaging every inch it traveled over. *What a waste*, he thought, pulling over to the side of the road to let it pass. A dozen or so tiny faces peeked out of the tractor's trailer. Tractors had become a main form of transportation to the Mennonites. It wasn't uncommon to see families loaded up in a trailer behind one, being dragged to church, the fields, the store—wherever. Horses were scarce; many colonists had sold them to the Mexicans. Where those had ended up, who knew.

The shift from horses to tractors had actually helped David, in a way. It had saved him and old man Hiebert from getting excommunicated for owning a car.

"Excommunicated," David muttered to himself as he passed houses and farms. The word had sounded so sacred in his youth, but he now understood it to be the clergy's main weapon to keep everyone in line. The colonists wanted a better life, but no one wanted to risk excommunication. Even David himself had found it difficult to push the boundaries at times, not wanting to think about what excommunication would mean for him and his family.

Since arriving from Canada, colonists had been excommunicated for having a sexual relationship with someone outside of marriage. Using rubber tires was another sin that had landed several men the ultimate penalty. David's use of rubber tires hadn't been noticed, although the tire tracks were fairly obvious in his fields. On the other hand, the fur collar on his new coat had been noticed, along with a new pair of boots. His parents were forced to return it all, so David could continue working way too hard and suffering more.

David knew of several farmers who had been disciplined for having gas stoves. Church discipline was a serious matter if you wanted to stay in the colony. He was told that his great-grandpa Johann Wiebe—an Ältester— had dealt with two very divisive issues shortly after moving to Canada in 1875. Both issues surfaced with the dedication of the first church building in Reinland, Manitoba, Canada, on September 17, 1876:

(1) Singing the hymns the old way or in a chorale tune. Since the congregation was made up of several different settlements from Russia, some of those people wanted to keep the long, drawn-out way of singing a hymn. Others, including Mr. Johann Wiebe, wanted the faster chorale tune.

(2) The Ban—when to use it to excommunicate someone. For the poor souls who were excommunicated, the punishment was severe. Besides getting a ticket to hell, the offender was prohibited from eating with their family; they were also banned from being intimate with a spouse. The offender was even punished in death, buried on the other side of the cemetery's fence facing west. The fear of this punishment usually kept everyone from breaking the rules publicly. And it had worked. Until now.

Mr. Johann Wiebe had survived his congregation's rebellion, but others weren't so fortunate. If David took a chance, he'd have to consider the possibility of excommunication. Yet David's grandfather had always talked of breaking away, planting the seeds in his mind at an early age. For years, David had kept his desire to leave a secret. He'd pushed the envelope more than a few times, but he'd always done it privately. Now, it seemed, the discontentment had spread. David had been talking to a lot of men in his generation. Many of them were disillusioned and secretly breaking the rules. They were bone tired of being poor. Tired of being hungry and sick. Tired of being told what they could and couldn't do. They wanted a better life. Like David, they had realized the steel paddle wheels on their tractor not only kept them from getting the work done faster, but also from leaving.

Yes, the seeds had been planted, and for the last twelve years, they had grown immensely. David had saved and scraped by, waiting for the day his plans came to fruition. He could see the light at the end of the long, dark tunnel. He just had to keep moving toward it.

David found the open gate he was looking for, pulling his car into the yard. The door to the barn swung open and a man appeared. David climbed out of the car, giving the stranger a wave.

"Hello. Are you Mr. Fehr?"

The man seemed friendly enough. He gave David a grin and held out his hand. "Yes. And you must be Mr. Rempel."

"I am," David replied, shaking the man's hand. "Are you still interested in buying my car?"

Mr. Fehr rubbed his jaw, glancing over at the car. "Might be," he said, "for the right price."

Mennonites were natural negotiators. David settled into the familiar rhythm, pulling out his favorite tactic first—silence.

"I heard that you're leaving for Paraguay," Mr. Fehr asked, since David said nothing. "Is that true?"

"That's true. I can't get much land here. No one will sell."

The man nodded. "Yeah, I know. My parents told me that every time we try to create our own society, it never lasts. Maybe this whole setup wasn't such a good idea. That's why I'm thinking about buying your car. I want to go into town to sell my goods and look for cheaper suppliers. I'm not worried about church discipline when I have a family to feed."

David raised his eyebrows. The rebellious attitude was spreading.

He went back and forth with Mr. Fehr before making a deal. David received some cash up front and agreed to accept two years of payments. After their business concluded, David handed over the keys and showed him how to operate it. David could tell Mr. Fehr had driven before, probably in secret, but he kept that observation to himself.

Mr. Fehr drove him home, dropping him off in his yard. David watched as he took off, dust kicking up behind the Volkswagen, and sighed. There was no turning back now.

A surprise winter storm ripped through the colony, causing sporadic damage—mostly downed branches, though some people had to face holes in their roofs when the wind ripped away some of their tiles. David's house made it through fine, but the shipping company dropping off the storage box was delayed due to the mud. David didn't mind. This gave him more time to secure a buyer for his farm. Again, he received some money upfront and agreed to accept payments.

When the box was finally delivered, David worked hard to load it all by himself. It was an interesting experience as he cleaned out every nook and cranny of the house and barn. He even found one of the plastic horses he'd brought back from Canada as a gift to each of his three kids—David, Elizabeth, and Tina. The mamma horse was connected to smaller foals with a chain.

He also packed up the gramophone and radio from Canada. Those were prohibited, but easy to hide. Anna would carry the beautiful alarm clock he'd given to her in her personal bag, one they'd carry on the plane. It would be their first ride ever—a long one—but with all they'd endured, he was sure they'd have no problem. After all, their new home would be on the other side. He could hardly wait.

As he cleaned out the barn, he found a wrench under a scrap piece of wood. He'd thought the thieves had taken it with the rest of the tools, but apparently they'd dropped it. A flame rose in his chest at the memory of the theft, making him angry all over again. He could still remember coming out to the barn the morning after it had happened, only to discover all his tools were gone. He had left them sprawled out after working on the tractor, never thinking someone would be so bold as to come in during the night and take them. He hadn't been able to track the two sets of boot prints, so the criminals got away successfully. They'd even taken his favorite tool box—one his grandpa helped him build. He couldn't replace that.

David shook his head, thankful to be leaving for Paraguay. He'd heard it was much different there, more lenient. As for Mexico, he was so tired of everything. The rules. The ignorance. The hypocritical preachers who smoked and drank yet pounded the lectern, extolling their listeners to do neither. And, of course, he was tired of the stealing. Practically everything he owned had been stolen: tools, chickens, eggs, pigs, and cows. Each one had been replaced, but not without financial hardship. The only two things that hadn't been stolen were his children and his wife—although his mother-in-law had sure tried hard at the latter.

David's angry thoughts rattled around in his brain. Then his grandpa shuffled in. "I guess I missed all the heavy lifting."

"You sure did," David said, laughing. "They took the box away two days ago. And that's late, on account of the mud. You're pretty smart to show up now."

"Not smart," Jacob said. "Just old."

The two men shook hands.

"You got enough money to make this work?" Jacob asked.

"Yeah," David replied, patting his pockets. "I dug out all my cubbyhole jars and feel like I'm in good shape."

"Just be careful," Jacob said, stroking his chin. "A rich man can soon turn into a dead man."

"They can try. But so will I."

Jacob chuckled, then his face turned somber. "You know, I wish I was going with you." He shook his head, fighting back the tears. "I'm just proud you were the one to actually make it out."

"Grandpa, you were the one who planted that seed."

Jacob wiped an eye. "I sure watered it a lot. I knew your dad would never leave. He's too important here. You were my only hope."

David moved closer and touched his grandfather's arm. "Thank you for teaching me my trades. I don't know what I would've done if you hadn't taught me how to work with my hands."

"I do. You'd have been a preacher. Like all the ones before us."

David grinned. "Probably right."

"When is your plane leaving?"

"In three days. Tomorrow, we take the kids to the village school where a nurse will be coming from Colonia Obregon to get their pox shots. Paraguay won't let us come without them."

"There'll be some crying for sure."

They heard a buggy coming into the yard. Jacob sniffled and drew his shoulders back a little. "I guess your dad's here. I knew he'd come after me—he's even less interested in getting his hands dirty."

They went outside to welcome the preacher, the generation between them.

"Son," the old man said, "we have some heavy lifting in the barn. You're just in time."

David loved it whenever his grandpa teased his much-too-serious father, silently laughing each time.

The preacher reined up the horse and stepped down from the buggy. "I didn't come for work," he said bluntly. "Besides, whatever it is, it can wait. I need to talk to David."

David tensed, wondering if his father had changed his mind about him leaving.

"Let's go back in the barn," his father said, his usually serious face a little darker than normal. "I don't want Anna or the kids hearing this."

David swallowed hard and followed his father back into the barn, and Jacob used his cane to keep up. His father pulled a letter from his pocket.

"This came in today," he said, handing it to David. "Ältester Schmitt received it and gave it to me."

"What is it?" David asked, turning it over in his hand.

His father eyed him carefully. "A letter from the Ältester in Paraguay. Somehow, they heard you had a Volkswagen. Now, they don't want you down there."

David stumbled back a few steps, the letter growing heavy in his hand. "How did they find out?" he managed, heart pounding in his ears.

"Obviously," the preacher said, "someone here wrote them about it."

David mentally thumbed through a list of suspects. Before he got too far, though, his stomach pitted as he realized all the implications the letter carried. "My shipping box!" he cried. "It has all of our dishes, blankets, clothes, and tools. If it ends up in Paraguay, I'll never get it back."

"You need to stop it before it leaves the country," his grandpa said, pointing his cane at David. "Do you know where it's headed?"

"The port at Tampico."

His grandfather shook his head. "That's almost a thousand kilometers. And it has a two-day head start."

David's eyes darted to his father. "Dad, can you take me to Jake's? I need to tell him about this and see if he still wants to go without me."

"I can't believe he will," the preacher muttered. "Not with our family name ruined."

Within an hour, David told his brother about the letter. Then they went to their cousin Jacob's house, explaining the situation to him. Without David, neither of the other men wanted to go, especially now that they knew Paraguay wasn't so lenient. They'd have to act fast to stop their boxes from being shipped there, and it wasn't going to be easy.

⊰◈⊱

The bus rambled on, swaying from side to side, its suspension long worn out. David stared out the window at the dusty roadside disappearing with each kilometer. After two days of being trapped in the confined space, the anxiety and exhaustion was wearing on him and his little band of men. In addition to his brother and cousin, two of the shippers had agreed to go with them for a fee, since they knew how to find the boxes.

The morning after talking with the shippers, they'd all climbed on board and ridden for hours to Torreón, where they switched buses. The second bus stopped at Saltillo, Matehula, and Rioverde before they'd caught a third one to Tampico. So far, the entire journey had taken thirty hours. Sleep was hard to find amid the constant rumble of the bus and its hardbacked seats.

David's stomach grumbled, the food Anna had packed for him long gone. He was hungry, but also worried. A large part of his family's wealth was tied up in that box. If he lost it, it would be a financial nightmare. He just hoped the shippers knew what they were doing.

A few hours later, the coastal town of Tampico appeared. Lakes, rivers, and marshes dotted the countryside, and strange birds filled the skies. It would've been interesting to watch had he not been worried sick. When the bus pulled into the station, they saw a sign directing travelers to the beach. It was only a kilometer away, but none of the men would even think to see it.

One of the shippers flagged down a cab and gave the driver the address. Fifteen minutes later, they all stood before a clerk. A massive shipping yard stretched behind the man in every direction.

"You want to find a box and turn it around?" the clerk asked, raising his eyebrows.

"Yes," one of the shippers replied. "Three of them. Here are the numbers and our papers."

The clerk thumbed through the documents, seemingly uninterested in helping them until a wad of pesos hit his desk.

"Let me see what I can do," he said, heading to the back.

Several hours ticked by, and with each passing minute David grew more worried. He straightened as the clerk reappeared, empty-handed. "We didn't find them, but I did learn that the boxes have not made it on the ship yet. They are here, but we are short of help. Perhaps you could help us look for it."

The two shippers agreed. They left with a second clerk, who took them out the back. David turned to his brother. "I guess we need to find a place to stay for the night—maybe longer. Do you and Jacob want to find us a place while I stay here and help them out?"

Jake agreed. He and Jacob left to explore the surrounding area and search for a cheap motel. David couldn't leave the yard. He wouldn't let himself—not until the box was safe and sound.

That evening, the exhausted shippers returned to the main office. After David bought some food for them, they called it quits for the night, staying in a motel a kilometer away. Even David fell sound asleep within seconds of hitting the pillow.

The next morning, they resumed their search and worked all day. Just as darkness was setting in, they found the three crates still on the train car that had arrived a day earlier. After ensuring the crates would be turned around and shipped back to the colony, the five men went to a decent restaurant and celebrated. They rewarded themselves with another deep sleep before the thirty-two-hour bus trip back.

Two months later, David watched his wife pour a cup of coffee in his mother's kitchen. After he'd sold the farm, they'd been forced to live with his parents. If anything, the experience made him more determined to leave.

Anna set the cup on the kitchen table. She sat down, staring at the coffee. He could tell she had something to get off her chest.

"Have you thought about staying here?" she blurted out.

David opened his passport. "See this?" he said, turning it around so she could see.

"What am I looking at?"

"These," he said, pointing to some stamps. "When I purchased the Paraguay visa, the clerk said my money included three visas total—so I also selected the United States and Canada. They're good for ninety days, and they have to be used within the year. That's why I've decided to take us to Canada."

Anna frowned. "My mother says there is no reason to go back to that sinful place. That's why we left. My sister wants us to stay here, too."

He sighed, rubbing his eyes. "I know. But your brother Henry is there, and he could let us stay with him until we get our permanent papers." His heart melted a little at the sight of Anna's disappointed face. She wouldn't meet his eyes. "Anna, please! There's nothing here for us. We have to leave, and that's that."

She remained silent, not moving from the table. He could hear her breath catch in her throat as she hesitated, finally glancing up at him again.

"Is there something else you want to discuss?" he asked.

"Yes. I'm pregnant again. The baby is due in October."

The news hit David hard, making him feel foolish. He had been so focused on leaving the colony that he had ignored his wife and her needs. He sprung up from his chair, hugging her. "That's wonderful!" he said, a smile making an appearance on Anna's face. "But you've been on birth control since we had Tina. The doctor said you'd never have any more children. How is this possible?"

"It's God. That's all I can say."

David stood there taking all this in. He wasn't sure what to say because after their third child was born, Anna took birth control. She had endured tremendous pressure and angst from his own sisters. They had made terrible comments like, "You really are a murderer," and "You might as well go chop off your baby's head because that's what you are literally doing. You're preventing future pregnancies!" It was harsh and damaging to his wife. Try as he might, he couldn't stop them. And he knew it had taken a terrible toll on Anna. That's why he knew his next comment had to be perfect. Though he wasn't an educated person, or even sophisticated—no Mennonite was—he did his best.

"My love, I promise you this: Our baby will have a life that we never had. It will be born in Canada."

<hr>

April 8, 1974

It was a Monday, a spring day in Mexico—one that lacked the green vibrancy of a normal spring. Without the July rain, the colors on the trees were mostly browns and grays.

David loaded the last bag into the buggy and lifted his three children into the back. Then he helped Anna take her place next to him. "Ready to go?" he asked his neighbor, who sat behind him on horseback.

The man nodded. Since he'd sold everything, David had borrowed the buggy from him. The man would take it back once they'd arrived.

David waved at his brother Jake, who sat in another buggy with his wife, Lisa, and their child. Jake gave him a wave back, elbowing their cousin Jacob to get his attention. Jacob's wife, Susana, rocked their child to sleep in the back of the buggy.

There was also Wilhelm Burg, the man in the colony who had arranged the car for David on his first trip to Canada. They'd hired Mr. Burg as the guide on this trip, with his expenses covered plus an additional $500 U.S. He had been to Canada many times and he spoke a little English. David and the others counted on him not only to get them through Canadian customs, but possibly to help them become citizens.

"Daddy," Tina said, "can I go get some more clothes from the box?"

David had let his family take a few things out of the box for the trip, but most of their belongings remained packed away. He wanted them to understand that staying in Mexico wasn't permanent.

"No, Tina," he said. "You have enough clothes. You'll be fine. Just sit back and enjoy the trip. It will be fun."

"Okay," she said, appearing satisfied by her father's answer.

David looked back to the road and urged the horses forward, his strong, calloused hands holding the reins expertly. His eyes were set on the horizon, taking on a distant look, like he was daydreaming.

Thirty minutes passed, and they reached the stop just as a large bus came rolling down the road. Once it stopped, David loaded the bags in a space below and handed the driver the tickets. When everyone had climbed aboard, the bus took off, with David noticing his five-year-old daughter glancing out the rear window, watching as the place they'd called home for their entire lives got tinier and tinier. When it disappeared, David lifted Tina up.

"It's okay, sweetie," he said soothingly. "We're going to a better place. You'll see."

The bus drove for hours, stopping at Ojinaga, a border town. There, the officials checked their papers before allowing them to cross into the United States. After boarding a new bus, they were off for Lubbock, Texas.

By now, the gentle rocking of the bus had caused his three children to fall asleep. David smiled, seeing Tina's head on Elizabeth's lap. Neither one seemed to mind.

At the airport, they all marveled at the large airplanes. They held hands as they made their way to one of them. After boarding and strapping themselves in, the Rempel family was about to have the experience of a lifetime.

No sooner had the thrust from the jet's engines pushed them back in their seats, than the children start crying. The pressure on their ears was intense. Yet, like the bus, they were soon asleep.

In Toronto, they landed safely, greeted by snow on the ground. This was rare for them to see, but there was no time to play in it. Mr. Burg hustled them to customs and immigration, handing their passports to some officers. Before long, they were pointing at David and his family. After more conversation, the officers returned the passports to Mr. Burg along with some papers, sending him on his way.

David, after crossing the official barrier, picked up his youngest daughter. "We're here, Tina," he said, kissing the little girl. "Canada!" Then he picked up David and Elizabeth, kissing each of them. He couldn't believe his dream had finally come true and the long journey out of Mexico was over.

Chapter Nineteen

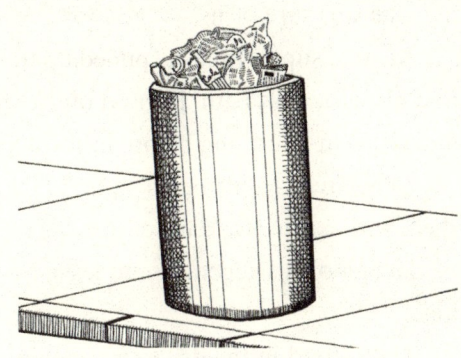

Aylmer, Ontario

David slowed the station wagon to a crawl, heart fluttering at the sight of the snow-covered sign. *Welcome to Canada.* He'd finally made it back. Gripping the steering wheel hard, he tried to focus on the road as his mind raced with all the possibilities. It was almost overwhelming.

Mr. Burg had helped him buy the used station wagon, which was a lot longer than his old Volkswagen. It was a good, sturdy car, but not quite big enough to seat all their families comfortably—five children and seven adults. It had been a cramped ride to Salem, where he'd dropped Jake and his family off, and then Jacob's family nearby. They each had friends to stay with until they found permanent places.

Now, Mr. Burg sat next to him in the passenger seat, his job as a guide nearly completed. David would drop him off at his sister's house in St. Thomas the next day, after they all spent the night at the Friesen's in Aylmer. After that, he didn't know if he'd ever see Mr. Burg again. The man planned on visiting his sisters for three weeks, then flying back to Mexico alone.

David caught sight of Anna in the rearview mirror. He could see her looking at the sign through tired eyes, as the children chatted excitedly—oblivious and too full of energy after their first airplane ride and road trip. She noticed him looking and gave him a weary, tight-lipped smile. Not for the first time, he felt his heart swell and break at the same time as he looked at her. Even with a baby on the way and her own reservations about Canada, her strength never seemed to fail. He was determined to take better care of her once they arrived. They would all have a better life—he was sure of it.

Around suppertime, he pulled up to the Friesen's house. Henry Friesen and his wife, Elizabeth, hurried out to greet them. Anna gave her brother and sister-in-law a hug before introducing the three children.

"My, aren't you three a sight," Henry said, bending down to inspect them with a grin. He'd never met his nieces and nephew, having been one of the first of his generation to leave Mexico. "You sure are good-looking kids!"

They stood in the driveway hugging and kissing, until Elizabeth ushered everyone in for supper. After a hearty meal, Henry showed David outside. Darkness had begun to creep over the land, and the temperature was dropping fast. David rubbed his hands together as he and Henry walked, trying to work some feeling back into his fingers. The cold would take some getting used to.

"How does it feel to leave Mexico?" Henry asked.

David shook his head, still not believing his good fortune. "I can't believe we're finally here."

"What did it for you?"

David took in the fresh air, the cold tickling his lungs. "When I was a child, just before church, all the preachers gathered in our barn and had themselves a cigarette and a stiff drink—or maybe some wine. I remember watching them and asking myself, 'How can they be one thing on Sunday, preaching what we should and shouldn't do, and another thing during the week?' After that, I was done. It was just a matter of time."

Henry nodded, clapping him on the shoulder. "Yeah, we all reach our breaking point. I just reached mine earlier than you."

"Are you glad you made the decision to leave?" David asked, hoping for a good answer.

"Absolutely!" Henry said. "You can't imagine. We're much happier here—at least, happier than most. What are your plans?"

"I'm going to look for some work while I get my permanent papers. My grandpa is a citizen. With our ninety-day visa, that gives me time to get everything straightened out."

Henry nodded. "I've got a list of people who might be able to help. I'll take you to them tomorrow, if you're interested."

"Yes, I'm interested. Thank you, Henry."

"You would do the same."

———◆◆———

David found a job at a construction company. They put him to work framing a house and hanging drywall. Before long, his pockets were full of money—at least, by Campo 101 standards.

A few weeks in, he found a place to stay. It was the basement of Mr. and Mrs. Reimer. They owned a restaurant and were gone during the day. The Reimers agreed to take in the Rempel family if David would pay for their groceries and help with some of the farm work. It was an easy decision. Life fell into a smooth routine.

By the fourth week, it was time to get his immigration status settled. He took the station wagon and rounded up Jake and Jacob. With careful instructions from his brother-in-law, they drove to Toronto—the location of the main immigration office. After waiting in line for an hour, they finally reached the clerk.

"May I help you?" the disinterested man asked the three Mennonites.

"Yes," David said, stepping forward, handing the clerk his passport. "We would like to apply for citizenship."

The clerk held up his hand, giving them a strange look. "Harry, these guys speak Low German. Can you handle them?"

"Sure," Harry said, taking the place of the first clerk. "What can I do for you?" he asked in David's native tongue.

"We would like to apply for citizenship."

"Are they part of your family?" he asked, pointing to Jake and Jacob.

"Yes," David replied. "He's my brother, and he's my cousin."

Harry held out his hand. "Passports, please."

The men produced them for his inspection and Harry scribbled down some notes. "Please excuse me. I need to check our records. I'll be back."

David rubbed his hands together. "I hope he comes back with good news."

"Me too," Jake said, watching the clerk disappear behind a mountain of filing cabinets.

The three men stood there for longer than they cared to consider. Finally, the clerk returned with several sheets of paper. After spreading them out on the desk, he held his hand out. "Can I see your applications?"

David glanced at his relatives. They looked as clueless as he felt. "What applications?"

Harry frowned. "At the airport? The officer gave you forms with big red stamps on them to fill out. Now is the time to give them to me."

"What?" Jake broke in. "We weren't given anything."

"Impossible," Harry said. "When they stamped your passport, they also stamped the applications."

"I don't know," David said helplessly, trying to remember what had happened in the chaos of the road trip. There'd been so much going on, so much paperwork, and so little time—but he couldn't recall ever seeing anyone stamp some applications.

Harry thought for a moment, tapping his finger on his chin. "Maybe you filled them out there and gave them to the officer. I'll send in a request. You three come back in one month. I'll have some answers for you by then."

David and his two companions left the immigration office, sharing a glance. Maybe becoming a Canadian citizen wouldn't be so easy.

———————

Life in the basement wasn't the best, but it wasn't the worst, either. The Reimers were easy to get along with. After working in construction for most of the day, David performed tasks around the house or farm after supper. He worked all the time but he didn't mind. He was making more money in a month than he would all year in Mexico. This was the life he'd been looking for.

And, his job was all he could want. He loved construction and was good at it—his grandfather had made sure of that. When he wasn't framing or installing drywall, he was shingling roofs and making cabinets. Even if the work stopped, there was plenty to do in this area of Ontario. He could join his brother and cousin who were working in the fields, picking tomatoes one day and tobacco leaves the next. David had done this seasonal harvesting work before and knew it paid well. But with construction paying even more, he was putting away money, hopefully to buy his own place once he gained citizenship.

The second week after their arrival, some friends invited them to a church. It was called the German Church of God. Attending a church like this was another big strike against him, but David didn't care. At this point he was so fed up with the old way—the whole colony system—that he didn't care what people said.

The German Church of God was different, looser. They allowed rubber tires on their tractors. A member could own a car, and many people had one. They also welcomed children to attend, instead of requiring them to be twelve or older. In fact, they believed it was never too early to start teaching children about God and the Bible. All three of his children attended Sunday school, where they met other children and made friends. They soon looked forward to Sundays—especially the candy treats David gave them for good behavior.

Even Anna began to enjoy going to church. She soon opened up to one of the friends who had introduced them to their new ways. "My mother and grandma told me how bad it was here, just a hotbed of sin," she said one day, shaking her head. "They begged me not to come. 'Our ancestors left this place for a reason,' Mom told me. 'You need to stay here.' That's all I heard. It was bad."

Her friend listened patiently. She'd welcomed several families from Mexico and had heard it all before. It was best to let them get it out of their system.

⸻◆⸻

When the two-month mark arrived, David, Jake, and Jacob made another trip to the immigration office and located the same clerk. "Did you find anything out?" David asked.

"Yes," Harry said, opening a file. "Jake Rempel was born in 1952, and that was the year we lifted the citizenship ban for Mennonites. Thus, he's actually a Canadian citizen."

"R-right now?" Jake stammered.

"Yes, right now. You need to take this paperwork and go to window seven."

Before the clerk could take a breath, Jake snatched the papers from his hand and was gone.

"What about us?" David asked meekly.

"Yes," Harry said, drawing out the word and sighing. "What about you?" The three men stood there, staring at each other. "It seems both of you were born when the restriction was in place. You don't have your applications from the airport and we didn't receive them, so it looks like you are out of luck."

"What can we do?" Jacob asked.

Harry crossed his arms, shrugging. "When you came here, you had to give an employment address. We have no record from any employer that you showed up to work. Thus, you'll have to leave when your visa is up."

A pit grew in David's stomach, endless and empty. He felt completely helpless. He didn't have the education or knowledge to deal with the rest of the world. That deficit was now apparent. Like a whipped dog, he and Jacob trudged out of the office, defeated and depressed.

An hour later, Anna dashed out from the Reimers' house to greet him, anxious for some news. She wanted to stay now. She'd changed her mind, having grown comfortable in their new surroundings. Once again, he was going to let her down.

David hunched his shoulders as he approached his wife, barely able to look her in the eyes.

"Did you all get your citizenship?" she asked nervously.

"Jake is a citizen now, because he was born in 1952." He grabbed her shoulders gently and sighed. "But I was born in 1946, and that means I can't be a citizen. We'll have to leave."

Anna drew her hands to her mouth, eyes widening. "Oh no!" she cried. "I can't believe it. Surely *you* can do something?"

He let her go, pacing the ground as frustration bubbled in his chest. "What?" he snapped, more at himself than at her. "Our parents never taught us anything. I feel so stupid speaking to these people. I'm not even sure what they're talking about. Now, we'll have to go back to the colony and listen to all the badmouthing. They'll complain about my station wagon and the church we're going to." He ran his hands across his face, feeling sick. He'd experienced freedom for a few short months, only to have it snatched away from him and his family. "It's going to be terrible. That's the only thing I can promise you."

Anna touched his arm lightly, stopping him. "I don't want you to give up."

"I'm not giving up, Anna," David said miserably. "I'm being forced out."

She hugged him tight. He brought his hands to her hair and smoothed it out, taking a deep breath, wishing the world was different. But it wasn't. There was nothing they could do.

When three months were up, David loaded his wife and three children into the old station wagon and drove to pick up Jacob's family. Together, along with a guide he'd hired to get them through the U.S., they made the long trip back to Mexico—by car, seriously used.

It was a warm June day when they crossed the Canadian border and entered America. The guide alternated with David, driving both day and night. Although David had made good money, he'd been living off his savings. He'd need every penny when he returned to buy a place and all the equipment they would need to restart their lives. It was going to be tough, especially since they'd tasted the good life.

The drive back was mostly uneventful, except for the oppressive heat wave sweeping through the middle of the U.S.—the area they happened to be driving through. Even with the windows rolled down, the car was cramped and sweltering.

After a stop in Oklahoma, David switched places with the guide and let him drive. He slid over next to his wife and tried to get some rest. That's when the stench hit him.

Turning around, it didn't take long for him to find the source. Jacob's son had messed a cloth diaper—several, in fact—each of which were stacked on top of the others. By now, the diapers were ripe, a foul odor wafting up from the pile. Adding to the disgust, he noticed his own son, David, was using them as a pillow.

"Tina," David said, "move his head off those diapers."

His daughter, apparently used to the nasty smell, followed his instructions. Her brother, unaware of what was happening, kept his eyes shut through the entire ordeal. David shook his head and turned back around. Between the heat, the awful smell, and the fact they were going back to Mexico, he wasn't sure the trip could get any worse.

It did, though. In El Paso, they learned that the Mexican officials wouldn't allow the car into the country—at least, not without a hefty bribe. The station wagon, completely worn out from the long drive, wasn't worth it. David parked it at a lot the Mennonites used for such purpose. A few weeks later, he found a buyer and received a small payment for it.

After a long bus ride, they arrived at his parents' home. His father drew him to the side to speak privately. "What happened?" he asked.

David searched his eyes, wondering if he'd see any triumph there. But Jacob's face revealed nothing. "We couldn't get the papers. I didn't understand what they wanted us to do."

Jacob pursed his lips and nodded, choosing to stay silent on the subject. Instead, he dropped another piece of bad news. "You've got another problem. That man you sold the Volkswagen to didn't make any payments. You'll need to go over and straighten that out."

David slapped his thigh, looking up at the sky helplessly. Nothing was going right.

⊷◆⊶

It took two weeks, but David finally got his forbidden Volkswagen back. Now, he had a car, but no place to permanently live. It was a rough situation, especially with a baby on the way and his savings slowly draining.

One day, as he was helping out in his parents' barn, a letter arrived for him. It was from his brother in Canada. He tore the envelope open with his teeth, his dirty fingers smudging the paper as he read it.

Dear David,

Great news! We have learned what happened with the immigration papers and believe we can fix the problem. At the airport, Mr. Burg was given an application from the officials for each of you to be filled out and sent in to the immigration office in Toronto. Please check with Mr. Burg and see if he has those papers. The big red stamps on them are important. The immigration officials need to see those.

Also, a tobacco farmer in Shedden named Mr. Hunter has been trying to reach you. Mr. Burg arranged for all of us to work for this farmer and he's been waiting for us to show up. He's been calling and calling the immigration office. They sent him documents to fill out so you could get your residency papers. Again, please check with Mr. Burg and find out what that is all about. Let me know, because once we have your application papers from Mr. Burg and talk to the farmer, I believe we can fix everything.

Your brother,
(and now a citizen of Canada)

Jake Rempel

Heart racing, David stuffed the letter in his pocket and fired up the Volkswagen, speeding to his destination. Mr. Burg lived twenty minutes away, but the distance didn't matter. He needed to get those papers.

After a mile or so, David forced his foot off the gas pedal, slowing down. There was no sense in getting into a wreck, especially when another few minutes wouldn't matter. His hands shook against the steering wheel. He didn't know if he should be excited or furious. Excited, because Jake's letter had given him a sliver of hope, or angry, because Mr. Burg should've given him the papers.

He found Mr. Burg digging a post hole. "Mr. Burg, how are you doing?" he asked, trying not to let his voice tremble.

Mr. Burg smiled and leaned his shovel against the fence, thrusting out his hand. "Ah, Mr. Rempel. You're back. Did you obtain your Canadian citizenship papers?"

"No," David said, wiping his hand on his pants and returning the greeting. "But we're close. Do you know something about a tobacco farmer in Shedden named Mr. Hunter? He has some papers for us."

Mr. Burg looked up at the sky, in thought. "Hunter... Hunter... Why, yes! I remember. I had seen some literature that he was looking for workers. Since I knew the Canadian officials would require an address of your employment and you had none, I called the farmer and arranged for you all to work there. That way, when I arrived in Toronto, I could fill out the papers with his address and get you into the country. Why? Is there a problem with this individual?"

"No, not really," David said coolly, despite the angry fire sparking in his chest. "The officials sent him a letter that we had arrived. When we didn't show up at his place, he called the immigration office looking for us. He had forms to fill out which would match up with our citizenship applications."

"Oh," Mr. Burg said sincerely. "I'm so sorry. I suppose I should've told you about him, but when you said you wanted to look for work around the Friesen's, I knew you wouldn't want to drive all the way to Shedden to pick tobacco. So I let the matter drop."

"I see." David took a deep, silent breath. There was no use blowing up at Mr. Burg, even if his oversight had cost him hundreds of dollars and a comfortable place in Canada. "Also, the immigration officers in Toronto said the airport officials gave you some papers with big red stamps on them. Do you know anything about that?"

Mr. Burg touched his chin with his forefinger and closed his eyes. "Hmm… let me think. Yes, I do. In the airport, they pointed at each of you and gave me some papers. They had big red stamps on them. They sure did."

David breathed a sigh of relief. "Wonderful!" he said, holding his hand out. "Could I please have those?"

"Why?" Mr. Burg asked, furrowing his brow.

Almost giddy, David chuckled. He was so close to getting his Canadian citizenship he could taste it. After all these years, money, and effort, he was knocking at the door of a new future. "Oh," he said, "I just want to keep them with my records."

Mr. Burg put his hands in his pockets. "Once again, I'm sorry," he said sheepishly, "but I really didn't think they were important—perhaps receipts or something. So I didn't keep them."

"What did you do with them?" David said, jaw clenching.

"I think I threw them in the trash," Mr. Burg said nonchalantly. "I didn't want to clutter up the car with unnecessary papers."

David dropped his head, anger and disappointment rolling into one. Instead of taking it out on Mr. Burg, David turned on his heel and walked away. It was a fact of life that most every Mennonite was in the dark—so completely ignorant—that they had no way of navigating the world. The key to overcoming their ignorance was knowledge—something that had not been taught. After all, they had four-hundred-year-old rules, school books, and sermons to tell them all they needed to know. It was tragic. Plain and simple. And painful.

David's stomach tightened as he drove toward home, his beautiful dream now a nightmare.

Oh Lord, what do I do now? Please help me!

Chapter Twenty

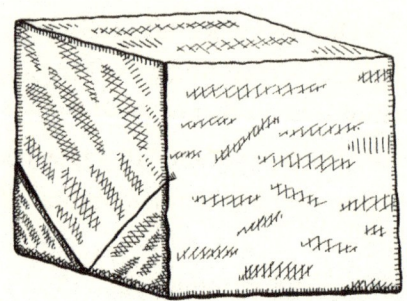

David rested his back against the old, ragged boards of his father's barn, taking a long drag from a cigarette. His life was a complete mess. He had gambled on getting a Canadian citizenship and failed.

Rubbing his forehead, he stared at the barren land before him. The July rains would come soon, and then planting could begin. It was land he didn't own—his father's land. A ripple of anger sliced through his chest at the thought. He'd sold his own farm before moving to Canada. Not only had he deprived his family of a place to live, but the buyer wasn't making the payments. Now, he'd have to go over there and beg, plead, threaten—whatever he had to do—to get paid or repossess the farm. And after his meeting with Mr. Burg, he was in no mood for problems.

A soft crying from inside the barn drew his attention. "What is it now?" he muttered to himself, shaking his head. Taking one last pull, he dropped the cigarette to the hard ground and crushed it out with his boot. There was no need to hide the evidence, not anymore. Instead, it joined the pile of butts that had been slowly building since his return.

He ducked in to find his daughter Tina sitting on a stump. Tears streaked down her cheeks, creating small rivers across her skin. "What's the matter?" he asked.

She gazed up at him, lip quivering. "I miss Sunday school with Mrs. Reimer."

David frowned. "Back in Canada?"

"Yes," she said, rubbing her eyes. "I want to go back."

David lifted the girl and set her down in his lap. "Why don't you tell me all about it?"

She put her arm around her father's neck and did just that. According to Tina, she loved attending the Church of God. The Reimers, the folks they'd been staying with, had taken them there. For Tina, it was not only different, but exciting. She had always wondered what happened every Sunday when her parents left. Now, she knew.

Like the other children, Tina had been placed in a classroom with Mrs. Reimer as her Sunday school teacher. On her first Sunday, Mrs. Reimer had given new attendee Tina an honor: She was allowed to pass the offering basket among the children. Tina had been so proud to be trusted with such an important job, her heart had almost burst.

The tears filled Tina's eyes again as she finished, voice shaking. "The last Sunday we were there—when class was over, Mrs. Reimer showed us all the little boxes on the table."

"What kind of boxes?" David asked, curious himself.

"They were wrapped with brown paper and just sitting there. Mrs. Reimer said we could each have one, but we had to be good during church. And we were."

"That's great," David said, bouncing her a little on his knee. "So, what was in the box?"

The tears plopped onto her red cheeks. "I don't know. You said we had to leave right away. We couldn't go back to the classroom. My present is still waiting for me... in Canada!"

Tina continued to sob as David gritted his teeth, that familiar anger returning in full force, burning deeper. He'd worked so hard to give his family the life they deserved, the life Tina now missed. And what did he have to show for it, besides trashed immigration papers? He tried his best to soothe his daughter, but she was hurting too much. For a child with very little, an unwrapped gift was like putting a freshly baked cookie to her lips and pulling it away before she could take a bite. It was hard to forget.

"Dad?" Tina cried. "Do *you* know what was in that box?"

"I don't, sweetie," he said, trying to keep the edge out of his voice. "I sure don't."

For the next few minutes, they sat together in silence. David searched his tired mind for a plan, something that would make sense.

———✦———

The Volkswagen raced down the dirt road, its driver tightly gripping the wheel, spinning it this way and that, all while dodging potholes and piles of horse manure. For the first time in five months, David finally had a chance to breathe—even if it was only for a short time. As the trees flew by in a blur of yellows and browns, he tried to let himself relax, but his mind kept whirring. It liked to do that, and it always had—especially when so much had happened.

If he'd been anyone else, he might have been content with the life he'd built for his family in such a quick amount of time. He'd convinced the purchaser of his old farm to make some payments, using that money to buy a small place in Bachfeld, a campo about twenty minutes from his father's place. It was an eighty-acre estate—with sixty acres to farm and twenty to live on—and a small house with just enough room for his three children, hardworking wife, and their newborn daughter, Nancy.

But it wasn't enough. The place was too close to the Old Colony, and his three oldest children—Elizabeth, David, and Tina—were suffering the consequences. They'd attended an Old Colony school in Bachfeld for four months, learning from the same old system he'd learned as a child, until a little church school in Burwald came to his attention. This school actually taught reading, writing, and math, with some Spanish and Bible lessons, too. This was real learning. The only problem was the distance. Burwald was three villages down from Bachfeld, an hour away by buggy. But David had his secret weapon: his red Volkswagen. He could take his kids there in fifteen minutes and pick them up, too. However, that didn't prevent the Old Colony from finding its way back into their lives. Anna had begun spending more and more time with her family again, listening to her mother's complaints about him and his principles, with her sisters piling on. Now, it was like everyone and everything conspired against him. Even Anna would drop subtle, disapproving hints about certain things he did—like driving that old Volkswagen.

His mother-in-law was less subtle. Every chance she had, she nagged David. "Now that you've come back, you've got to stay in the Old Colony ways." With all he was juggling, fighting this battle was something he didn't need. Yet his commitment to leave, to provide a better life for his children, still burned strong. He was determined they would not face the world with ignorance as their only weapon. They would be educated, one way or another.

I need to leave, he told himself again. *Enough is enough!*

The one bright spot was that his three children loved the new school. Run by the Evangelical Mennonite Mission Conference (EMMC), it was a much lighter version of the original Old Colony Mennonite teachings. EMMC had come down from Manitoba, Canada, and was led by Pastor Peters. Its members appreciated education, and didn't require metal tires on tractors. They spoke David's language.

David slowed the car and pulled off the road, navigating his way through a narrow opening in the fence, crawling slowly into a man's yard. Several buggies were already there, their owners inside the barn where the meeting was being held. David cut the Volkswagen's engine and took a deep breath. He desperately wanted to hear some good news and extinguish the vision of his mother-in-law, folded arms like an imposing wall, saying over and over, "I told you so!" It was a far cry from what his brother-in-law Henry, standing in front of his nice house, had said to him in Canada: "You can leave. And you can have a nice life." That was the one memory that kept him going.

David slipped past the barn door and introduced himself around. There were fourteen men who had come to hear the speaker of the meeting. Ten minutes later, the man himself climbed onto a stump and began speaking in English. David understood some of it, but was glad Mr. Reimer was translating.

"Gentlemen, my name is Bill Smith. I'm from Seminole, Texas. That's in Gaines County. I'm here to tell you that our county is ripe for farming. We have lots of good land. Our only problem is men. We need good, solid men to develop it. For a long time, we've been coming out of the 'thirty-two dust bowl, where land was poorly farmed. But now, the land is back. With all of your equipment dealings in Seminole, we've learned that Mennonites are good farmers. And good citizens. Mr. Reimer here has been to Seminole many times to check us out. I think you'll like what he has to say. That's why I'll turn it over to him so he can speak in your native language."

Mr. Reimer stood up and said he had been investigating the land, looking for sellers. He had talked with a lawyer and would report back in a month with what he found. He promised to hold another meeting when he knew more.

He stood around with Mr. Smith and they answered question after question. Eventually, the crowd thinned, leaving David with the two of them.

"Can a man make a good living there?" David asked.

"He sure can," Mr. Smith assured him. "I live there and I'm making a good living. Come and see for yourself?"

David nodded and shook Mr. Smith's hand. "I just might do that."

After this meeting, word spread fast. The colonists learned there was a group going to Seminole. Men who were secretly interested began seeking out those attached to it. And David was right in the middle of it all. The constant refrain he told them was, "If this comes to pass, I'm going to be in that group."

He kept quiet about the urgent thought constantly at the forefront of his mind. *This might be my last chance.*

Chapter Twenty-One

Two long years passed after that initial meeting. Of course, there were more meetings and more plans. During one of them, David found himself surrounded by a determined group of men interested in permanently leaving the colony for Seminole. This time, though, he would have to speak. His palms were sweaty and his throat was dry as he waited for his turn. Mr. Reimer went first.

He told the men he had been working with a lawyer in El Paso to process potential groups from the Old Colony and EMMC into America. He'd assured them that their children would be properly educated, the rubber tires would stay on the tractors, and other mandatory hardships would be done away with—the main point being that each man could live his life as he saw fit. This was what David needed to hear. No matter the obstacles, he was now fully committed.

"Gentlemen!" Mr. Reimer shouted. "We have another report to give you. Let me call your attention to Mr. David Rempel."

David rubbed his palms on his overalls before stepping onto the stump, unaccustomed to being the center of attention. He cleared his throat, swallowed hard, then started talking. "Four weeks ago, Mr. Schmitt and I hitched a ride with Mr. Reimer, who was driving to Seminole to pick up some farm equipment. We stayed in Seminole for three weeks, at the Teepee Lodge. I learned that the Reimer family has spent so much time in Seminole that the owners of the Teepee Lodge asked them if they would be interested in buying the motel, since the owners are ready to retire. Mr. Reimer agreed and is moving to Seminole to run it when the purchase goes through. I tell you this because it means we will have people from our colony in Seminole—people who know their way around. They speak the language and have connections. I don't know about you, but that makes me feel comfortable."

The group of men nodded at each other. David continued. "We stayed in Seminole for three weeks, at the same Teepee Lodge Mr. Reimer is purchasing. I spent the entire time looking around. Since Mr. Schmitt wanted to earn money for his way back, he had a chance to work at a machine shop there. Mr. Schmitt can tell you there is plenty of work because he found some and doesn't even speak the language."

"What's the land like?" an anxious man called out.

"The land is good," David replied. "It's dry, but there's farming going on. They need more of the mesquite land cleared and planted."

Several men smiled, apparently satisfied with the answer. David continued. "I want to tell you I liked what I saw. I told my wife that they have these machines for the dishes. No one has to wash dishes anymore. The machine does it all for you. And they have little houses for dogs. Imagine a place so rich that they build houses for dogs."

A buzz raced through the group with several men shaking their heads in disbelief.

"After three weeks, we hopped on a bus and came back here. I don't know about you, but I'm moving my family to Seminole. Are there any questions?"

One man raised his hand. "How do we buy some land?"

David was ready for this. "The Reimer family is putting together a joint purchase. They're looking for a large piece of land, enough for all of us. When they find some, they have a lawyer who will draft a contract and obtain financing for the first year. After that, we will make payments directly to the bank. The good news is we will only have to deal with the Reimers. They will handle everything."

Heads bobbed up and down, smiling and grinning, as the men realized how easy this entire plan was coming together. David answered a few more questions before stepping down and talking individually to several men. When everyone was satisfied, he climbed into his Volkswagen and headed home.

If only Anna was as agreeable as the men, he thought, setting his jaw. It didn't matter, though. He had waited two full years before putting his plan into action. It was past time they left.

Stepping through the door of his small house, David heard some splashing from the room containing the bathtub. With no running water, they took their baths in a small clawfoot tub in its own little room. The water was heated up outside and carried in, which his wife was doing right now. He thought back to Seminole, where the water came right out of a faucet. And it was hot or cold, depending on how the knobs were turned. The colony was so far behind that he now dreaded his daily trips to the outhouse, thinking of the nice commode and endless supply of toilet paper at the Teepee Lodge.

He walked up to the bathroom door and knocked. "Who's in there?"

"It's me, Tina."

He could hear her splashing around in the tub, something she loved to do. "Are you almost done?"

"Yes, Dad."

Tina took baths with her cheap plastic sandals on. They were one of her most precious possessions. Anna had told him that his daughter wore them directly into the tub to clean off the hard-packed mud from their soles. After removing all the mud and pebbles, she would bathe in the dirty water and somehow clean herself up. He smiled, amused by the little girl so attached to those sandals that she refused to take them off.

David checked on the other children, finding them scattered about the house, waiting for their turn at the tub. Then he spotted Anna—out back, tending the fire and heating up water for the next child. When she noticed her husband, she frowned.

"You've been at another meeting," she said.

"I have," he replied coolly.

Anna stared down at the boiling water. "I suppose you've made up your mind."

"You know I made up my mind when we left for Canada. I'm just sorry that didn't work out."

"When are you going to tell the children?" she asked, shoving more fuel onto the fire.

"Tonight, after supper. It's the best time."

She didn't meet his eyes. "It's going to be your job, not mine."

"That's fair," he said.

Anna and the girls put away the last dishes as David sat in his favorite chair, working over a toothpick, waiting for his wife and daughters to join him and his son. When the entire clan had assembled, he looked at them, sitting up a little straighter.

"Children," he said confidently, "I've got something to tell you."

Tina raised her hand. "We forgot to tell you about our turkeys. Remember?"

"Turkeys? Why… oh, yes. Go ahead," he said, unhappy with the delay.

Tina ran to her room and brought back three pieces of paper. Each one had fabric glued to it. David studied them as Tina explained.

"While you were away, we had a project at school. The teacher wanted us to make our own turkey."

"I see," David said. "They look nice."

"Yes," she replied, clearly not through with the story. "The teacher told everyone to bring some fabric to school, and the other kids had a few pieces in tiny plastic bags. But we brought a big cracker box of scrap fabric. When we pulled it out, the other kids laughed at us and said, 'What were you thinking?' But we had the scraps left over from all the dresses Mom makes for us." She lowered her voice. "The other kids don't dress like we do."

At EMMC, David knew that his kids looked different because of their clothes. He was hoping that would change in Seminole.

"Anyway," Tina continued, "David, Elizabeth, and I started making turkeys with all the scrap, and they were looking really good. That's when the other kids—the ones making fun of us—started coming over and asking if they could have some. We were very popular!"

David's face lit up. It was important for Tina to feel she could help others. She loved learning, and especially loved being asked to do important tasks—ones that required trust. There was something in her spirit that needed to be needed.

"That's wonderful!" David told her. "I'm so proud of you."

Tina beamed, nudging Elizabeth and David. They hid their emotions better than her, but David could tell that they were pleased by his words, too. Of course, two-year-old Nancy could only sit and listen.

David put his hands on his knees, looking at each one of their happy faces. "I have some news, too. Your mother and I have decided to move to Texas. The town is called Seminole."

Suddenly, the smiles disappeared. "Are we leaving the colony?" his son asked.

"Yes, we are," David told him.

"And our friends?" Elizabeth ventured.

"Yes, but you'll meet new ones in Seminole."

"Can I take my sandals?" Tina asked, ready to cry if the answer was not what she wanted to hear.

"Yes."

"And my doll?"

"Of course."

Before he could say more, the single lightbulb hanging from the ceiling dimmed. David got to his feet and trudged outside, switching out the car batteries. This was the only light they had at night, unless they pulled out the expensive oil lamps. He couldn't wait to leave this place and turn on all the lights simply by flipping a switch. What a day that would be!

<hr/>

A horsefly buzzed around looking for a place to land. David swatted at it then heard his father kicking some dirt clods out of the way as he shuffled to his barn, where David waited. This would be another goodbye, one that David hoped would be permanent.

Mennonite men liked meeting in the barn. It was the only place they could have privacy—especially if a tear or two appeared.

"Hello, son," Jacob said, shaking David's hand. "I guess you've said your goodbyes to Mother. She's in there wiping her eyes."

"Yes, I have. Now I need to tell you goodbye."

David was surprised when his father impulsively stepped forward as if he would hug him. But instead, he shook David's hand firmly, something he wouldn't have done two years ago. Then again, his father had done a lot of things David never would've expected—like laying down his title and giving up preaching. It had all come about when David's mother had left the Old Colony church and began attending the Church of God. She'd said she wanted to teach her youngest daughters something different—that they didn't have to live under man-made rules, but under God's grace and forgiveness. As Jacob had listened to his wife and seen the changes in his daughters, he had decided to go to a few services and started seeing the light. One day, his father threw everything out and announced to his family, and then to the colony, that he no longer wanted to be a preacher. David figured he could've been the Ältester, but instead, the Rempels' long direct line of preachers died right there. Or would future generations pick it up again?

David had learned that after his father's announcement, as Jacob was cleaning out his desk of old, recycled sermons, Jacob realized he'd preached 940 sermons, performed 142 weddings, and presided over 140 funerals. It had been his life's work. But now, he'd found true salvation. That was more important than numbers.

He released David with a sigh. "Have you said goodbye to your grandfather? You two always had a strong bond."

David recalled the day before, when Grandpa Jacob had visited him right here in this same barn. It was more of celebration than a sad goodbye. They had laughed and told stories, recalling all of the crazy ideas and failed attempts. At the end, his grandfather said how proud he was, and how he'd be waiting for a letter on how the world looked in Seminole.

"Yes," David replied. "We said our goodbyes."

Jacob nodded, clearing his throat to keep his emotions at bay. It was almost time to let his son go. "I noticed you're leaving your storage box here," Jacob said, pointing at the large wooden crate against the back wall.

"I don't have any choice. We can only fit so much in the car. I'll have to send for the rest of my stuff when I get settled."

"Do you have enough money?"

"I think so. I sold my place and all the furniture and equipment. I did move the kids' toys to my brother-in-law's house, since they don't have any children. They'll be safer there than with all the grandkids around here."

"Yeah," Jacob said, grinning. "What about your old farm?"

"I'm getting a few payments here and there, so I might need you to drop by and see if you can shake loose some money."

"Great," Jacob said. "My favorite thing to do." David picked up the sarcasm. "How many families are going?"

"Fifty—five hundred people total. There'll be more once we get settled and show them it's okay."

His father sat down on a stump and picked his teeth with a piece of hay. "I'm sure you're right. We need more land, and no one wants to give us any. We tend to eventually outnumber the native people wherever we go. Did you sell the car?"

"Yes. It made Anna's mother very happy."

"Speaking of them, how are they taking the news?"

"Not good," David said, pushing his cowboy hat back. "Anna is very upset. I just need to get her across the border and seal the deal."

A comfortable silence settled over them for a time, as they spent these last moments together. Finally, Jacob stood. "Okay, son. I wish you the best. And I'll be praying for you, too. I hope this move is the last one."

"It's going to have to be," David said, pulling his father into a tight hug. "Goodbye, Dad. I'm not sure when we'll be allowed to come back."

His father nodded, then hung his head. That was the last thing David saw as he turned away and walked through the barn door, leaving his father behind. When he fired up the Volkswagen and drove off, he wasn't around to see Jacob swipe at something in his eye and sit back down on the stump to rest for a while, before going back into the house.

The sun was just peeking above the horizon as David tied a small piece of luggage to the roof of the camper. "There," he said. "That should do it. Anna, are you ready?"

"Are we leaving for good?" Anna asked, her eyes filling with tears.

"Yes," he replied, pulling her away from the car and lowering his voice. "I know I've failed so far, but you must believe me. This is it. I just know it. That's why I'm certain we will probably never come back."

Anna's tears fell to the dry dirt. "Wait a moment. I just need to say goodbye to my father."

David nodded, watching her as she stepped away from the pickup and stared out over the field. She did this sometimes, praying about a sick relative or talking to her father. Jacob J. Friesen had died April 4, 1962, before David had started dating Anna, depriving him of a chance to meet his father-in-law. Later, Anna had painfully detailed her father's last days of suffering, how he'd barely been able to breathe due to bad lungs from smoking and working in the fields trying to make a crop. When he'd become unable to feed himself, he shrunk, getting thin and weak. That's when they knew the end was near. According to Anna, his death had been an act of mercy.

After a few minutes, Anna turned back to him with swollen eyes and allowed herself to be escorted to the pickup truck, where she was loaded in the front seat with Mrs. Schmitt. He and Mr. Schmitt had hired a driver, Mr. J. Dyck, to take them to Seminole. With only room for three adults up front, David and Mr. Schmitt climbed into the bed of the truck, a camper shell above to protect them from the weather. Packed around the two men were four of the Schmitt's five children, and three of David's four. Each family had a child just over two named Nancy, who rode up front in their mothers' laps. To say the car was stuffed was an understatement.

"Daddy, will my doll be safe?" Tina asked, her back against the tailgate.

"What?" David said, confused.

"My doll. Will it be safe?"

"Oh yes, your doll. Of course, it'll be safe. Don't you worry."

He had been forced to pry the doll from her hands and store it with the rest of the toys. If he had allowed just one child to bring a toy, the others would want one. And they had absolutely no room in the truck bed. David had his back up against the cab, with clothes and boxes crammed all around his body. His neighbor, Mr. Schmitt, was no better off. If there would be an accident, the authorities would take forever locating their bodies among all this stuff.

Hearing his response, Tina gazed at him with a doubtful expression. "Okay. But I miss my doll."

He pulled his daughter into his lap. "I know, sweetheart. But I'll get someone to bring your doll to Seminole. You won't have to leave her behind." He hoped this wasn't another promise he couldn't keep.

The pickup truck rolled through the colony, giving its occupants one last look at the place they had called home all their lives. When they crested a slight hill, David saw the familiar vendor trucks underneath a large tree, trading fruit and fish for the Mennonites' eggs and butter. There, on a hill, David spotted the exact place where Fiex, his precious black-and-white sheepdog, had died—crushed by the wheel of one of those trucks. His throat tightened at the memory of that loss. They had been such close friends. Not only was he leaving his family behind, but he was leaving a lot of sad memories, too.

⟫◆⟪

The heavily laden pickup truck arrived in Juarez just after two in the afternoon, giving David several hours to get the paperwork from the El Paso lawyer and enter the United States of America. He couldn't wait.

"You stay with the car," David ordered the driver. "And keep these children from getting lost. We'll be right back."

Everyone climbed out of the truck to stretch their legs as he and Mr. Schmitt looked around for the other families. Several cars had beaten them to the U.S. immigration office, while others were just pulling in. Regardless of when they had arrived, all of them waited for the men-in-the-know like David to tell them what to do. He signaled the men to huddle in an area to the side of the office and told them that the Reimers had arranged for a lawyer to have the papers ready. David suggested he and a few men go inside to find the lawyer, get the papers, and come back outside to distribute them to the fifty families now waiting. With the plan set, David hitched up his overalls and went inside.

On one side of a long counter that took up most of the room, immigration officers sat at stations tending to lines of people on the other side. There had to be hundreds of people in line, each immigrant holding both paperwork and money. David scanned the waiting area and didn't see anyone who looked like a lawyer. In fact, every person in line was Hispanic and dressed like a worker—just like him. David swallowed hard. This was not what he had expected.

He walked the length of the office to make sure the lawyer wasn't obscured or hidden behind someone. He wasn't.

"I guess we'll stand around here and see if he shows up," David said to Mr. Schmitt and two other men. Then he tapped Mr. Schmitt on the shoulder, pulling him aside for a moment. "Will you take a pass outside and see if you spot a man dressed like a lawyer?"

"Sure," Mr. Schmitt replied. "I'll be right back."

A few minutes later, he returned. "Nothing out there but a bunch of Mennonites and Hispanics."

David rubbed his chin. "Hmm. Maybe the lawyer was delayed."

The men nodded in agreement. That had to be it.

At five o'clock, two immigration officers approached the four men and said something in English that no one understood. Finally, one of the officers held up his hands and said, "*Cerrado*," making a sweeping motion to shoo them out.

Outside, David frowned. "I guess we'll have to stay the night and come back in the morning."

One of the men complained. "I thought the lawyer was going to be here today. Tomorrow is Tuesday."

"I know," David replied, trying to calm him down. "But what can we do? They're closing the office. Let's find a place to stay, and I'll call Mr. Reimer to see what's happened."

A short time later, David hauled his family's luggage into a small motel room a few miles from the immigration office. The driver, familiar with the area, had recommended it. Ten other families joined him while the others found another motel, one that was cheaper. Money was tight, so a few families even slept in their cars. During a spare moment, Anna pulled David aside. "What happened?"

"I don't know," David told her. "The lawyer was supposed to be there, but he wasn't. I'm going to make a call and see what I can find out. Go ahead and pull out the food and feed everyone. I'll eat something when I return."

Anna nodded and did as she was told. She could see her husband was stressed, and didn't want to add to it.

David returned an hour later, a grin creasing his face. "I talked with the Reimers. The lawyer will be there tomorrow. He was delayed in El Paso."

Anna smiled. "That's wonderful. Did you tell the Schmitts?"

"No," he replied. "Let me tell them. I'll be right back for my supper. Suddenly, I'm hungry."

The next morning, David and his group of men returned to the office before it opened. To his surprise, there was a line outside. They waited at the end of it until the doors flung open precisely at eight, and followed the immigrants ahead of them who were all rushing in. Once inside, he looked around to find the lawyer, but he wasn't there.

"He'll be along shortly," David said, reassuring the men. "He's coming from the American side, so he's probably going through the line over there."

By noon, though, there was no lawyer. David sat inside the office on a bench, a sick feeling rising in his stomach. When the office closed at five, he lost all appetite.

Back in the parking lot, he talked with the men trying to keep their spirits up. Several of them had checked out of their motel and would now have to re–check in. That meant unloading everything again. Wisely, David had left his family at the motel, so he didn't have to go through that. Still, it meant another night of expenses, including a room for the driver, Mr. Dyck, and his meals too. With the food they'd packed mostly gone, David would have to take Anna to buy some groceries tomorrow. Hopefully, they'd be shopping in Seminole. He forced himself to stay positive, but it was getting hard.

Wednesday evening, he returned to the motel with no lawyer and no papers. He was in a foul mood. That's when Anna told him there was a big problem. All the children were restless. Like their trip to Canada, every-thing was new and wonderful. This led them to make noise and explore the building, both of which were driving the manager crazy. But the final straw was when Tina gained access to an electrical closet and pulled some switches, cutting off the electricity to the entire motel. She got away with it several times before the manager caught her red-handed.

"He wants us to leave," Anna said. "Now."

David pounded a fist into his palm. His first reaction was to spank the life out of Tina. Instead, he calmed down and went to speak to the manager, where he spent thirty minutes using his broken Spanish to convince the manager it wouldn't happen again. Eventually, the manager relented and let David stay. When that was done, David found Tina and briskly escorted her to their room.

"Listen here," he said, trying hard to control his anger. "You'll have to stay in this room until we leave this place. Understand?"

Tina nodded, her lip quivering. She could see her actions had caused a lot of harm. David left the room in a huff, grabbed his wife, and took her to buy more groceries. This was not how they had planned to spend their week.

Thursday morning, David set up shifts in the immigration office. This put two men inside, with the rest looking for the lawyer and smoking cigarettes outside. Several of the men complained about money. No one had counted on these extra expenses. Then one of them said something they had all been thinking. "What if this entire thing is a scam? We've made a down payment for the land. How do we know the land is there?"

Another man added to their fears. "Is it even true that if you own one acre of land in the U.S., you can enter and become a citizen?"

David shook his head, trying to stop this talk. "I don't know the answers, but I'm sure everything will work out. Mr. Reimer told me the lawyer had the papers and he and his immigration man would show up to help us. I called him last night and he said today is the day!"

"But tomorrow is Friday!" the man spat back. "Then it's the weekend and the office is closed. If the lawyer doesn't get here tomorrow, I'll have to go back to the colony. I don't have the money for this."

"Me too!" another man chimed in.

David's chest tightened. "Let's all pray for a miracle tomorrow," he said, holding his hands up. "Okay?"

The men nodded and moved away, mostly wearing frowns. David understood. They had sold everything. There wasn't anything to go back to. For David, it would be yet another failed attempt to leave—his third. He couldn't see making a fourth. This would be it for him. Something had to happen tomorrow or he'd be headed back too, with the money he had put down on the Seminole land gone. He couldn't believe Mr. Reimer would do that to him.

It was Friday afternoon when David took over his shift inside the office, sitting on a rickety bench. The scene didn't look good. Despite Mr. Reimer again saying today is the day, it wasn't. There was no immigration man anywhere. In a few hours, time would run out.

The words of his grandfather echoed in his ear. "Leave this place, David. It's no good here. You must find a way out."

Once again, I'll have to go back with my tail between my legs, David thought, shaking his head in disgust. Everything had seemed to line up this time. But it had just been another dream, another failed attempt. And he'd have to go back to both his father and grandfather and admit his failure for the third time. How had he gotten everything so wrong?

A large immigration officer appeared, one David hadn't seen before. The man stood on the other side of the counter staring at David, as if he was trying to burn a hole right through him. Suddenly, he barked an order in English and waved him to the counter.

"Yes?" David said, in Low German.

The officer said something in English, which David couldn't understand.

"*Qué?*" David tried.

Sure enough, the officer spoke Spanish. David let him know that he wasn't fluent, and to speak slowly. The officer nodded, then asked, "Who are you people and why have you been here all week?"

David blinked a few times. He thought about lying, which could possibly gain his passage into America. Yet if he told the truth, he'd probably get denied. It was in that moment, he thought of everything he stood for: his life, his dreams, and his desire to leave the colony. Then he made a decision.

If I can't cross with the truth, I want no part of this country.

David told the officer everything. The promise that if they bought land, they could become citizens. The down payments they had made. The lawyer who was supposed to show up with an immigration man. The papers they were waiting on, day after day. The confusion. When he was done, the officer stepped back and shook his head. He walked a few steps down to another officer and spoke with him in English. That officer shook his head too and whistled. They both exchanged words before the officer came back to David.

"I'm going to process you. Let me see your Mexican papers and we'll get this going."

David handed him the papers before he could change his mind, mesmerized as the officer filled out the paperwork before pounding on several pieces of paper with a large stamp.

"Here you go," the officer said, handing David a stack of documents. "You can enter now."

David stared at the papers in disbelief.

"Call the other men in, and have them bring their papers," the officer said. "Hurry now. We close soon."

David was too shocked to move.

"*Rápido!*" the officer barked.

In minutes, the Mennonite men had formed lines in front of three officers who hurriedly scribbled on their papers and stamped them. By five o'clock, all of the men had their papers. David couldn't believe it. A miracle had indeed happened. They were going to make it.

The dirty pickup truck rumbled along State Highway 62, having just cleared Hobbs, New Mexico. Its headlights cut through the vast darkness of West Texas—the Llano Estacado—and continued east toward its destination. Most of the passengers were asleep, unaware of how close they were to ending this long journey. But one person knew: He could smell it. After all, he'd spent three weeks there and could sense the place from miles away.

This man gazed through the front windshield, seeing a glow on the horizon. Just as the vehicle came over a rise—the beginning of a long draw, the same one that saved the men of the Tenth Cavalry so long ago—he woke everyone up and told them to look at the lights of the town ahead. Once each passenger had their gaze fixed on the lights, David said something that came from deep within his heart. "We're home. Now, we're home!"

Chapter Twenty-Two

The sound of a slamming door shook David awake. Without the rooster crowing or the typical farm sounds, he felt disoriented. He stared at the white stipple on the ceiling as if it held the answers. He hadn't felt like this since that morning after his wedding, when he'd woken in a strange bed in a distant farm—lying next to the woman who was his wife.

A door slammed again. Now he remembered. He was in the Teepee Lodge, his entire family stuffed into one room and the Schmitt family in another. He and Anna slept in one bed, while all four kids slept in the other. It was a tough scene.

David rubbed his eyes. The exhaustion from the previous day—no, the previous *week*—had worn on him. He'd slept past six, nearly oblivious to the ruckus of four pairs of little feet scurrying across the room, slamming doors as they darted in and out of the room, and occasionally the bathroom. With the chaos beginning, it was time for him to get up.

Anna reached out to touch his arm but missed. He was dressing too quickly. "Where are you going?" she asked.

"We have to pay the driver so he can head on back to Mexico. When we're done, we'll find some breakfast."

Ten minutes later, David stood next to Mr. Schmitt watching the pickup's dust trail heading west, back toward the place they used to call home. Once it was out of sight, David rubbed his hands together and drew in a deep breath, allowing the butterflies to settle in his gut. He'd finally cut his ties to Mexico. There was no turning back now.

"I'm hungry," Tina announced when he got back to the room.

"I am too," David said. "Let's get everyone rounded up and head to Jo's."

Tina pursed her lips, brow furrowing a little. "Who's Jo?"

He couldn't help but smile. "You'll see."

The sun was hot on their backs as the two families made their way to the restaurant, a bell announcing their presence as they opened the door. David had eaten here on his last trip to check out the town, so he knew how it worked. "Let's take that table over there," he said, leading the large group to the corner. They pulled over another table and enough chairs to accommodate everyone.

A waitress came over with menus and surveyed the strangers. Fortunately, she recognized David from the year before. With some patience, she was able to understand enough of his broken English so he could tell her what everyone wanted. As she left, David's children scanned the restaurant, mouths agape as they observed the large windows and cozy decorations.

Tina's eyes widened as she picked up a packet of jelly, examining it closely. "What is this?" she asked.

David explained everything on the table and how the place worked. The children listened in fascination. To them it was such a delightful place.

When the food arrived without their mother having to lift a finger, they dug in. He watched them, his family, eating and chatting with excitement. All the worries of the past week slowly faded away, leaving him with a lump in his throat and tears in his eyes, which he tactfully hid by lowering his gaze. *This* was what he'd been working toward his entire life. *This* was what his grandfather had wanted him to pursue, planting the seed of determination within him. A life without the pointless restrictions and never-ending backbreaking labor that he'd endured growing up. A better chance for his children. Right now, he simply savored the feeling of accomplishment, taking a bite of his food as a grin creased his face.

The moment might have lasted the entire meal, had Mr. Schmitt not leaned over and spoke into his ear. "Well, we finally made it. Can you believe it?"

David continued smiling. "Yes, I can. God is watching over us."

"Yes, He is. We're all here and safe." Mr. Schmitt set down his fork, making sure the women and children were preoccupied with their own conversations before turning back to David. "But I have a question."

David shot a glance at him. "A question? What is it?"

Mr. Schmitt rubbed the back of his neck, shrugging. "Well, we're here. Now what?"

David swallowed hard, setting down his own fork as he tried to find some words. After the confusion of the past week, and all the obstacles they'd run into so far, he didn't exactly know how to answer Mr. Schmitt's question. The truth was, he had his own doubts about the situation, but he wasn't sure that voicing his concern would do any good. And going back now wasn't an option. He cleared his throat. "Uhh…"

Tina held up the tiny square of jelly, waving it in front of his face. "Dad, can I take this with me?"

He mustered up a smile for her, feeling Mr. Schmitt's quiet stare on his opposite side. "Sure, Tina."

Turning back to Mr. Schmitt, he rubbed his jaw. *Nothing's ever easy, is it?*

The crowd of men gathered around the main organizer, Mr. Reimer. It had only taken a full day for everyone to get settled into a motel room somewhere in Seminole—and for word to spread about a meeting downtown, across from City Hall. Mr. Reimer had told the men he was ready to explain everything to them, and they were more than ready to hear that explanation.

After what seemed like an eternity, Mr. Reimer climbed onto a milk crate and shouted to the men to quiet down. It didn't take much for them to listen.

"First, let me welcome you to Seminole," Mr. Reimer said in Low German. "You've finally made it." Some applause, though hesitant, rippled through the crowd. "I want to apologize for the lawyer not meeting you at the border. There was some miscommunication, which may be due to our different languages."

Several men shook their heads and frowned. Mr. Reimer kept his face neutral, looking out over their confused stares. "The paper you received at the border is a temporary visa. You can only stay in the U.S. for sixty days."

Loud murmuring threatened to turn into real anger. Mr. Reimer's lip twitched a little as he raised his hands. "Wait a minute! Wait a minute!" he said. "I *do* have the lawyer working on your permanent papers. He's working on everything right now."

The chatter in the crowd died down as some of the men crossed their arms, waiting for him to elaborate.

"Now, as you know, lawyers cost money." The men exchanged looks among each other. "If you and your family want to stay here, I'll need fifty U.S. dollars for you and your wife, and each of your children."

A quiet shock settled over them, especially the men with large families. David stood among them, unable to stop from gaping at the absurd sum. He leaned over and whispered in Mr. Schmitt's ear. "With five hundred of us, that's twenty-five thousand dollars for the entire group."

"Must be a really good lawyer," Mr. Schmitt whispered with a crooked grin, but there was no humor in his eyes.

"When do we get to see the land we purchased?" one of the attendees yelled out.

"Soon," Mr. Reimer said. "We're still finalizing the sale from a potato farmer. We have a real estate man working on it, too."

Finalizing? David thought, gritting his teeth. Around every corner in this new land, something seemed to require his money. Paying for a lawyer *and* having to wait for work would do more than cut into his savings.

"Any questions?" Mr. Reimer asked.

"Yeah," a man up front said. "We were told—no, *promised*—that by purchasing land in Texas, we'd be granted citizenship. What papers do we need, and why do we need to pay money for a lawyer?"

"That's how things get done in this country," Mr. Reimer explained. "The Englanders have a system and you have to work within that system. They have buildings full of records that keep track of everything, unlike back in Mexico, where we journeyed to a wide plain and just staked out our lots. It's very different here. Believe me, when the paperwork is complete, you'll each have a document that gives you title to your land. Please, just be patient."

"And pay fifty dollars a head," someone said under their breath, loud enough for the men to hear.

A couple of them nodded in agreement, but David held his peace. *It's just another setback*, he thought, mind already working toward a solution. He knew from experience that brooding wouldn't get him anywhere. *I'm thirty-one years old with a thirty-five-year-old wife and four children to feed. The only thing I know for sure is I need to get some work right now.*

Mr. Reimer ignored the remark and stayed around to answer more questions from some of the men while David stood with a separate group.

"I hope this all works out," one man offered, turning his worried eyes to David.

"I hope so too," David said. "I have ten acres with my sisters and father. I need to get on that land and start farming so I can make some money. After all, I have four children to feed. The three hundred dollars he needs will take a chunk of my money."

"I have a feeling this is going to get worse before it gets better," Mr. Schmitt mumbled, drawing no response mainly because everyone knew he was right.

<hr/>

There was a rhythm to Seminole. It wasn't the hustle-bustle of a large, modern city, but more of a country town filled with friendly folks who always put in a full day—at least before the sun went down. Cars rumbled here and there, citizens intent on getting their work done before the day was over. It might have been comforting, if the motel manager wasn't still frustrated with the Rempels and the Schmitts.

Five days after they'd arrived, the angry manager finally hit his breaking point and called David in to speak with him. Their struggle to communicate just made things worse.

"You can't hang your laundry to dry on the bushes. You just can't!" the manager barked at him.

David was confused. He knew Anna was washing the clothes in the bathtub by hand and then placing them on the bushes in front of their room. It was the only way to dry them, even if they did have a nice layer of dust when they were done. Why was this man so upset?

"Sir, how do we dry them?" David asked several times, using different words to try and get his meaning across.

When the manager finally understood his question, he led David to a room on the far end of the motel and pointed to a machine on the wall. "There! You use that." The manager produced a quarter and placed it halfway in a slot. "See?"

David walked up to the machine and studied it, opening the door and looking inside the large drum.

"This is a dryer," the manager said, pointing at the drum. "It'll dry your clothes. Your clothes go in here."

David nodded several times before grinning. "Yes. I understand." He couldn't wait to show his wife. She would be thrilled. He turned his attention to a freestanding machine. "What's this for?" he asked.

"That's a washing machine. You put your clothes in here with some soap, and the machine washes it. See?" Again, the manager demonstrated everything. And again, David grinned, but this time he could hardly contain himself. He was now absolutely positive Anna would be in a terrific mood when she learned how to use these machines.

For one short moment, he forgot about his troubles and jogged back to the room, grabbing Anna, Mr. Schmitt, and his wife, and leading them all to the laundry room. It took a few minutes, but David was able to show them how to wash and dry clothes. Everyone was thoroughly impressed. They would no longer need to hang their laundry over the bushes.

Mr. Schmitt exchanged a grin with David, clearly mirroring his excitement. "Living in America is going to be better than we thought!"

That afternoon, David and Mr. Schmitt located a mobile home to rent. It had one bathroom and two bedrooms. Although tiny for Seminole standards, it was a mansion compared to the two small motel rooms they'd all been living in for the past five days.

Anna was in for another surprise, too: The stove didn't need wood, instead running on electricity. One turn of a knob and before she knew it, the heating element was red-hot ready for a pot of water to boil. And although the trailer lacked a dishwasher, she couldn't hide her smile at the thought of doing laundry and cooking chores in a fraction of the time she was used to. She might even have some leisure time one day. Maybe.

While she cooked away, David spent time in private counting his money and he wasn't happy. He'd watched his roll diminish at a rapid pace—certainly faster than he'd planned. To save money, both he and Mr. Schmitt bought the cheapest food they could find. They shopped at a nearby convenience store, believing they had the same prices as the large grocery store a mile away. It wasn't as if they could've shopped somewhere else. They lacked transportation.

Every few days, he and Mr. Schmitt walked to the convenience store and loaded up on their mainstay: pork and beans. The two families consumed gallons of the stuff. An occasional treat was Beanee Weenees. The kids looked at the tiny wieners with amazement, savoring the sauce as if it had been sent from heaven. Sandwiches were also served for one of the meals each day—a concoction of dry white bread and baloney. Coming from their limited selection in Mexico, everyone's palate was thrilled with the new choices.

David soon made friends with a neighbor who had a car, often hitching rides with him. Finding a job was the top priority, so he traveled wherever the neighbor would drop him off. With the influx of so many Mennonite men, jobs in Seminole were temporarily tight. That's where the Reimer family came in. They owned two sections of choice land and hired David and Mr. Schmitt to plow it, paying them $1.50 an hour to work day and night. David didn't mention that ten acres of this land belonged to him, his father, and sisters.

The rubber-tired tractors they provided gave David a lot of time to think about his situation, and his worries threatened to crush him. At such a low pay, he'd never get ahead—much less keep up with his current expenses. He needed to find a car so he could look around for another job. But his cash was still short, especially with the heavy fees he paid the Reimers for the lawyers. The payments from the land in Mexico weren't coming in either. Soon, he'd be in real trouble.

Each day, as swirling dust enveloped his tractor, his fears ate at him. Money, immigration issues, everything weighed heavily on his mind. He could only pray for help from God. It was just too big for him to handle.

God had a plan. Hopefully.

The morning breeze drifted through the old house, cooling its inhabitants. March was a great time to be in West Texas—not too hot and not too cold. A woman sat at the kitchen table, feeling the cool air on her skin, listening to the yellow curtains dancing back and forth as she thumbed through the day's newspaper, hoping to find a coupon on steak or pork—two staples in her household. A man crouched in a corner nearby, rolling marbles around, lost in some imaginary adventure or game—it was hard to tell. Suddenly, he jumped to his feet and sprinted to the front door. The woman watched him go and pushed back from the table, grabbing a mirror from a kitchen drawer. This early warning gave her a chance to check her quality—a phrase her aunt had often used. Satisfied, she straightened her dress and moved to the front room, certain that the man's intuition would be accurate. It was.

A minute later, a strange man in overalls cautiously stepped up to the porch, creaking across the boards until he reached the front door. It was already open.

"Can I help you?" the woman asked.

"Yes," the man said with a foreign accent. "Miss Rose?"

Rose nodded. "That's me. And who might you be?"

The man grimaced as if he was confused, so she repeated herself slowly. Finally, he understood. "I'm David Rempel. Do you have a car for sale?"

Rose picked apart his broken English until she understood. "Why, yes. It's a four-door Buick. Let me show it to you."

She removed the keys off the hook and took the man outside to a sandblasted car. A few brown patches of color still lingered here and there. After introducing Melvin, who hung back studying David, she started the car and let him listen to the engine. David climbed in the front seat and turned it off, examining the dashboard. Then he crawled underneath the car for a more detailed inspection. After twenty minutes, he appeared satisfied.

"How much?" he asked.

"Two hundred dollars," she said. "That's a fair price."

David scratched his arm and hesitated. "One hundred fifty?"

Rose shook her head. "No, I need two hundred dollars. I'm on a fixed income."

"One hundred eighty?" he offered.

"No, sorry."

David pulled out his money and counted it out. Rose could tell it added up to $180. "Here," he said, handing it to her.

She handed it back. "The price is two hundred dollars." This wasn't her first negotiation. Selling tractors to strong men had trained her well. And even if this man was from somewhere else, haggling was the same everywhere. Surely, he'd find the other twenty dollars tucked away somewhere.

He did. Reaching in the middle pocket of his overalls, he produced the final bill. As she took it from him, she noticed his face darken. Perhaps this wasn't all a show.

Rose took him inside and filled out the title. After completing a bill of sale, she handed him the documents and the keys and said, "Congratulations, David. You now own Old Blondie. Take good care of her and she'll take good care of you."

He furrowed his brow, staring intently at her.

Rose laughed. It was doubtful he understood anything she had said. "Well anyway," she chuckled, "it's all yours. Let me show you out."

Melvin bounded up the steps, having kept watch on the car while they were inside. He brushed past David, who still looked confused. But it didn't take long for him to start up the car and take off.

Rose placed her hand on the man's shoulder. "Melvin, there goes Old Blondie. She served us well. I guess it's time to look for another one. You want to help me?" He stood there, expressionless. "Good. Come on inside. Let's look through the newspaper and see what we can find for the lawyer to buy for us."

David gripped the steering wheel of the Buick and guided it through the streets. He was deeply worried about what he'd just done. That twenty dollars was it. No more. He'd planned on using it to buy groceries. Now, he'd have to wait until his next meager paycheck to feed his family. They had some food in the trailer, but how long would that last? A day or two? This was a real problem.

He stopped at a light near the Teepee Lodge, spotting the room they'd stayed at when they'd first arrived. It had been less than two weeks and already it seemed like a lifetime. He and his family had come so far. But now, things looked grim. No money meant more hunger—and, of course, the inevitable frustration from Anna. She still missed her mother. This would add to her anger and his stress.

David peered at the light, which was still red. It was hard to see it clearly with the angle of the sun. He shaded his eyes, but that didn't work. Then he remembered to lower the visor. When he did, something drifted into his lap. He glanced down and couldn't believe his eyes. It was a twenty-dollar bill. Smiling, he closed his eyes and prayed. *God, thank you so much. It's exactly what I need at the exact right time.*

A horn behind him blared. He twisted around to see a motorist angrily waving at him, sounding the horn again. He looked up at the green light, hit the accelerator, and took off. Food was back on the menu, and his family would never know how close they'd come to starving.

Chapter Twenty-Three

April 18, 1977
Seminole, Texas

D avid pulled the suspenders up over his shoulders as he watched his wife place sandwiches in three brown bags. Stifling a yawn, he bent down to peer out the window. It was still dark outside, the sunrise nowhere in sight. His family's day was beginning before even the sky had woken up.

Down the hall, a toilet flushed. David couldn't help but smile. This two-bedroom trailer was all his. That was, his and Anna's—and their four children's. And then there was Mr. Schmitt, his wife, and their children. They were crammed in too. But one small trailer was luxury living compared to the Teepee Lodge and Mexico. After all, they had an electric stove that Anna put to good use, making her famous bread. And a toilet that flushed next to an indoor bathtub. Adding to that the privacy of their own bedroom, the American dream he'd been hearing about was looking like a real deal.

"Come on, kids," he said, straightening and stretching out his back the best he could. "Time to load up. Don't want to be late on your first day."

Mr. Schmitt mumbled something under his breath, searching the tiny living area for his ballcap. His wife moved in behind Anna to start making breakfast for their children. The toilet flushed and the bathroom door flung open, nearly hitting Elizabeth as she pulled on her shoes.

"Hey, Tina!" she snapped, shutting the door behind her eight-year-old sister. "Watch it!"

Tina ignored her, bouncing across the trailer and heading for the living room to slip on her cheap rubber sandals. "I'm ready, Dad!" she yelled.

"Hold on a minute," Anna said, handing Elizabeth, David, and Tina their lunches. "Take these and don't forget your water jugs."

Each of the children grabbed the reused glass bottles, already heading for the front door. Their Buick was the next stop, bare metal showing in patches between the original brown color. David turned to kiss Anna goodbye, trying to muster up a smile for her. When she didn't smile back, he decided to keep his mouth shut.

He climbed into the Buick as Mr. Schmitt took the passenger seat. Five minutes later, David stopped at the edge of a barren field so he could let his children out. Tina, the last one to emerge from the backseat, tapped on the driver's window and David rolled it down. "What's the matter?"

"How long do we have to hoe weeds?" she asked.

"Until I come and get you. It will be later this afternoon."

"Is this just for one day?"

"No," he said, growing frustrated. "It's for every day but Sunday."

She frowned. "Am I ever going back to school?"

David took a breath, trying not to snap at her. "Yes, Tina. It's just that we need the money right now. I'm blessed to have found you kids some work. Now, run along." He started to roll up the window, but she wasn't done.

"Where are you going?"

He ran his hands over his face. "I'll be plowing the fields for Mr. Reimer. It's where I've been the last eight days. Come on, you know that."

"For how long?"

"Until they show us the land we've bought. Then I'll be farming that, just like I did back in Mexico. You'll see. Get to work before the others leave you behind."

Tina set the water jug and sack on the ground, taking her time to push a wide-brimmed straw hat down over her light brown hair. Finally, she picked up the food and water again before running off to join her siblings. In the gray dawn, David watched her dancing among the rocks, trying not to trip. Her flimsy sandals had caused more than one fall back at the trailer.

As they headed toward the highway, Mr. Schmitt eyed him. "Do they know you're going to keep their wages?"

Biting his lower lip, David pulled onto the road. "Yes, but they don't know I'm keeping all of it. We have so many things to pay for. I have no choice."

"Like that phone line we put in?"

"That, I think, has already paid for itself," David said, triumphant when Mr. Schmitt chuckled. A week earlier, they'd had a heated discussion about the cost of the phone line. Mr. Schmitt was against it, but David prevailed because he said a phone would help them get more work. The investment had paid off when a farmer called to offer him a job hoeing weeds in his fields. David had said he was tied up plowing land for Mr. Reimer but offered up his children. The farmer took the deal.

The car slowed, crushing clay rocks as Mr. Schmitt pointed to the field. "Which side do you want?"

"The side with less rocks." They both laughed.

With the first rays of sun peeking over the horizon, David climbed up on his tractor and started down a row, rubber tires propelling him like they had in Mexico. Here, though, no one hassled him. The issue of the ridiculous metal paddles was long gone.

What wasn't gone was his wife's longing to go back to Mexico. Anna had made a few calls to her mother, each time hanging up the phone in frustration. She was seriously doubting this move. *I just need to get on the land we bought and she'll settle down*, he said to himself, thinking of the meeting in town later this afternoon. Hopefully he'd get his land and be able to move onto his own place. A warm tinge of excitement rose in his throat at the thought of it. *Just a little while longer*. The excitement faded as he lifted himself up to find the end of the row. He had another mile to go.

———

"Gather round, men!" a loud voice yelled in Low German. "Gather round!"

At least fifty overall-clad men pushed forward to hear the speaker—a Mennonite standing on an apple box. "For those of you who don't know," he barked, "this is John Shepherd, the lawyer working on the immigration matters." He pointed to a tall, slender man who thrust up his hand and waved as if he was in a parade.

"And this is Seth Woltz," the speaker continued, "the real estate agent." A second man, somewhat nervous, waved at the crowd.

"Mr. Woltz arranged for the purchase of that land southwest of town by the Old Colony from Canada. He's helping all of us." A murmur ran through the crowd. "Now, I need to explain something very important. Each of you received a tourist visa when you crossed from Mexico into the United States. Your visas expire at the end of May. That's one month away. Mr. Shepherd is working hard on your immigration problems, so I want you to plan ahead. We will need another fifty dollars per head from your family."

Dozens of men groaned. David grimaced and lowered his head. He was barely making it. With four children and a wife, he'd owe another $300. The thought made him nauseous.

Seeing the crowd turn, the speaker held up his hands. "Listen, the expenses in this country for papers are high. But we believe this is it. Once you make the payment, our lawyer can submit the proper paperwork."

The crowd studied the lawyer, who was clueless about what the speaker was saying. Sensing they were talking about him, he smiled.

"Now," the speaker said as the men quieted down, "let me answer your questions about the land you have purchased."

<hr />

"What's going on out there?" Mayor Bob Clark said, peeking through a metal window blind. "Bernice, do you know what's going on?"

"I've seen them out there before," the secretary replied. "I think Seth has something to do with them."

Mayor Clark squinted. Sure enough, they were standing on Main Street near the real estate agent's office. "What's this all about?"

"I don't know, Bob, but I saw a few men hanging out at Mr. Shepherd's office too. Do you want me to go find out?"

"No," he said, backing away from the window. "I'll call Marcus up. He always seems to know about what's going on in the good ol' town of Seminole."

Marcus Crow was the county judge. He didn't hear court cases, but instead managed the finances and affairs of Gaines County with other commissioners. Seminole, the county seat, just happened to be where his office was located.

"Marcus, good afternoon, it's Bob Clark here," he said when the judge answered. "Listen, there's a bunch of strange-looking men standing on Main Street. I can see them from my office. It looks like John Shepherd and Seth Woltz are involved with them. Do you know anything about this?"

The voice on the other end sighed. "Not a whole lot, but probably more than you."

Mayor Clark picked up a pen and began writing. "Well, let's hear it."

The county judge cleared his throat. "Seems they're called Mennonites. There's two groups: one from Mexico and one from Canada. I first saw them at the bank when a Mr. Froese walked in wearing all black. He was with an American and they were trying to establish some credit. This Froese fellow carried a suitcase with him. I don't know what was in it, but I heard it was lots of money."

Mayor Clark clicked his tongue. "Yeah, some of the men outside my office are dressed in black. What did this Froese need the money for?"

"I heard he was trying to purchase some land owned by Odessa National Bank. Some rancher had a farm on the southeast side—two sections, I believe—and they wanted to buy it for a bunch of Mennonites in the Mexico group. Apparently, they pooled their money to come here and farm. After some of that property went back in foreclosure, the bank was trying to sell it to them."

"I think I know that property," Mayor Clark said. "It's on Telephone Road—a half a mile wide, running two miles down Lamesa Highway."

"That's it. I think they brought fifty or so families to live and farm on it. But they've hit a snag, something about their immigration papers. I heard the name Reimer several times. In fact, some Reimer in the last century must have had a hundred children because everyone seems to be named Reimer. Anyway, I think there are several Reimers involved somehow. These other Mennonites may have to leave the country because they don't have the right papers."

"That sounds like a big problem brewing in my town, the kind that'll suck me in," Mayor Clark said. "Thanks for the information. I'm going to get to the bottom of this."

"Okay, Bob. Call me when you know more."

The mayor placed the phone back on the cradle and sat in his high-backed chair, turning this over in his mind. When he went to the window again, he saw the men were still there.

"Bernice, I'm stepping out. Tell anyone who calls I'll be back in an hour." He set a stiff gray fedora on his head. "Maybe."

<hr />

The sandblasted Buick cruised down South Main Street. When SE Ave L appeared, David turned left, still listening to his children moaning and rubbing their calluses. Each child had bright red splotches in place of their usual fair German skin. Their water jugs, long since empty, reminded them of their heavy thirst. The question was, who would be the first one to reach the faucet?

David pulled the car to a stop and cut the engine just before the exhausted children flung open the doors and ran to the trailer. Tina was first up the steps, pulling open the screen door then the front door and inhaling the smell of freshly baked bread inside. Anna had several loaves waiting for the hungry workers, along with a gallon of pork and beans. During a moment of hesitation, Tina's brother pushed past her and made it to the faucet, sticking his mouth below it to take in a dangerous amount of water.

Tina waited, staring at the pork and beans. It was so cheap, it was almost all they ate for supper. She didn't care. Compared to the food in Mexico, this was a new exotic delicacy to be enjoyed.

Each night, the Schmitts and Rempels dined together. This time, after the children had been stuffed with food and water, the adults shooed them outside so they could talk. With the trailer to themselves, David spoke up. "The papers we received at the border are expiring in late May. If the lawyers don't do something, we'll lose our land and everything else."

"What are we going to do?" Anna asked sullenly.

"Save every penny," David replied. "They told us today we need to pay another fifty dollars a head for the lawyer."

"We don't have that kind of money," Mrs. Schmitt said, the anger in her voice clear.

David glanced at Mr. Schmitt, who looked at him helplessly. "I know. We're looking for more work. But in the meantime, if you don't need it, don't buy it. Save every penny you can."

Silence enveloped the group.

Anna grabbed the pork and beans can. "We're already buying the cheapest food we can find. And I'm making fresh bread each day instead of buying it. What more can we do?"

David grimaced. "Just do your best and pray."

"Yes," Mrs. Schmitt said, nodding. "Praying is something we can do."

The four sat there for a while, each lost in their own thoughts. After some time, David fished around for his pack of cigarettes and tapped Mr. Schmitt on the arm. "Let's go outside."

Leaving the women behind, he passed a cigarette to Mr. Schmitt and lit up. David took a long drag. "With the kids whining and my wife wanting to go back to Mexico, I might not make it until the end of May."

"What will you do back down in Mexico?" Mr. Schmitt posed.

David nudged his hat back, exhaling a cloud that covered the horizon. "Starve."

Tossing his fedora on the rack, Mayor Clark patted the red sand off his suit and stepped into his office to find Bernice facing him. "Did you find out what's going on?"

"Yeah, I did. And you can hear all about it when I make this call." He picked up the phone and dialed. "Marcus, I know what's going on."

"Good, tell me."

Mayor Clark loosened his tie. "Seems most everything you told me was right—especially about all the Reimers. And there *are* two groups of Mennonites. But it's the ones from Canada who are buying that Nix property—the sixty-four hundred acres—that are in trouble."

"What kind of trouble?" the county judge asked.

"I don't know who, but somehow the Mennonites were told that if they purchased one acre, they could be U.S. citizens automatically!"

"Uh-oh. That's a problem."

"It's a huge one because they plunked down four hundred forty-five thousand dollars against a one-point-seven-million-dollar purchase price."

County Judge Crow whistled. "That's a big briefcase of cash."

"Actually, it isn't," Mayor Clark said. "I think the briefcase you saw had to do with the ones from Mexico. They put down two hundred ninety-five thousand dollars against five hundred fifty thousand dollars for A.C. Ward's twelve-hundred acres off Telephone Road. And their visas expire at the end of May."

"Man, what a mess. You and I don't have anything to do with immigration. What do you suggest?"

"I'm going to call our representative in Washington. That's why we elected him, after all."

"Washington?! That's going to take a miracle. Good luck, and let me know how I can help."

"Will do, Marcus." Mayor Clark hung up the phone and leaned back in his chair, picking at something in his teeth. "Bernice, do you have the number for George Mahon?"

She raised an eyebrow. "You want to talk to Mr. Chairman? You'll never get him on the line."

"I have to try. I may be these folks' only hope."

She scribbled a number down on a piece of paper and handed it to him. When someone finally answered the phone, the mayor sat up a little straighter.

"I need to speak to the Chairman."

"May I ask what it's about?"

The voice on the other end sounded skeptical, maybe even resistant. *Not good.*

"I'm Bob Clark, the mayor of Seminole back here in Texas. We have a problem in town with some strange folks called Mennonites."

The voice hesitated. "Did you say Mennonites?"

"Yes. Why?"

"Congressman Mahon is aware of the situation. Hold on, he may want to talk to you."

He lifted his eyebrows and pressed the phone against his chest. "Bernice, I think I'm actually going to talk to him."

Bernice gaped. "Really?" she mouthed.

He nodded, holding up a finger as a booming voice came through the receiver. "Mayor Clark, how are you doing?"

"Pretty good, Mr. Chairman. Certainly better than this large group of Mennonites outside my office. Your staff told me you are aware of what's going on out here."

The Chairman didn't hesitate. "I think I am. David Langston and Larry Siegel have been working on it. But go ahead and summarize it for me."

"They all bought a lot of land out here and they're about to be deported. That means they'll lose north of seven hundred thousand dollars. It's going to be a train wreck if we can't do something."

The silence on the other end made him frown. Bernice shifted from foot to foot, watching his reactions carefully. Just when the mayor thought he'd hung up, the Chairman spoke. "What do you think I need to do?"

Mayor Clark considered his words carefully. "Sir, I think you need to send out representatives from the labor department and the immigration service to explain to these people what their status is and how they can fix it—you know, apply for citizenship."

"Labor, too?"

"Yes," Mayor Clark replied. "Some folks in town have placed ads in the paper looking for specialized labor. It's some kind of requirement to get these people jobs without taking them away from Americans. The labor department must certify all this to the immigration folks, and somehow, it's all supposed to work out. If not, these folks will be deported and lose north of seven hundred thousand dollars!"

"Hang on," the Chairman said. Mayor Clark waited for a few seconds until the congressman returned. "Sorry, I have to go vote in a minute. So, labor and immigration need to come to Seminole. I'm writing it down. If I can't make that happen, I guess I'm not good for anything."

Mayor Clark chuckled. "Oh, I think you're good for a lot of things. After all, you're chairman of the appropriations committee. I'm sure both of those departments need you for funding. I'm guessing they'll listen to you."

Congressman Mahon laughed. "Yes, that's true. I've been known to tear down a fence or two to get what I want."

"That's why we keep sending a big ol' bull to Washington. In a china shop, sometimes a bull can make things happen."

"Or break glass trying," Congressman Mahon said. "I'll let you know what's going on. Gotta run." With that, he was gone.

Mayor Clark leaned back and grinned, already expecting a handful of questions from Bernice. *I sure wouldn't want to be in that china shop.*

———◆———

"Where are we going now?" Tina asked, hands on her hips. It was late in the afternoon, and this was very unusual.

"Into town," Anna replied. "You like going there, right?"

"To get some ice cream?" she asked, knowing that was unlikely.

"No. The immigration people are here and they want to talk to us. Maybe they'll give us our permanent papers." Anna glanced at David, who was bent over Nancy, fastening a small bonnet under the two-year-old's chin.

"Don't worry," David said. "Your father has everything under control."

The group got organized and piled into the car with the Schmitts. It didn't take long to get to town, and less than a second to feel sick when they did. Parked there, bumper to bumper, were five long buses with writing on the side. Because it was in English, no one knew what it said. Still, the buses looked ominous.

David parked a block away, the car pointed in the direction of their trailer. He made sure no one could park in front of him in case he had to drive off fast. Leaving the keys in the ignition, he turned to his wife and said, "You and the children stay here. We'll see what this is about."

Out on the sidewalk alone, Mr. Schmitt whispered, "Are these buses for us?"

"I don't know," David replied nervously as they walked.

Mr. Schmitt grabbed his arm and pulled him to a stop. "Do you want to turn around right now and head for the border?"

David shook his head. "No. We're going to do right by these people."

The pair spotted John Shepherd and Seth Woltz talking to several animated Mennonites. For avowed pacifists, these religious men were waving their arms wildly, forcing the lawyer and the real estate agent to try and calm them down.

As David approached the crowd, a government official pointed for the Mennonites to get in line. Another official—standing with Mr. Reimer—asked David for his name and yelled out something in English. David stood in front of Mr. Schmitt, who endured the same process. Before long, a woman came running with a sheaf of papers. When the official handed it to David, he asked, "What is this?"

Mr. Reimer said happily, "It's an extension until June seventeenth. Now, you don't have to leave at the end of May."

David beamed. "Wonderful news! *Danke schön.*"

When Mr. Schmitt had his papers in hand, the two men milled around with the others, talking excitedly about the new development. A few minutes later, the agitated Mennonites David had seen approached their group.

"Why are you angry?" David called out. "They just gave us an extension." The men around David nodded.

One of the agitated men snatched the documents from David and pointed to one of the papers. "It isn't an extension. This is an order to leave the country by June seventeenth!"

A man next to David said, "But they brought out the buses for us."

"That's right," the angry Mennonite replied. "They were going to deport everyone today. The writing on the bus says Border Patrol. They're here for a celebration because they were about to get rid of us!"

The group turned solemn. Several of them stared at their papers, trying to make sense of this news.

By now, David was red hot. Breaking free from the men, he walked briskly to where Mr. Reimer stood and noticed a man they called the mayor. Behind him, Mr. Shepherd and Mr. Woltz nervously rubbed their hands.

"Tell them," David said, pointing forcefully, "if this country doesn't want me, I'll load my family in my car and drive us back to Mexico!"

Mayor Clark, upon hearing the translation, grew agitated and pulled Mr. Shepherd and Mr. Woltz away from the others. The three began talking, with Mayor Clark using quick gestures.

"Do you think that man will do anything?" Mr. Schmitt asked David.

"I don't know if anyone can do anything," David replied. "But what I do know is that we don't have papers to be citizens, we don't have our land, and we're out a lot of money. If we can figure out who has our money, we might find the answers."

As they turned to leave, Mr. Reimer came up behind them. "Don't forget the fifty dollars per head. We need that money to keep the process going."

David said nothing, blankly staring at him. With no response, Mr. Reimer turned and went back to the group. David took ten steps toward his car and spit on the ground. "I'm not giving up," he muttered just loud enough for Mr. Schmitt to hear. "I'm not giving up!"

Chapter Twenty-Four

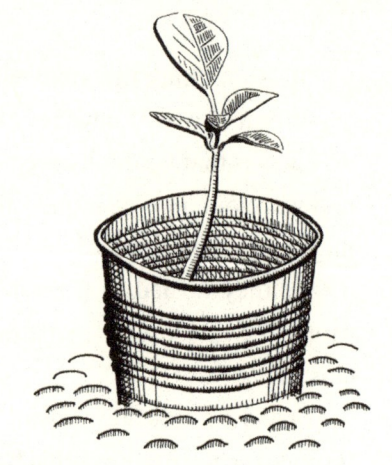

June 1977
Seminole, Texas

It had been seven long weeks since the Border Patrol buses had lined the downtown streets. For Mayor Bob Clark, it seemed like a lifetime.

"Well, we're famous!"

Mayor Clark swiveled his chair around just in time to see Bernice toss a *Newsweek* magazine onto his desk.

"What's this?" he asked.

"The beginning," the secretary said. "I think."

He grabbed the magazine and thumbed through it. Sure enough, there they all were. "Say, this is great." he said, staring at the color photos of their town. "And look at the children. They're precious. Those large straw hats and colorful bows grab your attention."

Bernice grinned. "Yes. Those photographers sure know who to take pictures of. Nothing melts your heart more than seeing little blonde-haired, blue-eyed girls with their hands folded, praying to God they won't be deported."

The bell on the front door jingled.

"Marcus," the mayor called out. "If that's you, we're back here."

Marcus Crow, the county judge, stepped into the office to find them hunched over the magazine on Mayor Clark's desk. "What's so interesting?"

"We're a national story," Mayor Clark replied, sliding the magazine over. "See for yourself."

Judge Crow picked it up, turning a few pages. "Well, I'll be. There's no turning back now. I'll bet this gets some action."

266

"No doubt. Grab your hat and let's talk about it over lunch."

The two men walked to Jo's Café, nodding at the occasional passerby. After ordering, they resumed their conversation.

"Listen," Mayor Clark said, "this whole thing is about to get very ugly. Now that we're in the national spotlight, we have to figure out a way to fix this mess or these people will be out close to a million dollars."

"Is that how much it is now?" Judge Crow asked.

"Yeah, when you add up the two land buys plus the money they've sunk into it since they've been here. And, to make matters worse, these Mennonites just received a new letter replacing the June seventeenth deadline with September twenty-second. One of them came in and showed it to me with that interpreter who follows them around like a puppy dog. When I told him it meant that he really had to leave by September twenty-second, he just smiled. I think the interpreter either misunderstood what I said or gave him the wrong message on purpose."

"I have to admit, they don't seem to understand much of our way of life—I mean, the rest of humanity." Judge Crow waved at a man leaving the café. "That's Rayford Bates. He's made a haul at his store. They all seem to shop there."

"You're right," Mayor Clark said. "I needed to talk to one of them, so I went to H&D Grocery at quitting time. Sure enough, they showed up. They all buy gallons of the cheapest stuff like pork and beans, sweet corn, and green beans."

The waitress set their sandwiches on the table, giving the men a chance to take a breath. Judge Crow studied his BLT before taking a bite. "Any update from Seth Woltz?"

"Sure," Mayor Clark replied, holding up his ham and cheese. "He continues to say he never told them they could become citizens by purchasing an acre of land. He swears he took their leader, Mr. Reimer, to the library and gave him a copy of the Bill of Rights *and* the Constitution. I don't know if that's true or not, but I do know these folks are going to leave all that land behind."

"And money," Judge Crow said, swallowing. "Any progress with Congressman Mahon?"

Mayor Clark chewed slowly. "He's sending the agencies out to talk to these people. I'm also talking to Senator Bentsen."

"What did he have to say?"

"Only that there are twenty thousand Mexican visas allowed each year and they're all used up by June. And, there's a ten-year waiting list. The immigrants from Mexico are in big trouble. Senator Bentsen said he'd have to introduce a private bill to grant them citizenship."

Judge Crow frowned. "I've often said it would take an act of Congress to get me to pick cotton, but I never thought our county would be involved in a real-life act of Congress."

Mayor Clark set down his sandwich. "Don't count your chickens before they're hatched. The senator said there'd be resistance, especially when so many people are fighting any immigration from Mexico. But these Mennonites are not welfare people. That new church they're putting up refused tax-exempt status and demanded to pay their fair share. I think our county could use hardworking folks like these."

"I agree. I told my daughter, Shelby, that even though the children aren't going to school yet, she had better get used to seeing them around. She was asking me about the women who look so different—the scarves and straw hats and dresses. I'm probably going to hire a few to work my ranch."

"Careful," Mayor Clark said. "Their tourist visas don't allow them to work."

Judge Crow chuckled. "So, all the cars they've fixed, and barns they've erected, and crops they've planted are illegal?"

"Yes," Mayor Clark said, smirking. "But no one is stopping them. The government knows about it and wants them to at least bring in their crops before they leave. Too bad no one told them this Brownfield loamy fine dirt we live on has been nicknamed 'blow sand' and is not well suited to dry-land farming."

"And too bad no one told them they didn't have the water rights."

"But at least they saw a copy of the Constitution," Mayor Clark replied as the men shook their heads, staring at what was left of their sandwiches.

David bent over and attempted to scrub the filth off his pants, trying hard to remove the raw sewage so he could get in his car and go home. He wasn't succeeding.

This was the second week of his new job for the Reimers. He had spent the last month plowing the fields and planting cotton. Now, he'd been tasked with the job of irrigating those same fields. The problem was the water source: raw sewage. Rainfall was almost nonexistent on the Llano Estacado during the summer months, and even though this portion of the field had water rights, the Reimers didn't want to spend the money drilling for it when there was perfectly good water nearby. Unfortunately, that source was the sewage that pooled from the surrounding homes—untreated and raw. It was a nasty job, but he needed the money.

After receiving his first paycheck, he had hurried his three-hundred-dollar payment to the lawyer, Mr. Shepherd, hoping it would be the last time. Then, he had paid off some rent and other debts, using a few leftover dollars to purchase five bottles of brown spray paint. Since most nights he was too nauseous to eat supper, tonight he had plans for those cans.

"I put the pipes up," a voice called out from behind. It was Mr. Harms. He had taken the sewage irrigation job when Mr. Schmitt declined. Right now, as he rubbed the mess from his pants, David wondered how Mr. Schmitt had gotten himself out of this one.

Mr. Harms slapped David on the back. "It kind of sticks to you, doesn't it?"

"It does," David said, straightening. "Like it was melted into the fabric."

David put his tools away and drove straight home. The kids were already there since they worked a field nearby and could walk to their new house. Actually, it wasn't new. And it wasn't a house.

David had purchased a tiny two-bedroom trailer from a dealer in Hobbs, New Mexico, before moving it to a rent-free lot belonging to Mr. Reimer. Perhaps its biggest selling feature was that the Schmitts and Rempels had more living space. The Schmitts remained in the other trailer, continuing to pay rent there. David figured that with the payments he was making to the dealer, it was almost a wash. Now, his family had more room to spread out. He and his wife enjoyed their own bedroom while the children occupied the second bedroom and living room. With a full tub in the bathroom and a water-cooled air conditioner, they were living large—Texas-style.

The stink from the sewage followed David all the way home. Despite that, he was in a good mood. The letter he had received from the immigration department told him he and his family would be staying for good. Of course, he couldn't understand the language on it, but the Reimers had interpreted the letter and assured them everything was just fine.

David guided the Buick to a stop and shut off the engine. He fetched the bag of spray cans from the passenger seat. He wasn't going inside just yet, because he wanted to return his car back to its original brown color. Then he'd be a proper citizen like the rest of the folks in Seminole.

Tina, standing at the door, watched him work. "Mom, is Dad coming in to eat?"

"I don't think so," Anna replied as she dried a large pan. "That's why we ate without him. He doesn't feel hungry after working at his new job."

Tina watched her father kneeling at the front fender of the Buick. She opened the door and yelled, "Dad, can I help?"

David waved at her. "Sure, come on. Just ignore the smell."

Behind Tina came two of her siblings—Elizabeth and David. Their father showed them how to hold the spray cans; the long drips from holding it too close to the metal was accepted as part of their learning experience. Eventually, they each figured out how to get the most paint on the car without creating drips. It was a rare family project, one that David deemed important. He simply could not stand driving a half-painted car around his new town.

The children worked well together and followed his instructions. At some point, Tina was out of paint. With no bottles left to give her, she went back inside where little Nancy and her mother relaxed.

"Mom, I heard Dad say something about Uncle Jake. Is he coming to visit us?"

"Yes, he is. He's bringing his whole family from Canada but traveling to Mexico first, for a visit before they will come to Seminole to stay.

Tina excitedly clapped her hands. "Will he bring my toys? I've missed my doll so much. I can't wait to hold her again."

Anna wiped her hands on a towel and removed her apron. "Well, you'll soon be holding your doll all you want."

Tina touched her chin and stared at the ceiling. "Umm, why is Dad painting the car? Won't it just get like that again?"

"He wants to fit in with these Englanders. Their cars all have paint on them. Or most of them."

"Oh," Tina said, hesitating. "Will we be able to go to the new church soon?"

"I think so. The Canadian Mennonites with the Gospel Mennonite Church have moved a small building to a nearby lot and are busy fixing it up so we can have services there. I hear they will hold evening classes to teach English. You kids will go there when you get in from the fields."

"Maybe I'll meet some new friends."

"Perhaps. At least you will learn to speak like Englanders—one day, you'll have to attend their schools."

"Do they even want us at their schools?" Tina asked, rubbing her temples.

"I'm sure they do." Anna gave her a reassuring smile, then grew serious. "Did you know I had headaches as a child?"

"Really?"

"They were so bad that sometimes I couldn't complete my chores. And my brothers and sisters thought I was lazy and spoiled. When I did do a chore, my sister Margaretha told me it had been done wrong and she redid everything."

"But you work hard now," Tina said.

"I tried to learn from Mother, but she put it off. One day, I was determined to learn sewing, so I started a dress. Mother came in and told me to go outside and do my chores. When I came back inside, she had finished my dress. And after your grandpa died, they thought I got away with less work."

"Did you live in a trailer like this when you were my age?"

"No," Anna said, tilting her head back a little as she remembered. "It was a nice, big house that we lived in back in Mexico. Mother had a large garden where we grew fresh vegetables. I remember Mother sitting on the

271

porch sewing baby blankets for the other ladies in the campos, waiting until the sun dropped and the air cooled. Then she'd spend an hour in her garden. At night, the breeze would carry in the smell of ripening fruit from the nearby trees. People came from all over to buy her fruits and jams."

Tina drew herself up. "You know, I'm going to grow a fruit tree myself. Then you can make jam from the fruit I bring you."

Anna reached over and patted her hand. "You do that, Renie. You do that." (Renie was a nickname that Anna sometimes called Tina.)

Tina noticed a hint of doubt. "I will. You'll see. Just be ready to make that jam!"

Anna smiled. "Let's go check on your father and see which has more paint: your father or that car."

⟫◆⟪

It was a full week before Uncle Jake and his family appeared, kicking up dust behind their sagging station wagon. Tina was the first out the door, greeting them before the engine had shut off.

"Uncle Jake!" she yelled out. "Did you bring my doll?"

A tired man emerged from the vehicle, opening the other doors and releasing his wife and three children. "Hello, Tina. I have two boxes of stuff in the back that your father can sort out."

The rest of Tina's siblings swarmed the new arrivals, anxious for news from home. It took an hour for David and Jake to unpack his station wagon and bring the belongings inside. That's when David pulled his anxious daughter aside.

"Tina," he said, gritting his teeth. "I have some bad news."

Tina's lower lip quivered. "Where is my doll?"

David gave it to her quick and clean. "It's gone."

"What?!"

"I'm sorry, but your cousins got into the box and played with all the toys. They broke your doll." He didn't add that its head had been ripped off the body and tossed about.

Tears streamed down Tina's cheeks as she tried to form words, yet nothing came out.

"And the rest of the toys—David's tractor and Elizabeth's doll—they're all gone too. Whatever we brought with us when we first moved is all we have to remind us of Mexico. I wish I could make it better. Just know that our new papers allow us to stay here. We'll soon be citizens in this country, and then we'll have the money to buy you another doll."

Hearing this, Tina turned and ran away, crying hard. That doll had been her best friend when times were tough, comforting her during stormy nights. Now, she was gone and with her, the last bit of her life in Mexico. To an eight-year-old child, it was a devastating tragedy.

———◈◆◈———

The U.S. Border Patrol station slowly swung its door open, signaling it was ready for the daily crush of eager immigrants. Some of them needed paperwork to establish citizenship, while others needed it for prospective employers. Boyd Robinson, a longtime agent, had seen it all.

"Tim," Boyd said, "we're going to El Rojo's for lunch. Are you joining us?"

"Sure," he replied. "I'm already picturing that enchilada special inside my belly."

The other agents laughed.

"Hey, Boyd," another agent said. "There's two of those German whatever-you-call-them Stan was talking about last month. Meteorites, I think he called them."

The agents watched as two blue-eyed farmers ambled up to the counter and began speaking in a foreign language.

"Mennonites," Tim said. "They're called Mennonites. Boyd, can you come and handle these guys?" Tim asked. "I don't speak Mennonite."

Boyd pulled up his belt and stepped down from his perch, sliding past Tim to rest his elbows on the counter. "What can I do for you gentlemen?"

The words coming out of the lead man was mostly gibberish. But the seasoned agent was able to pick up a few scraps.

"Are you saying you want something for this fellow next to you?"

The farmer grimaced, reached into his overalls, and produced a paper. Boyd picked it up off the counter and read the contents.

"What is it?" Tim asked. "What's it say?"

"It's a mandatory depart letter from the Dallas office." Boyd studied the two men closely. "But this one seems to think it's something good."

"What are you going to do?" Tim asked.

"I don't know. I guess try to make them understand." Boyd held the letter out and pointed to the second man. "This is bad news for you. You must leave this country on September twenty-second. Do you understand? It's bad news."

The lead farmer pointed frantically at his companion. The word "same" was uttered several times.

"Hey," Tim offered, "I think he's saying he wants one of these letters for his friend."

"Yeah, that's the impression I'm getting," Boyd said, rubbing his jaw.

Boyd shouted, "Sir, this is a mandatory depart letter. If your friend here gets one..." Boyd pointed with his finger to the companion, moving the letter to the man's chest. "...he will have to depart too. Do you understand?"

The first man nodded excitedly. "*Ja! Ja!*" he repeated with a large smile.

Boyd stepped away from the counter and looked at his fellow agents. "Well, I'll be, gentlemen. I thought I'd seen it all. But apparently I haven't." He moved back to the counter and faced the two Mennonites. "Sir, you want him to receive a mandatory depart letter? Is that what you want?"

"*Ja! Ja!*" the man said again confidently.

"We're here to serve," Tim blurted out before laughing. "Isn't that what you've always said, Boyd?"

Boyd shook his head. "I guess. But I'm not giving up." Squinting his eyes at the first man, he said for a third time, "Sir, if I give him a letter like this, he'll have to depart with you. He will not be able to become a citizen. Is that what you want?"

The two farmers huddled together, speaking in their native language. When they finished, the first man nodded, saying, "*Ja!*" over and over. The second man smiled and nodded, holding his hand out for the imaginary letter he wanted to receive.

Boyd sighed. "Okay. If your friend here wants us to deport him too, we are willing to oblige."

"Serve and deport," Tim said. "Isn't that our motto?"

The other agents laughed. Boyd simply shook his head as he pulled out some paper, set it in the typewriter, and began typing.

Thirty minutes later, the two farmers sat content in their freshly painted Buick as it rambled along State Highway 87.

"I told you this country wanted us," David said, one hand on the steering wheel. "And now you know the truth."

"Boy, you were right," Jake said. "I can't believe my luck. And he added the names of my family, too. With this letter, we're going places. We're really going places."

Their ignorance overwhelming, neither man had any idea what had just happened to them.

<hr />

Sunday finally arrived, and with it, the commandment of doing no work. Church was over and the lunch dishes had been put away. As with most every day, Tina had snuck out an extra can of Del Monte Green Beans and consumed it with gusto. Between her desire for those green beans and the spoonfuls of pork and beans slopped from a large can at lunch and supper, she couldn't imagine any other food giving her that much happiness. And when the can of green beans was empty, she would usually take it outside and throw rocks at it. But today, she had a different use for it.

Tina picked her way through the weeds and brush, reaching the abandoned pig barn at the back of their property. Tina eyed the ripe apricot she had in her other hand, her uneaten dessert from lunch. She thought, *Where can I plant this seed?*

She moved to an open patch of ground halfway between the pig barn and the trailer. Then she sat down and ate the apricot. The dark brown pit, sticky in her hand, was all that was left. So she set it down and began digging into the hard ground with the edge of the tin can. When the can and her fingers had turned enough earth, she dropped the pit in before covering it back up. With a nearby rock, she pounded on the bottom of the can until it came loose, leaving a hollow metal cylinder. Twisting it back and forth in the dirt, she pressed the can down, around the pit.

Getting to her feet, she ran to a hose and filled a bucket halfway with water. With the bucket's handle cutting into her hand, she carried it back and poured its contents over the freshly planted pit.

"There," she proclaimed, slapping the dirt from her hands. "You will be my tree. My doll is gone, but I will have you. Now, grow strong and put down deep roots. Grow, little apricot, grow."

Standing over the wet can, she said a prayer. With the harsh climate and impending deportation, it was a near certainty that this would be nothing more than a waste of time. Yet young children have one thing many adults don't: dreams.

Chapter
Twenty-Five

July 1977
Seminole, Texas

"Come on, get up!" A hand jostled Tina's shoulder. "It's time to get up." Tina blinked a couple times. It was Elizabeth, her older sister.

"Go away!" Tina said, pulling the pillow over her head and drowning out all light and sound. But the smell of fresh bread and the fact that she had to go to work made her toss the pillow aside and swing her legs to the floor. At least this made Elizabeth leave her alone.

Sitting on the edge of her bed, Tina rubbed her eyes. Yesterday—Sunday—had given her a pause in her six-day work week. She actually felt rested. But she didn't want to go to the field and hoe weeds. *The field.* Just thinking about it was both sickening and exhausting. The endless rows of mounded dirt were dotted with weeds that constantly played tricks on her, teasing her as if one day she might actually finish the job. She'd hacked down thousands of the pests, only to return the next day to find more in their stead. For an eight-year-old girl, it was a cruel prank.

Dressing quickly in a long flowery dress and rubber sandals, she stumbled to the kitchen. Her mother had been up early cooking. A slice of bread and a cookie awaited her. It took her less than five minutes to consume the measly breakfast along with a glass of milk, before plucking a wide-brimmed straw hat from a hook and fastening it to her head. Grabbing a plastic lunch bag and a glass bottle of water, she headed to the door.

"Have a good day," her mother called out as the three children left the trailer and stepped into the darkness.

Tina felt the dust settling between her toes and sandals as she glanced at the sky and frowned. The stars were out and that was bad news. The past four days had been overcast, with most of their time in the fields shaded by dark, heavy clouds. No rain had come, though. Even a light rain would cool the earth, keeping the dust down for the day. But there hadn't been much since they'd arrived. Since this was her first summer in America, she couldn't imagine how people lived in a place like this.

Walking in the darkness, Tina was last in line. Her brother, David, led the way, with Elizabeth close behind him. No words were spoken. There was nothing to say. They would work for twelve or more hours and then march home, where they would do more chores and go to bed. They needed their rest so they could do it all over again the next day. With very little leisure time and even fewer toys, work and sleep were pretty much all they had to look forward to.

They walked for twenty minutes, until a pale orange filled the horizon. It was just enough light for Tina to see the field up ahead. A local farmer had hired them to hoe weeds, paying them $1.25 per hour. It didn't matter to Tina what he paid them. She never saw any money. It all went to her father, who spent it on groceries and some lawyer in town. But it did give her immense satisfaction that she was contributing to the family and helping with their immigration status. Her presence here mattered.

The small group stopped at a bush, one of the only spots with some shade. Though it was still dark, Tina shoved her plastic bag and water bottle under the bush, bending some branches around it. A few rays of sun would still hit her cache, but at least it would stay cooler than out in the direct sun.

While she was doing this, David located the hoes that he had sharpened with a steel mill file and passed one to her. He didn't have to tell her where to go, since the weeds were everywhere. Picking a spot to begin, she bent at an angle, lifting the hoe about a foot off the ground before letting it fall. The blade hit the weed just behind its root ball. Pulling on the hoe loosened the weed, causing the tough plant to fall over. Moving a few inches backward, she spotted the next weed and repeated the sequence. She'd repeat this same lift-drop-pull process thousands of times each day.

Occasionally, she'd stop and straighten her back, bones popping and muscles complaining. Then it'd be back to work.

Somewhere along the morning, the sun rose high. Having been under clouds for the last four days, the rays quickly burned Tina's fair skin. After thirty minutes, though, she didn't feel it at all.

Tina worked hard for two hours before dropping the hoe and walking back to her water bottle. The water was cool against her lips, and for a moment, she drank greedily. She wanted more, but needed to make it last the twelve-plus hours she was out here. Returning the bottle to its place, she went back to her hoe to start all over again.

Shade, she thought as she brought the hoe down on a stubborn weed. That's what she wanted right now, along with a never-ending supply of air conditioning. Maybe a couple gallons of pork and beans too—or even a lifetime supply of ice cream. She had been introduced to ice cream one day when her father returned from the store to celebrate some good news. They had dug into the gallon with their spoons, fascinated at this new dessert. Near the bottom, Tina had clashed spoons with Elizabeth and David for the last bites.

"Lunchtime," David said from a few rows over, interrupting her daydreams. Since none of them had a watch, he used the position of the sun to guess when it was noon. Tina dropped her hoe and walked with her siblings to the bush, digging out the plastic bags and water bottles.

She formed a mound of dirt to lean her lower back against and opened the bag. It contained two slices of the white bread her mother had made that morning. Between them were a few pieces of meat and a tomato. Due to the heat, the sandwich was soggy, falling apart between her fingers. Tina had to eat it slowly, putting pieces in her mouth before they fell to the dirt. It had happened before.

After the tasteless sandwich was gone, she pulled out an apple. It was hot, but at least this made it easy to sink her teeth into. After that, a melted cookie with icing made its appearance and disappeared. She used her napkin to wipe her face clean, smearing the morning's dirt and sweat on her cheeks.

With a few spare minutes, she leaned back and gazed at the cloudless sky, a blistering sun behind her. High up, a black dot circled the field, looking for its next meal. Tina wondered if it ever found anything to eat.

At some point, Elizabeth stood up, followed by David. Tina thought about it for a moment then got to her feet. No one said a word. They just trudged down a row, found their hoes, and went back to work.

At 4:30, with long rows of cut weeds behind them, Tina trudged home with a water bottle in one hand and her empty sack in the other. Elizabeth led the way just in front of David, both of them kicking up dust for their little sister to swallow. Sure, she could walk faster and get ahead of them—but she didn't feel like it. She had no energy.

When they reached the steps to the trailer, they dusted themselves off and went inside, the cold air slapping them in the face. It should have felt good, but instead, their burning faces stung.

"I'm first!" shouted Elizabeth as she raced to the bathroom. David set his empty bottle on the kitchen counter, grabbed a glass, and filled it up with water. He drained it, then another. Tina waited her turn at the faucet and took her fill. With that over, she plopped down at the table just in time to see David head to the living room (also his bedroom), where he would nap until Elizabeth finished her bath. Then he'd have his, leaving Tina to wait.

"Even though it's a bit past four," her mother said, "I'm making some coffee. Nancy is sleeping in our bedroom. Why don't we have *faspa*?" Anna brought the pot of coffee over and poured herself a cup. "Would you like some?"

Tina frowned. "I guess." The last thing she wanted was something hot, but it was a chance to spend some time with her mother without David and Elizabeth butting in.

Anna set a plate of cookies on the table. "Would you like one of these?"

"I don't feel good," she uttered, especially since the cookies lacked icing. For some reason, a cookie needed icing.

"I understand. You've been outside in the sun. Maybe the cold air will cheer you up."

When a few minutes went by and Tina still felt bad, Anna tried a different subject. "You know, I've never told you about the time I was born.

The midwife and some family members stayed with my mother because they wanted to console her."

"Why?" Tina asked. "Didn't they want her to have a baby?"

"Yes, they did. But when they looked at me, they were sure I was going to pass."

Tina set her cup down. "What?"

"Yes. The skin covering my tummy was so transparent they could see my intestines. I was tiny and frail. And your grandma was forty-five when I was born. I was the last of eleven siblings. So, they waited. And waited. After a full day, they went on with their chores, thinking about the funeral they would have to plan. A few days later, they decided I might actually live. Of course, I did live, thanks be to God."

Tina had been hanging on every word. Realizing her mother was finished with her story, she said, "Tell me another one."

Anna sipped her coffee, showing a hint of a smile. "Okay, but have a fresh piece of bread with some jam." She pushed the plate over to Tina. "Let me tell you about when I was nineteen. My mother and father traveled from Mexico to Saskatchewan to visit my father's sister. Her husband had been unfaithful, and she had gone through a divorce. After the divorce, she couldn't cope with her new life, so they had to put her in an asylum."

"What's an asylum?" Tina asked.

"It's a place where people who have mental problems go. Some get better. Unfortunately, she didn't and had to live there."

Tina nodded so Anna continued.

"Since the asylum provided her clothing, my parents went through her things and brought back some beautiful Victorian dresses. It was good fabric, certainly nothing we could get in Mexico.

"My mother took the dresses and altered them for me and my sister Margaretha. When my father came inside from work, he asked me to try on the dresses so he could remember his sister the way she had been before they'd moved to Mexico, before she'd lost her mind. As I came into the kitchen wearing one of the beautiful dresses, my father, who was sitting at the table, started crying. Thinking something was wrong with me, I assured him the dress fit me perfectly. Then I told him since it was a beautiful Victorian style, it would look wonderful at special events."

Anna shook her head, eyes growing distant. "But Dad just kept on crying. I didn't know what he was upset about. My mother pulled me away and ordered me to take it off. The next day, she cut up all the dresses and made baggy conservative dresses out of the fabric. The white socks that had been in with the clothing had to be dyed with the gray ashes from the stove because it was a sin to wear something so flashy. And that was the end of that."

Tina reached for some water. "Mom, that's a good story. Tell me another."

Anna gave her a grin, pulling herself out of her memories. "All right."

Tina sat with her mother until it was her turn to bathe, feeling a little lighter than before. That was, until she lowered herself into the bathtub and the lukewarm water made her sunburn feel even worse than before. She splashed around, slowly acclimating to the temperature. But as her skin cooled to a dull ache, hot tears stung her sunburnt cheeks.

Her problems seemed endless. Her neck was so burnt that trying to scrub off the red sand was extremely painful—if it would come off at all. The red splotches on her forearms still stung, and the sandals she always kept on her feet were caked with dirt, which meant she'd have to spend time trying to clean them. Her heart sunk a little more as her mind slipped back into a tired funk.

Tina continued to cry. Nothing was going right. When she thought about her broken doll in Mexico, the tears flowed harder. It was simply one of those sad days.

"Hey, what's going on in there?" It was her father knocking at the door.

"Nothing," she cried. How could he understand that the sand wasn't coming off and the pain wasn't going away?

"What's wrong?" he demanded.

Tina ignored him.

"Are you almost done?"

"No," she managed. "I have a lot of sand on my neck, but it's so blistered that I don't know how to wash it off."

"I see," he said. There was a moment of silence. "Listen, if you hurry up, I'll take you to the grocery store and get some ice cream for everyone."

Tina jerked upright, her tears stopping. "Ice cream?"

"Yes. But you need to be out of this bathroom now."

"Okay, Dad!" she squealed, bursting into action. "I'm washing up."

It was like a miracle. Instantly, she was reinvigorated. The pain from scrubbing the sand off her neck was bearable. The caked dirt on her sandals somehow disappeared. Instead of thoughts about the broken doll, she remembered the beautiful necklace she had found in this very trailer the day they were cleaning it out. No one else had seen her slip it around her neck. It was her special treasure, one she kept in one of the empty margarine bowls she had scavenged from nearby dumpsters. She loved playing with the bowls, pretending she was having her own four o'clock *faspa* with friends.

With the water swirling, carrying the day's dirt down the drain, she quickly dressed in fresh clothing. Suddenly, the world seemed different. Better.

Staring out the windshield of their beat-up old car, Tina was all smiles as the H&D Grocery Store came into view. In fact, she was out of the car before her father could remove the key from the ignition. She heard him chuckle as she ran ahead, already thinking about which flavor of ice cream she would choose.

"Mr. Reimer!" David called out suddenly. "Can I talk to you a moment?"

Tina slowed and fell in behind her father, who was walking over to a man she had seen once before. She could sense the sudden change in her father's attitude.

"Mr. Rempel," the man replied. "What can I do for you?"

David stood before the nicely dressed man and put his hands on his hips. "I'll tell you what you can do for me. I'd like to see where my land is."

Mr. Reimer gave him a tight, polite grin. "Of course. Unfortunately, we have not surveyed it yet."

Her father shook his head. "That's what you said last time. My family is getting tired of waiting."

The man was unfazed. "I understand, but you are living on my land without paying rent. Isn't that fair while you wait?"

David stood his ground. "But I want my land. And my father wants his land. And my sisters want their land. When are we going to get it?"

With David's voice rising, Mr. Reimer raised his hands. "Soon. You will have your land soon. Just please, be patient. We are spending all of our time and money on the immigration matter."

At the mention of the word "immigration," David's shoulders sunk. Humbled, he lowered his voice when he spoke next. "Okay. Thank you for your time."

Taking Tina's hand, David tugged her along toward the store. He was no longer smiling, and the slight bounce in his step had disappeared. "Come on. Let's get the ice cream and go home."

The brown Buick pulled up to the trailer, giving Tina a chance to pose a question. "When Mr. Reimer said the land hasn't been surveyed, what did he mean?"

David looked away, unable to meet her eyes. "It means they don't want to give us our land."

Tina nodded, unsure of what all this meant.

"Let's get inside before the ice cream melts," he said, mustering up a grin for her.

Two minutes later, three spoons clashed as David, Elizabeth, and Tina fought for every bite. Anna slipped in to carve out bowls for herself and David. Even little Nancy got a bowl. Tina glanced over at her father and noticed he was still bothered. Whatever was going on, she sensed it wasn't good for her.

⋙◆⋘

Bernice gathered up several newspapers and magazines and went to see her boss. As was her usual habit, she dropped the stack on his desk. The loud *thwack* caught his attention.

"What is this?" the startled mayor asked.

"More fame and glory."

Mayor Clark glanced at the pile. "*New York Times. Wall Street Journal. Dallas Morning News. Houston Chronicle.* And what's this? *Los Angeles Times*? I can't believe it!"

"Believe it," Bernice said. "Our little town is nationwide for good."

Mayor Clark studied one of the articles. "For a people who shun the outside world, these Mennonites are great at getting publicity."

Bernice pointed to a blonde girl praying. "I think that's their secret weapon."

Mayor Clark chuckled. "It worked last time. Why not again? I just wish I could get back to selling insurance. I'm about to go broke dealing with this twenty-four/seven."

The phone rang and Bernice answered it. Pressing the phone to her chest, she whispered, "It's Mr. Chambers with the immigration agency."

Mayor Clark nodded as she handed him the phone. "Mr. Chambers, what can I do for you?"

Bernice listened in, trying to pick up the gist of the conversation. After a few minutes, she could tell it wasn't going well. When the mayor hung up, she learned the truth.

"Well," Mayor Clark said, "the immigration folks are sending out another letter—one that tells the Mennonites in no uncertain terms that they must leave the United States by September twenty-second. Even though that's the date they've already been given, this letter will be harsher and easier to understand."

"Oh my," Bernice said. "And I thought we were clearing up this Mennonite mess."

"Mennonite mess," Mayor Clark repeated. "That's a good term for it, though I've actually grown to like these people. They're hard workers. But the ones from Canada who planted their crops late have had almost no rain. Now, I'm pretty sure they're doomed—on both fronts."

Bernice tapped his desk with a finger. "You're always saying how we could use more workers to develop this county. Too bad they can't stay and help us turn this place into something special."

"Yeah, too bad," he said, doodling with a pencil, his gaze fixed on the wall. "I wish there was something I could do about it."

"Me too," Bernice said sadly.

Mayor Clark looked through his Rolodex of phone numbers, stopping at one of the cards. "Maybe there is something," he mused, reaching for the phone.

Tina looked down at her paper, scanning the Low German phrases next to strange words.

"Listen up," Miss Eva said. "We are going to say, 'How do you do?' in English." The teacher repeated the phrase in English and waited for her students to mimic her. Tina focused on the words and said them as close as she could.

"Very good," Miss Eva said. "Now, let's move on to the next phrase: 'I'm doing fine.'"

The class followed her lead. Tina repeated the words, but nothing made sense. How she was ever going to learn this new language, she had no idea. It was all so foreign.

As the teacher went on, Tina rubbed her aching forehead. Her scalp hurt, a byproduct of her hair being pulled back tightly. Ever since she could remember, her mother had wetted her hair down with sugar and water—a natural hairspray to keep her hair in place. She'd pull Tina's hair back tight, making sure it stayed that way all week. Every Saturday night, Tina would undo her hair and wash it, allowing her forehead a moment's relief from the strain. Her mother would then coat her hair with the sugar-water solution again, pulling it tight and braiding it for the next seven days. And if the pain of each hair being pulled back wasn't enough, the occasional fly or insect that buzzed around was an added nuisance. She wasn't sure she'd ever get used to it.

Two hours crawled by before class was dismissed. Tina, Elizabeth, and David ambled home as the sun sunk below the horizon. It was almost nine, and they were exhausted. After twelve hours in the fields, a supper, and two hours in class, Tina couldn't even imagine how people lived to be twenty years old.

Pulling the door open, Tina was the first in. Her father sat at the kitchen table, eyes trained on a paper in front of him.

"First, they won't give me the land," he spat. "And now, they are making me leave. I just can't take it."

Tina tried to get a glimpse of the paper sitting on the table, but she couldn't make it out. "What happened?"

Anna pulled them into a back room and explained the situation. "Your father just received a letter. He took it to a neighbor instead of the Reimers and they read it to him."

"What does it say?" Elizabeth asked, eyes wide.

"It says we have to leave this country by September twenty-second. Apparently, the last letter said the same thing, but in different words."

"So, we aren't going to be citizens?" Tina asked, thinking of all her future plans. If they left America, there'd be no more ice cream, or pork and beans. And the apricot tree she had planted and watered daily would never grow without her help.

"I'm afraid not," her mother said. "It would take a miracle from God."

The children said nothing.

"So, please be kind to your father. He's having a hard time."

"Are we going back to Mexico?" Elizabeth asked.

Anna whispered, "I think so."

The group went back to the kitchen as David rose from his chair and headed outside. Tina hurried to join him. "Father, are you okay?"

David pulled out a cigarette and lit it. "Yes. I just got some bad news."

"I know," she said. "Mom told us."

David's jaw clenched. "What a fool I've been. And I made Jake go to that place so he could get the same letter. Now I know why they were laughing at us."

Tina tugged on his arm. "I don't understand. Is Uncle Jake going to be staying with us?"

David removed the cigarette from his mouth. "No, I'm afraid not. I just ruined his chance to stay here. All because I'm ignorant and don't understand this language or how the world works."

Tina tried to grab his hand, but he was too angry to pay her much attention. In the red glow of the fading light, David raised his hands and exhaled. "I just bought this trailer, and now I have to leave! Why? God, why is this happening? Why?!"

Chapter Twenty-Six

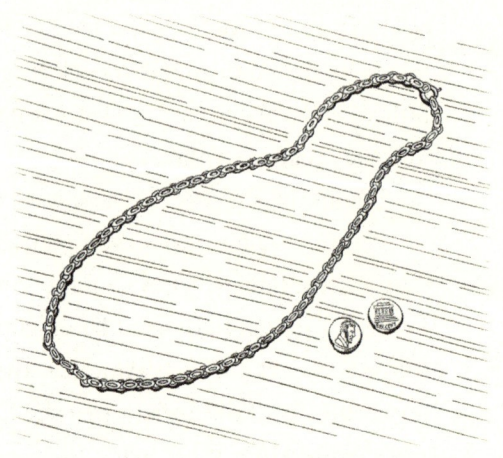

The week dragged by as David thought miserably about the prospect of returning to Mexico and its poor living conditions. While America had presented a fair share of challenges, nothing compared to the desolate land and slow technology he'd grown up working with. *Our children need a better life than that*, he thought, over and over again—as if that would somehow avert the disaster. But he had no options.

Just when he thought all hope was lost, a call from Mr. Reimer sent him skyward.

"Finally!" he shouted, hanging up the phone. "I get to see our land this evening."

Anna looked at him, her face unreadable. "Does that mean we are moving again?"

"Yes. Mr. Reimer told me that since my land is now available, I can't stay here—especially without paying rent."

Anna remained silent.

"And you thought we'd been taken," David said, glaring at his wife. "It's only been four months since we arrived. Sure, it took some time for the survey, but it was worth the wait."

Before she could respond, he grabbed his jar of water and lunch bag and bounded out the door, ready for another long day plowing the fields.

"Good afternoon, Mr. Rempel," Mr. Reimer said. "Let me show you your property."

David practically skipped along the shoulder of State Highway 180, following Mr. Reimer to a set of stakes. When his guide stopped, David gazed out over the land, his enthusiasm somewhat checked. The field was full of rocks, tumbleweeds, and mesquite brush. The amount of work to get the land ready for crops would be huge, but at least he could have a home for his family—assuming they could remain in the country.

"These stakes here show your plot," Mr. Reimer said. "To provide everyone with some frontage on Highway 180, we had to make your property deeper."

"What's this other stake here?" David asked, his face darkening a little.

"That's the eastern edge of your property."

David stared hard at the stakes, blinking several times. "I don't understand. That's what? Twenty-five feet wide?"

"Twenty-eight feet," Mr. Reimer corrected. "And don't forget, your land goes all the way back there, at least a half a mile."

David studied Mr. Reimer's face to make sure he wasn't being played for a fool. "But that means I'll have to install over a mile of fencing."

"Okay." Mr. Reimer coughed and looked away.

Hot anger rose in David's chest. "Over a mile of fencing for just five acres?!"

Mr. Reimer smiled nervously.

"Did you hear me?" David said, his voice loud. "And what about my house? If I put in a ten-foot driveway on this side, I'll have only eighteen feet for a house."

"That's right. You just need to make your house deeper. It's not a problem."

"Are you crazy?!" David shouted, his anger taking hold. "I can't build against the property line. My neighbor's house will be right up against it. Or maybe their driveway."

Mr. Reimer stepped back, color draining from his cheeks. Somehow, he kept his voice steady. "Just offset it five feet from the property line. If your neighbor does the same, you'll have ten feet of space between you. Of course, your home will only be thirteen feet wide."

David shook his head in disgust.

"And don't forget," Mr. Reimer added, "your father and sister will be next to you. Maybe you can work it out with them? Design the property so everyone has a nice house."

David gritted his teeth, heat rushing to his own cheeks. "I see what you're doing."

To make sure he fully understood the situation, David paced off the width between the stakes several times. When he was done, he came and stood less than a foot from Mr. Reimer. Mr. Reimer watched him carefully, taking another step back just in case the pacifist ideals ingrained in every Mennonite got lost in the moment.

"Listen," Mr. Reimer said, "everyone's property is like this. The surveyor laid it out so we could avoid anyone being landlocked."

David lowered his head. Then, without another word, he spat contemptuously at the ground, spun around on his heels, and jogged back to his car. His mind whirled, already cooking up a new plan.

<hr />

A hot, dry breeze flitted though Tina's dress. She stood there under a bright sun, fidgeting with her necklace, the one she'd found in the trailer when she'd been cleaning it out. With her doll gone forever, it was her most favorite thing—along with the rubber sandals that never left her feet. But another one of her prized possessions was on her mind today. "Are you going to leave my tree behind?" she asked, her eyes filling.

David took one look around the bare property. "What are you talking about?"

"My apricot tree. I've been watering it and taking good care of it. I can't just leave it behind. My little tree will die!"

David frowned. "Oh yeah, I remember now." He asked his daughter to show him where it was.

Tina led him to a green bean can sticking up from the dirt. "It's right here," she said. "See?"

David leaned over and saw the tiniest of sprouts coming from the center of the can. His definition of a little tree was far different than his daughter's.

He lifted his head and scanned the property again. When he didn't see what he was looking for, he turned to his daughter to give her the bad news. "Tina…" He didn't have a chance to finish, because tears welled in her eyes again. "Okay, okay. Just give me a minute while I look for something to dig it up with."

Getting to his feet, he headed to the abandoned pig barn, where he found a rusted piece of metal. Using it, he pried the can from the dry land as well as the land beneath it and put the entire package in Tina's hands. "Here's your little tree. Let's go and plant it at the new place."

As they walked across the dusty field, a jubilant Tina took the opportunity to get some much-needed information from her father. "Dad, why aren't we moving to our land?"

"That land's no good," he said. She could tell he was trying to stay calm, but a hard edge crept into his voice. "We can't use it. Just forget about it. That's why I bought six acres from Mr. Neudorf, the preacher."

David left off the part about how he was only picking up the payments because Mr. Neudorf had gotten fed up with everything and was heading back to Canada. To David, it was no more than paying rent—with the possibility that, someday, it might turn into ownership.

"So, are we going to get to stay here?" Tina asked.

"I sure hope so," he replied, the looming date of September 22 always at the forefront of his mind. "We have to trust God that it will all work out."

It only took a two-minute walk to arrive at their new backyard. David took his time selecting a spot inside of the fence he hoped to build one day. He grabbed a shovel and dug a hole as Tina watched over her little seedling, cupping it in her hands like it was a baby animal. When the hole was large enough, she gently lowered it into the earth, helping her father pack the dirt in around the can.

"There," David said, inspecting their work. "That should do it. Why don't you go get some water and take good care of it from here?"

"Don't worry, Dad. I'm going to make sure this tree gives us big apricots one day. Mom will make apricot jam for our bread. You'll see."

David smiled. "I can't wait, Tina. And speaking of bread and jam, I'm hungry. Let's see if we can get your mother to hurry up supper."

———◆◇◆———

Even though it was almost eleven in the morning, the downtown area was unusually quiet. With not much work to do, Bernice watched as a car slowly pulled up to the curb outside their office and stopped. A man wearing a suit jacket got out, grabbing a briefcase from his passenger seat. "Bob," Bernice said, "I think that man you were looking for is here. Who's he again?"

Mayor Clark leaned forward in his chair and got to his feet. "Some heavy hitter who used to work for the Chairman in Washington. He's a problem solver of sorts. All I know is that the Chairman trusts him."

"Do you want me to hold any calls from your clients?"

"What calls?" he said. "Dealing with this Mennonite mess and all of the governmental agencies and news media inquiries have just about put me out of business. Maybe one day I can get back to selling insurance. But I guess today's not that day."

His last words were stopped by a bell. The tall Texan sauntered in, stopping at the front desk. "Howdy," he said to Bernice. "Can you direct me to Mayor Bob Clark?"

"Here I am," the mayor said, coming out to meet him. "What's your name again?"

"Brown. Bo Brown. Congressman George Mahon sent me to look over this Mennonite situation."

Mayor Clark grinned. "We call it the Mennonite mess. But situation sounds better."

"I see," Bo said, setting down his briefcase in a chair and removing his fedora. "What can you tell me about it?"

Mayor Clark filled him in on the latest developments. "I have a lunch appointment in town with some folks. Come with me and they should be able to give you the entire lay of the land."

"Sounds great. Let's get to it."

292

Four hours later, Bo Brown loosened his tie and picked up the phone in his hotel room. When George Mahon came on the line, Bo made his report. "Well, Mr. Chairman, I met with the mayor, two Mennonites, a lawyer, and another businessman today over lunch. Afterwards, we all drove out to check on the property they have. One thing I can say for sure is that I learned a lot."

"Great," Congressman Mahon said. "What's the situation?"

"It appears everything is going fine. The Mennonite group from Canada is making payments on the land—although they're having more and more participants dropping out. This adds to the payments of the remaining members. But, so far, they're making the payments on time. The group from Mexico is just getting their land so that seems pretty stable, at least right now. "

"What about their immigration problems—both groups? That's what worries me the most."

"I thought it would be worrying them too. But the two Mennonites I spoke to were unconcerned. They said INS was working to get everyone their papers, and so far, no one has been deported. The only real problem is that the land the Canadian group bought lacks water rights. Of course, I'm sure you know that already, what with the news media reports and everything. Some of the land the Mexican group bought has water rights. It's still getting sorted out."

"Yes, I knew that. Anything else?" the Chairman asked.

"Uhh…" Bo Brown glanced at his notes. "One of the Mennonites told me that when his grandfather was seven, he was put on a train in Russia and shipped to Canada."

"What does that have to do with anything?"

"I guess he wanted me to know that these folks have been constantly on the move since the 1500s."

The Chairman hesitated. "Well, if we don't make sure they get their papers, they'll be on the move again, and it won't be a train. You know we can't have that. Sure can't."

"No, we can't," Bo said. "But really, sir, I think things are well in hand. Otherwise, the two Mennonites in charge would have told me."

When the two men finished their conversation, Bo Brown donned a casual shirt, intent on finding a proper restaurant for a nice supper. Later that night, when his head hit the pillow, he had no idea how bad things would get.

⟜•⟝

Another Sunday had arrived and church was over. During the service, David prayed hard that his family would be allowed to stay in the country. But when it came to the land and money he had lost, the concept of forgiveness was a struggle.

His father and sister had taken the news better. They were upset that their money was gone too, but David had detected relief in their voices. He could understand why. They hadn't sold everything and moved to Seminole, only to discover that they might have to move back and start all over again with no land, no money, and no future. Every time David thought about it, he got depressed. So, the game became keeping it out of his mind and trusting God. That was all he could do—except in church. Church reminded him of it and the feelings returned. He was supposed to feel refreshed after worshipping, but instead, felt drained.

After eating their lunch, the family split off in different directions. Elizabeth and her brother, David, took Nancy to visit a neighbor. David, lacking a barn to hide out in, went to his bedroom for a well-deserved nap. That left Tina and her mother alone in the kitchen, the dishes cleaned and put away. It was an opportunity Tina couldn't pass up.

"Mother, can we have another *faspa*?"

Anna glanced at the clock. "It's not four yet. But since we have some time alone, I suppose we can. Let me brew some coffee."

With a steaming cup in front of her, Anna studied her daughter's features. Tina was growing, but still had a long way to go. The English lessons the church provided at night didn't seem to be making a difference, although Anna had no way of knowing since the only three words she knew were "pork and beans." All she could do was hope that Tina was catching on.

"What would you like to talk about?" Anna asked.

Tina didn't hesitate. "Some stories about Grandpa. I never saw him. What was he like?"

"Oh, your Grandpa was an interesting man. It's too bad your father never had the chance to meet him. He died two years before we met."

Tina's eyes widened. "Was Grandpa like Dad?"

The corners of Anna's eyes crinkled. "On some things. On others, they are quite different. For example, your father takes good care of his animals. So did your Grandpa Friesen. Oh, how he loved his horses. After every ride, he brushed and brushed them till their coats shined. You could see how happy they were. And they treated Grandpa well."

Anna took a sip of coffee. "And his harnesses were the best around. Everyone knew that he was a true horseman. He had brought from Canada all the tools and leather to make his own bridle and straps, which Grandma Friesen gave to your dad after we were married. Your dad, too, was very talented at making bridles and harnesses. But where your grandpa differed from your father was that I sometimes thought he loved his horses more than he loved us—his very own children."

"You mean like Dad and his car?"

"No. Although your father spends a lot of time making that car look good, your grandpa was overly doting on his horses."

"Was Grandpa smart, like Dad?"

"Oh yes. And wise, too. I remember one time I was about your age and wanted to get his attention. So, I decided to take his pocket watch and put it by the sidewalk outside our house. I left it there for an entire day."

"Was it still there the next day?" Tina asked excitedly.

"Yes, it was. No one else had seen it. I pretended to find it so my father would be proud and spend some time with me. Running inside, I showed him the watch. When I handed it to him, he said, 'Go and put it where you found it in the first place.'"

Tina's forehead creased. "He knew what you had done all along?"

Anna's face brightened. "Yes. He was wise like that. But he was also very demanding and harsh. I often wondered if he wouldn't have lived such a hard physical and stressful life, perhaps he wouldn't have died so young. But God only knows."

She noticed Tina rubbing her necklace. "You know, if you would've worn that in Mexico, the church would not have let you keep it."

"Why not?" Tina said, covering it up with her hand. "I didn't take it from anyone."

"They were very strict, not like the church here. Anything that displayed pride was forbidden."

"Pride." Tina considered the word. "I'm not prideful. I just miss my doll."

"I know you do, but your necklace belonged to someone else and I'm sure they are missing it right now, just like you miss your doll."

"But I *didn't* lose my doll. They *broke* it!"

Anna released a deep, quiet sigh, determined to change the subject before this *faspa* dissolved into tears. "Pretty soon, you'll get to go to school. You'll like that, won't you?"

"Yes," Tina replied, letting the necklace drop against her chest as her eyes lit up. "I'll get to meet new friends and learn so much. And I'll get out of the hot sand and sun." The light in her eyes died a little. "School has already started, you know."

"It has," Anna said soothingly. "But we need the money you make from working those fields. When the hoeing is done, you'll be going to school. Maybe two weeks more. Your father can tell you."

"Where does all the money go?" Tina asked. "Are the lawyers taking it all?"

"Yes, and I'm sorry about that. They charge so much we can barely afford anything else. Without the hard work of you, David, Elizabeth, we'd be in trouble."

Tina stuck out her chest. "I'm glad to be here and helping us. The work is hard in this country, but I know it's for the best."

"It is." Anna paused for a moment, a soft smile playing on her lips at her daughter's strength. "Why don't you go play with your friends while I join your father? I need a nap too."

"I'm going to water my apricot tree." With that, Tina grabbed her straw hat and bounded down the steps, in search of a bucket.

Two weeks had passed, and yet another Sunday rolled around. Tina had been playing outside all afternoon with her siblings and several other local girls when Anna called to them. "It will be time for supper soon. Come in and wash up. I need your help."

Tina managed to grab the bathroom first and bathed as fast as she could. When she was dry, she slipped on fresh clothes and went to the kitchen. There, she saw a man who was a Mennonite sitting with her father at the kitchen table. Tina hung back, saying nothing.

The man finished looking over the letter in his hands. Turning to face David, he delivered the news. "It says that your application for alien employment has been denied. I'm sorry, Mr. Rempel."

Anna stood near the sink, listening. "What does this mean?" she asked.

"It means," David replied, "that unless we receive an extension, we'll have to leave on September twenty-second."

"I'm sorry," the man said again. "If you need anything else, you know where to find me."

Before he could get out the door, another man appeared. Tina had seen this man before. He was an Englander who employed her father to plow his fields. He said something in English to the first man, then left without making eye contact with any of them.

"What did he want?" David asked, a look of concern heavy on his face.

The man frowned, eyes lowering to the ground. "He said that this is one of the driest years ever. It looks like the crops are lost. He is giving up and doesn't need you any longer."

"Oh," David said. Tina could see him set his jaw. "Did he mention my pay?"

"Yes. He said he will bring it by later this week, when his bank is open."

David nodded. "Thanks again for your help."

"I'm sorry this has turned out to be such a bad day," the man said, trying to console David.

Tina's heart was heavy. Her family was getting nothing but bad news. She needed some happiness.

Tina headed to the drawer in her bedroom where she kept her most treasured items—especially her precious necklace. As she pulled out the drawer, she could tell something wasn't right. A frantic search ensued, with clothes tossed about. When the drawers were empty, there was no doubt in her mind. It was gone. Someone had *stolen* her necklace!

Tina dropped to her knees and tried to scream. Instead, no sound escaped her mouth. The only special possession she had left was gone.

Chapter Twenty-Seven

Tina ran her fingers along the bottom of the drawer for what seemed like the thousandth time, hoping she'd overlooked the necklace. She hadn't.

She grabbed her sandals instead. With their cheap rubber soles and thin plastic straps, they were the last of her valued possessions. Even her tiny apricot tree in the bare backyard couldn't compare with the necklace and her sandals, since she'd probably have to move before it started producing any fruit. No, the sandals were really all she had left—the only thing she could take with her, always.

She heard her mother call from the kitchen. "Children, are you dressed?"

With a sigh, she plopped to the ground to tug on her sandals. There was no use complaining about her missing necklace to anyone. They wouldn't understand. No one else could possibly know what it had meant to her.

Besides, she had bigger things to worry about. With the summer hoeing over, her father told them they needed to go to school. The sad news the man had brought hadn't made her father any less adamant that his children be properly educated. If anything, it had made him more determined to see them succeed.

"Dad, do we have to go to the public school?" Elizabeth had asked, the day before.

"Yes," he had replied, giving her a serious look. "Your mom and I want you all to learn English, and the private school on the ranch doesn't teach it. We want you to be able to speak the language as we make this

299

our new home. Besides, I understand there are several other Mennonite families who have sent their kids to the public school." When he saw the long looks on their faces, he added, "I grew up with next to no education. Our people have been bound in ignorance for too many years. When I was a child, I made a decision that if I ever had a chance to escape, I would. And I would get educated. It's too late for me. But it is not too late for you. I've come too far to let you be raised in ignorance. You *will* learn the ways of the new world and have the life your mother and I can only dream about. If I give you nothing more in life, *knowledge* and teaching you to work will be enough. According to your mother, Grandpa Friesen always said that the best thing parents can give their children as they grow up is the value of hard work."

Butterflies filled Tina's stomach as she pulled a piece of paper from her pocket and read the few English words and phrases she had learned at night school. *Will* this *be enough for my new school?*

"Tina? Elizabeth? David? Are you dressed?" Anna shouted again.

"Yes ma'am," David called, buttoning up his shirt.

Tina followed him into the kitchen, watching as he stood before their mother so she could verify he was telling the truth.

"Let me check you out," Anna said, grabbing his shoulders and straightening his store-bought snap-button white shirt. Spinning him around, she brushed some lint off his navy-blue slacks. Then she bent over and was pleased to see he had followed her instructions by wiping off his cowboy boots. "Well, at least one of my children will look good."

David grinned. Next up was Tina. Anna took her time picking the lint off her daughter's hand-sewn polyester dress, smoothing the dark blue fabric so it hung down mid-shin, just over the knee-high white socks Tina wore. Tina's dusty sandals brought a frown to Anna's face, but nothing could be done for those.

"Elizabeth?" Anna called out, ushering Tina toward the door. "Where are you?"

Elizabeth ran into the kitchen, undergoing the same process as Tina and David. With a final clap, Anna shooed them out of the house. "You three look just fine. You'll fit in well."

Tina wasn't so sure. Her insides felt like a gallon of nervousness with an ounce of excitement mixed in. At least her big sister and brother would be going to the new school, too.

The three hurried down the steps and walked over the bare, dusty land to the road's edge. Anna remained at the trailer's entrance, holding on to little Nancy's hand while keeping a watchful eye on the rest of her brood.

It wasn't long before the yellow school bus rumbled down the road, stopping in front of the three children. Elizabeth, the tallest and first in line, anxiously glanced back at her mother. Tina and David followed her gaze. Anna, with tears in her eyes, waved for them to get on the bus. Tina swallowed hard and followed her brother and sister up the tall steps and down the narrow aisle, eyeing the other children already onboard. It was scarier than she had imagined. This wasn't like the little night school they'd attended. Here on the bus, no one looked like her. She tried not to make eye contact. The bus driver, Mr. Love, got up from behind the wheel and ushered them to an empty seat.

Elizabeth slid over to the window and David sat next to her. This left only a few inches for Tina. Tina thought briefly of finding another seat and glanced around. The other children glared at her, so she snapped her gaze back down to her tiny space, bumping up against David with her right hip, *hard.* He muttered something under his breath as he scooted over, nudging Elizabeth a few inches closer to the window so Tina could take her seat. Mr. Love, watching all this, reached behind David's ear and pulled out a dime. The Rempels were fascinated with the trick. He smiled and went back to the front of the bus.

Letting out a sigh of relief, Tina reached up to run her fingers over her hair. With the sugar water her mother applied the night before—Anna's own recipe for hair gel—and the tight braids that pulled back her forehead creating the famous wide-eyed look all Mennonite girls had, the hair felt less like hair and more like a hard, waxed surface. *Hopefully the flies will leave me alone for today,* she thought, as she rubbed her sore forehead.

The bus stopped abruptly and the door swung open. No one said a word. The children at the front already knew what to do, since they had been coming to school for two weeks. Before she knew it, Tina was standing in front of the large school with Elizabeth on one side and David on the other.

"Come on," Elizabeth said, sounding a lot braver than Tina felt. "Let's go."

David and Tina followed her to the elementary school. "See that number four?" Elizabeth asked David. "You go there. Tina, you go to that three."

"Where will you be?" David asked.

"At number five."

"I'm not sure about this," Tina muttered, playing with the end of her sticky braid.

"Me too," David chimed in.

A tall man in a suit appeared and said something in English—not one of the phrases Tina had picked up at night school. None of the three understood him. He finally motioned for them to follow him.

Inside, the school hustled and bustled with all sorts of children. Tina felt her head spin with all the noise, footsteps, and laughter. *What is this place?* she wondered, struggling to keep up with her siblings as they followed the man through the chaos.

The man stopped and looked at a piece of paper he carried. "Elizabeth?"

Tina's older sister stepped forward. The man said some more words and pointed inside. Elizabeth hesitated and walked into a classroom. The man followed her in and beelined for a woman standing at the front of the room. After he said something to her, the woman nodded and started talking to Elizabeth. Before Elizabeth could say goodbye, the man pulled Tina and David to the next stop.

He repeated the scene with David, but found the teacher gone when he went to Tina's room. He motioned for her to stand by the front desk and left. This gave the children already seated a chance to gawk and whisper. All Tina could do was stand there and take it, her palms growing sweaty. She squeezed her eyes shut, trying to imagine being anywhere but here.

A woman's voice reached her ears, but Tina didn't understand anything she was saying. "Mrs. Gray," the woman finally said, pointing to herself. She took Tina's hand and led her to an open desk.

She could feel the stares as the children around her went silent. Not a single one was dressed like her.

It seemed like an eternity before the lady, Mrs. Gray, went to the front and began talking. Tina could only sit there and try to absorb a few new words. This was going to be hard.

Several hours drifted by, with a break in between. Suddenly, a bell rang and the children jumped up from their desks, fleeing the room. Tina got up slowly from her desk and was happy to see Mrs. Gray coming to lead her to the next place. It was lunchtime.

The large cafeteria held hundreds of children, all buzzing around with excitement. Tina fell in line and waited for her food, handing the cashier a few coins. The tray held strange food and a small milk carton. Finding an empty seat at a long table, she ate alone as everyone gave her a wide berth.

When she finished, she followed the flock of children who were taking their empty trays to a counter. Watching their examples, she emptied the trash off her tray and handed it off to a woman, who sprayed the tray down. Then she let herself be swept up in the crowd of students headed outside.

Tina came to a halt as the children fanned out across the field, climbing on ladders, slides, and swings, among other things Tina had never seen. All the equipment seemed to have been created just for children, but Tina wasn't in the mood to go exploring. Instead of joining her peers, she found a spot to stand and simply waited for whatever came next.

At some point, another bell rang and Tina followed two of her class-mates back to class. Mrs. Gray spoke a great deal more, mixing her lecture with drawings on the chalkboard. Somehow, more hours disappeared. At the sound of yet another bell, Tina stood. She knew enough to follow her classmates.

She soon found herself in a large gymnasium, trying to follow the instructions of a grown-up with a whistle around his neck. A few minutes later, she noticed David and Elizabeth come in, and they quickly gravitated to her.

"How's it going?" Tina asked her sister.

Elizabeth shrugged. "I don't understand anything, but at least it's cool here."

"Yeah," David chimed in. "This beats the fields anytime."

"Where are your boots?" Tina asked him, staring at his white socks.

"Some man made me take them off before I came into the gym."

The whistle blew and the coach pointed to David. Her brother ran over, nodding obediently as the man with the whistle pointed to the other boys. They were on the ground, pushing themselves up and down with just their arms and legs—pushups, Tina would later learn. David dropped to his belly and thrust his arms out. He had no idea what a pushup was, but he was determined to try. Twenty pushups into the set, he collapsed while the boys next to him did more than a hundred. He couldn't believe it. He'd worked outside all his life. How could he not do this?

While Tina and Elizabeth watched this tragedy unfold, the coach pointed for them to get in line with the girls. The other girls were all doing cartwheels, and Tina narrowed her eyes, trying to follow every movement they made. When it was her turn in line, she lowered her hands and lifted her legs sideways. To her surprise, she did all right. It was only after Elizabeth did her cartwheel that she understood why all the other kids were laughing. Since they were the only girls wearing dresses, they exposed themselves to the entire gymnasium every time they did a cartwheel. Tina tried to hold her dress down, but cartwheels needed two hands. It was an impossible task.

The coach saw that this was unacceptable, so he told the pair to stand on the side. A few minutes later, he handed Elizabeth a note. He kept talking to them, but they had no idea what he was saying.

When a whistle blew, the class ran outside to the track. David, arms aching, quickly put on his boots and followed his sisters. The three Mennonites were in for yet another surprise: running was hard.

They tried to keep up with the group but couldn't. Even if he'd had the strength, David's boots hurt his feet. Tina and Elizabeth, having run no farther than a few feet—perhaps chasing a chicken or playing with their friends—felt like passing out. Unbeknownst to them, their almost exclusive diet of sugar and white flour left them unable to perform even the most basic physical exercises. The sit-ups almost caused them to throw up. And all this made the Rempels stand out even more.

An exasperated David cried, "I wish I was back out in the fields. I never felt like this when I hoed weeds."

"Me too," Elizabeth said.

Tina gulped air, hoping she might be able to speak—but she couldn't catch her breath.

After P.E., Tina staggered back to class and took her seat. Strangely, everyone was at the back of the room doing something. When the children took their seats, Mrs. Gray tapped her on the shoulder. Tina followed her teacher to the back of the room. Without saying a word, Mrs. Gray turned on the water and ran it over her hands, using a liquid from a container to create bubbles. After she rinsed her hands off, she grabbed Tina's hands and showed her what to do. Slowly, a smile spread on Tina's face. *She's trying to show me how to do something*, Tina thought. *She actually cares about me.* This gave Tina the strength to finish the day.

Staring out the window, Anna heard the bus coming and opened the door to see her children bound off the steps and run to the trailer. "How was school?" she asked them.

"It was hard," David said. "They made us do things that we can't do." Elizabeth gave her Mom the note.

"Come on inside and tell me."

After getting an earful, Anna called one of the Mennonites who knew the Englanders' ways. When she hung up, she called another Mennonite from Canada who could write and read English. She learned that they wanted her daughters to bring shorts and running shoes for all three kids. By nightfall, she had three letters asking the school to excuse her children from gym. "They cannot be allowed to expose themselves nor have they ever performed the exercises in P.E. class."

The next day, they gave it to their coach. It worked, because when P.E. class started, they were separated from the rest of the students. Unfortunately, their newfound freedom came at a cost: bullies.

Tina felt it first. Dozens of kids made fun of her. Although unable to understand what they were saying, she was sure it was mean. The laughing and pointing made it clear. To get away from them, she walked toward the building and leaned up against the brick, hoping they would leave her alone. They didn't.

It was three boys who decided to make the first move. One boy moved in close, sizing her up. Tina avoided his eyes, looking only to the ground. *Go away,* she thought, but the words died in her throat as he loomed even closer. Then, *pain*. He picked a spot on her shin and kicked it hard.

The tears came next as Tina collapsed to the ground, screaming. The boy retreated, only to be congratulated by his fellow bullies. When the bell rang, the fields emptied of children—all except Tina. She remained on the ground crying, assuming she would be in trouble if she went inside. Or maybe she'd even be hit again.

Minutes later, Mrs. Gray found her, crying and hurt. She helped Tina limp inside, making sure she was safely at her desk. Then she talked to two girls at the front and left the classroom.

Ten minutes passed until the door creaked open and Mrs. Gray stood there. "Tina!" she said, motioning to her. Tina's heart pounded fast, sure she was in serious trouble. When she made it to the hall, there stood the three bullies, waiting for her. Tina cowered, assuming this was a trap. But Mrs. Gray laid a reassuring hand on her arm and pushed her up against the wall to watch. What happened next was hard to believe.

Mrs. Gray pointed to one of the bullies to bend over. The boy reluctantly complied, gripping his ankles with each hand. Another teacher handed a piece of wood to Mrs. Gray, who positioned herself behind the bully. Mrs. Gray gripped the long paddle tightly and drew her arm up. The bully, obviously not a first-timer, clenched his jaw and prepared for the nightmare that was coming. As the paddle sliced through the air, Tina heard something she couldn't quite make out. When it hit the bully's backside, the loud thwack made him yelp and step forward. But Mrs. Gray was not done. The paddle sliced through the air and smacked the bully again. This time, Tina could hear the word the paddle was singing—*justice*. It was a word she would understand well in later years.

Each bully received three swats, with the one who'd kicked her getting an extra two. As they raised up, rubbing their backsides, Tina could see them fighting tears. Mrs. Gray, a satisfied smile on her face, dismissed the three bullies and led Tina back to her desk, where she patted Tina on the shoulder. It was at that moment when Tina fully understood Mrs. Gray would take care of her. All she had to do was focus on learning, which was made easier by the complete cessation of bullying or laughter at her expense.

That evening, Tina recounted the entire day's activities—including handing her mother a note.

"What's this?" Anna asked.

"A note from school," was all Tina could say.

By now, they had a close neighbor who could understand English. After a quick trip to her trailer, Anna broke the news to Tina. "You need eyeglasses."

Tina sagged in her chair. "How will that make me look? The kids already think I'm strange. I'll never fit in now."

"Let's sit down and have a *faspa*, and discuss it."

After the coffee had brewed and Anna had taken a sip, she started in. "I haven't told you, but when I was about twenty-two, I had trouble with tapeworms. No one knew what they were. I had to be hospitalized for it."

"What are they?" Tina asked.

"Nasty worms that grow inside you. They're very long, and they take nutrients from the food you eat. It was embarrassing. Everyone wondered what was happening to me."

"Oh, that's terrible," Tina said.

Anna nodded. "And, before my wedding, I knew I needed glasses really bad, but my mother had never taken me to get some. While your father and I made the rounds, visiting relatives and such, he pulled the buggy up to an eye doctor so I could pick up my glasses. When we came out, a police officer had written your dad a ticket."

Anna's face brightened as she got lost in the memory. "We were shocked. However, your dad convinced the officer to accept a box of eggs. The next day, when he received the eggs, he took the ticket back."

"How did you feel getting glasses?"

Anna chuckled. "Strange, but I was so excited with all I could see. It was like a whole new world opened up to me. You'll see—literally."

"Will Dad be mad we have to spend money?"

"Of course not. We both live to make your lives better. One day, you'll do the same for your children. They will be all you care about. That's why your father works so hard. It's for you, and David, and Elizabeth, and Nancy. You four and, God willing, several more little Rempels."

Tina smiled. These times with her mother seemed to make all her worries melt away. If she ever had a daughter, she would have *faspas* with her too.

After supper, Tina and Elizabeth helped their mother put away the dishes and straighten up. The light outside was fading when their father dragged himself inside, collapsing on the couch and waiting for his wife to bring him some cool water. It took him a good thirty minutes to revive before he could move to the kitchen table, where Anna had a precooked meal waiting for him.

This had been the scene the last few nights. After losing his job plowing the fields, he had gone to the tractor supply place in town to see if they had any work. David and his fellow Mennonites had purchased hundreds of John Deere tractors from them over the years. They didn't have any work for him but had recommended a tractor repair shop in Lamesa—a forty-minute drive. David, along with Peter Harms, had traveled there right away. Much to their surprise, Nix Implement Co. hired them on the spot. For $2 an hour, they repaired old farm equipment. This was perfect for David. He had worked on farm equipment since he was a boy. And Nix Implement Co. saw how quickly he could make the equipment valuable again—equipment they could sell to the Mennonites down in Mexico. It was a unique circle for David, having been on the receiving end in Mexico, and now on the sending side.

When his day was done at Nix Implement Co., David drove Mr. Harms home. To make extra money, they both ate supper, then went to work at SME for an eight-hour night shift. SME, or Seminole Mennonite Enterprises, was a factory set up by locals to provide legitimate jobs to skilled men like David. They had a machine shop and other trades with Mennonite men manufacturing parts and products local merchants could sell. Early in the morning, he would come home and briefly sleep, constantly reminding himself that the day of their departure was drawing nearer and nearer. All he could do was pray that God would come through.

"What's this?" David asked as Anna showed him the paper Tina had brought home.

"A note from school," Anna replied. "It says Tina needs glasses."

"How much is that going to cost?" David said, his voice lowering an octave.

"I don't know. I'll take her into town Saturday to an eye doctor and find out."

David sighed. With so much money going to the lawyers, there wasn't enough light left in each day for him to make more—even if he'd had the strength to do it. At some point, the children might have to start earning money and sacrifice their education. It would be a tough choice, one he prayed he wouldn't have to make.

—————

Mayor Clark was sitting at his desk sifting through paperwork when Bernice walked in, a receipt in her hand. "Bob, don't you think you should charge this airfare back to the city? I mean, it's a city expense. Right?"

Mayor Clark studied the receipt. It was a roundtrip ticket he had taken to Dallas to talk to immigration officials. He frowned, leaned back in his chair, and sighed. "Nah. I'm spending my own money on that. My religious training says to be kind to the aliens among you. And my heart goes out to them. They picked our town because of the availability of land. The price was well within what they thought was reasonable. And now, it's all collapsing on top of them. I can't stand by and let that happen."

"I agree," Bernice said, cocking her head, "but isn't that a city expense—you know, because you're the mayor and supposed to do stuff like that?"

"No, I'll eat it."

"We'd better get some business in," she mumbled as she turned around and went back to her desk.

"I heard that," he said.

The doorbell dinged as attorney John Shepherd walked in. "Mayor, do you have good news from Dallas?"

"Well, I have some news. I'll let you decide what kind of news it is."

Bob explained that he had met with immigration officials in Dallas and this had led to a proposed meeting in Seminole. Every Mennonite family needed to be there to hear from three men: Troy Cargill with the

Department of Labor, Jerry Goodman with the Immigration and Naturalization Service, and Tim Mitchell with the Texas Employment Commission. Mayor Clark told John he needed to get a German interpreter since they could no longer rely on Mr. Reimer, the leader of the Mennonite group from Canada. There were rumors that he was distraught and not well. And that group had gone in different directions since the GMC church opened.

"What's the purpose of the meeting?" John asked.

"The families will hear a better explanation about their status, the flow of paperwork, and all the legal problems they are facing."

"That's a full slate," John said. "I'll get busy and put it together."

A week later, 104 families gathered in a large community building in Seminole. After they heard from the officials how the church they had set up to buy the land failed to qualify the transaction as an investment, and how a jobs workaround entity created by some local citizens had been rejected, grumbling commenced. That's when Mr. Wall, a prominent Mennonite leader, stood up and read a letter that was translated for the Englanders.

He explained how they were a landless people, seeking only a place to work and raise their children while living out the beliefs of their chosen religion. He asked for forgiveness and a chance to bring in the crops. "We want to sell out, clear our debts, and pay what's owed. We'll depart from here at our own expense."

When he stepped down, tears dotted almost every eye—including the government officials'. The officials quickly huddled and announced they would try a few more options. Despite this, the meeting ended with long faces.

Outside, a TV station from Lubbock waited to interview the officials. Over to the side, a collection of Seminole citizens gathered.

"What are we going to do?" a nervous John Shepherd asked. Next to him was an equally nervous Seth Woltz.

"I don't know," Mayor Clark replied, "but there's a man the Chairman sent over from Lubbock. He might be the right tool for this job."

"What's his name?" Seth asked.

"Brown. Bo Brown."

"Here, you must eat more," Mr. Bergen said. "Please. Eat."

Bo Brown stared down at the cabbage broth, a staple of the Mennonite diet, then glanced back at his extremely thin hosts. With a piece of bread in his left hand, he took another spoonful.

"This is tasty," Bo said sincerely. "I've never had this before."

Mrs. Bergen poured him more soup. Bo lapped it up, waiting for the thin broth to fill him up. It didn't.

Eventually, they assumed Bo's hunger was satisfied and drove him to a meeting being held in a newly constructed wooden barn off Frankel City Highway. Inside, eighty people waited along with several translators. Bo maneuvered to the front, where he stood on a stump sizing up the Mennonite crowd. Because Mr. Bergen had hired Bo to help with the large tract of land they'd purchased, he assumed this was what they wanted to hear about.

Clearing his throat, he gave them the news. "I have reviewed all of the legal papers and discovered several things. As you know, you made a sizable down payment with the next payment due in one year. That date is almost here."

The crowd murmured as he continued. "There's very little value to the land without the water rights. The only thing you can do is drill water to use for household and stock purposes. That's it." He let that soak in. "Next, we had one of the worst years for crops. With the sand blowing the way it has been, crops just can't be made." Heads nodded as the translation reached their ears.

A loud bang sounded. It was the barn door slamming shut. Through the cracks, Bo noticed sand filtering through.

"Oh no," Bo said. "That can't be a good omen."

"What's an *omen*?" one of the Mennonite translators asked.

"Nothing," Bo replied. "Pretend I didn't say that."

"The biggest problem is the nature of your transaction," Bo said, shouting over the increasing noise from outside. "The Old Colony Mennonite Church purchased the land from the owner. Unfortunately, the Old

Colony Mennonite Church was not legally incorporated in Texas. So, that makes the contract void."

"Can we get our money back?" one of the Mennonites asked.

Bo shook his head. "Very doubtful, since you would have to sue and be liable for the use of the land from the time you took possession. The landowner might claim fraud and countersue you for damages. Of course, you'd need to be in the states to prosecute this lawsuit—not to mention have money to pay the lawyers."

This comment led to more murmuring. Bo discussed a few more items before stepping down and mingling with the crowd. Before he knew it, sand and dust hung heavy in the air. Bo looked at the back of the barn yet couldn't make out any faces. The thick smoke from the Mennonites' cigarettes simply added to the enveloping fog. Suffocating, Bo pulled out a handkerchief and covered his mouth. He needed to get out of this place.

Bo decided to make a run for it. Knowing where his car was, he dodged all obstacles in his path and somehow found it. Fumbling with the lock, he ducked inside as the sand blasted his body. He couldn't slam the door fast enough.

Not surprisingly, an inch of sand coated his windshield. He started the car and flipped on the wipers, giving them time to clear a patch of windshield to see through. When his headlights lit, they mostly illuminated the powerful gusts of sand. Somehow, he managed to get on the highway, where growing sand dunes awaited him. Fortunately, this wasn't his first sandstorm on the Llano Estacado.

By the grace of God, he made it safely home, shaking out in his garage and leaving his clothing and shoes there on the floor. When he was clean and dressed, he snatched up the phone and called an old friend. "Mr. Chairman, I figured you'd still be up."

"Someone has to run the government," Congressman Mahon said. "What do you have for me?"

"I'm afraid this Mennonite mess is getting worse. The Canadian group didn't incorporate their church properly and the seller could void the transaction. So far, that hasn't happened. Then there is a large one-year payment that's coming due on the land, and unless it's made, they'll be out on the streets."

"Hmm. I've been talking to that mayor out there in Seminole—Bob Clark? He put together a big meeting a few weeks back and it's looking like we're going to need a private bill."

"Is that doable?" Bo asked.

"Maybe, maybe not. The Mexican groups are up in arms. How can we allow the Mennonites to stay when we deport them?"

Bo sighed. "Let me guess—they say it's only because the Mennonites are blond and blue-eyed."

"And white."

"Gosh," Bo said. "This is a sticky situation."

"Yes, it's a big mess. Then factor in that our citizens may have basically scammed them out of seven hundred grand, and it makes all of us look evil."

"What are you going to do?"

The Chairman was silent. Eventually, he coughed and said, "Mayor Clark has been pushing Senators Tower and Bentsen. I'm going to talk to them to see if we can work out a private bill. I guess we'll have to let the chips fall where they may."

"Okay, Mr. Chairman. I'm working on getting an extension from the note holder—maybe give them another year to make the payment so long as he doesn't void the sale. I'll let you know what I can work out."

"And tell the note holder how bad this is going to look if he forecloses."

"I will," Bo said. "Goodnight, sir."

"You know the government never sleeps."

Mayor Clark sat in a large chair next to a reporter, watching as a technician adjusted a light to shine directly on him. The reporter cleared his throat and said, "Just pretend we are regular people and speak directly to me. Don't look at the cameras. Just forget they are there."

"And forget you are with *60 Minutes*?" Mayor Clark asked, picking at an invisible wrinkle in his pant leg.

The reporter chuckled. "Yeah, basically. Ready?"

Mayor Clark nodded.

"How did the Mennonites get an extension from that September twenty-second deadline?"

Mayor Clark shifted in his chair. "There were several factors. Media coverage in the state of Oregon swamped all the phones in Senator Bob Packwood's office. The same happened in various congressmen's offices up there. The media coverage has been relentless."

"And the other factors?" the reporter asked.

"On September twenty-first, Congress authorized thirty-nine million dollars in aid to those fifteen thousand Indochinese refugees. The money is going to buy them homes and so forth. Suddenly, citizens began asking, 'What about the Mennonites?'"

"I see. What happened next?"

"Senator Bentsen sent his staff assistant Robert H. Block, Jr., to check on the situation. He met with me, and then we filled in Senators Tower, Goldwater, and DeConcini. Oh, and don't let me forget Congressmen Morris Udall and Jim Wright. When a fresh *Washington Post* article hit with pictures of those cute Mennonite girls praying and those little bonnets tied around their braided hair—why, I don't know what to say. I guess a picture is worth a thousand votes."

The reporter suppressed a smile. "So, that's why they got an extension to January thirty-first of next year?"

"Unless you have a better answer, I would say so—along with a big amen!"

The reporter finally let loose a laugh, before continuing with an interview that lasted longer than sixty minutes.

—————

The land was bare as a cold wind blew, lifting dust and tumbleweeds into the air. The debris circled David, who stood still and alone, gazing southward. He could hardly believe his good fortune. And he could barely understand his situation.

Three weeks earlier, it had been October 31—a Monday—when he'd once again dragged himself up the steps to his trailer for another late meal and a very brief time with his family. But there'd been a man waiting for him—an old friend, Mr. Schmitt. He'd been there to tell him something. David had poured himself a glass of water and plopped down on the couch. When Mr. Schmitt finished, David's life had changed.

A private bill had been introduced in Congress specifically for adding citizenship to all the Mennonite families. Incredibly, all their names were on it—even his brother Jake and his family. Their foolish trip to the immigration office in Big Spring had not gotten Jake deported; instead, it had accidentally added him to the list of families seeking U.S. citizenship. Standing there in the cold wind, David could do nothing but smile with gratitude at God's miracles.

To add some icing on the cake, David had received a raise at Nix Implement Co. and was making $4 an hour. The extra money allowed him to keep his three children in school instead of making them work. It was still hard to believe—a victory snatched from the jaws of certain defeat.

However, the bill hadn't passed, and the leaders continued asking for more money for the lawyers. It was impossible to get ahead with that ever-present expense.

But today was time for celebration. David was pleased to discover that this country took time off each year to celebrate everything they had, and he was planning on joining them. All German families had unexpectedly received an offer from Seminole's First Baptist Church to join them for a Thanksgiving dinner. Rev. Gerald Tidwell was the man in charge. Yet, to the reverend's surprise, there were few takers. The Rempels were one of them, though. David made sure of that.

He looked at his watch and smiled. It was almost time.

Back inside the trailer, he found his wife pulling Tina's hair back to start the braids. Elizabeth's hair was already done, braided and tied up neatly.

"Stop," he commanded, his loud voice scaring Anna.

"What are you saying?" she asked.

"We are now in the states, and our daughters are not going to have braided hair anymore. Undo them and leave their hair loose. That's the way the culture is here."

Anna, her mouth hanging open, had rarely seen her husband so demanding. Both Tina and Elizabeth matched Anna's expression.

"Take them out now!" David said again.

Anna undid the few braids on Tina's hair and combed it out, letting the tresses fall past her shoulders like fine permed hair. Tina, stunned, rejoiced as her forehead relaxed and her eyelids came back. It was a luxurious feeling, one she'd only felt when her hair was being washed.

No sooner was Tina's hair undone than Anna loosened and combed out Elizabeth's hair. The two girls were giddy. It was like an early Christmas present.

Thirty minutes later, Anna and David strolled into a large dining hall with their four children clinging to them. Rev. Tidwell stepped forward and greeted them, speaking with words that neither Tina nor her siblings understood. When he showed them to the buffet, they could hardly believe their eyes. The reverend picked up a plate and showed the Rempels how to serve up their food. Then, after each family member held a loaded plate, the parishioners took them to their table.

A few other Mennonite families joined them, sitting amongst the kind Baptists. For Tina, it was like a dream. Her hair was loose and the plate in front of her was loaded with all sorts of delicacies. The day's normal meal of pork and beans and bread was replaced with three kinds of meat, five kinds of salad, and a dozen different fruits. No sooner had she finished off a plate than they encouraged her to go back for seconds. She did, only to find her brother and sister right behind her. Not to be outdone, her father and mother loaded up too. In fact, they put so much food on their plates that the Baptists insisted on placing the leftovers in a small pouch she learned was called a doggie bag. Upon hearing the news, David touched Anna's arm and said, "This country is so rich that they take food home for their dogs."

"Not in my family," Anna said. "And don't tell them we don't have dogs. This will be for us."

"I think they understand that," David said, laughing.

With bellies full and toothpicks in their mouths, the Rempels hugged everyone who came close. They shook Rev. Tidwell's hand while clutching the doggie bags, before making their way to the car.

"I can't believe what we just had," Elizabeth said.

"Same here," her brother added.

David slapped the dashboard happily. "I can't believe how great this country is. I just can't forgive myself for not trying to get here sooner."

Tina, sitting in the backseat, noticed him wipe something from his eye. As he started the car, Anna moved closer and rubbed his arm. Soon, they were back home.

That night, as the light faded in the western sky, Mrs. Schmitt came to visit and see how everything had gone. When Anna showed her all the food, she was speechless. But she was sure smiling when Anna loaded up two bags for her to take home.

"We might as well spread our blessings with our friends," Anna said. "Of course, it's always easier to share on a full stomach," she added, laughing.

David, his eyes misting over again, put on a jacket and stepped outside. Watching her father, Tina grabbed a jacket and joined him. Together, father and daughter walked over to Tina's tiny tree—the size of a twig now. David knelt and studied the rusted can. It was still protecting the plant—barely.

"Dad, do you think my tree will make it?"

"Only time will tell," he replied, wiping his eyes again. "And, speaking of that, I think it's your time."

"Time for what?" Tina asked, kneeling next to him.

"Time for you to tell the rest of this story. I'm getting older and too tired to do it. Besides, you're learning English and will do better than I ever could."

"I don't understand," Tina said. "What story?"

David placed his hand on her arm. "For hundreds of years, our family has been moving to different countries, trying to survive. But along the way, we've always kept our heritage and history up here—in our head." He tapped his temple. "We passed down some of our history to each generation, but not as thoroughly as we should have. I would've liked to write our story for the next generations, but it's your time now."

"I'm not sure I'm ready," Tina pleaded.

The corners of his lips turned up. "That's what I said when my grandfather Jacob Braun Peters Rempel told me it was my turn. I didn't know

317

what he was talking about, but I do now. I'm thirty-one years old and dead tired each night. We need someone young like you. Believe me, you can do this."

Tina touched her tiny tree. "But I'm scared."

"Don't be," David soothed. "They want to hear from you, anyway."

"Who?"

"Our family. Your children. Your grandchildren. Their grandchildren. The endless generations of Rempels to come."

Tina looked down at the ground and considered his words. Lifting her head, she gazed into her father's eyes. "How do I start?"

"Just talk in your own voice. If you don't say the right word, they'll be patient. You'll see."

"Okay, Dad. I'll do my best."

"That's my girl," David said. "Make me proud."

I loved my father and I wanted to make him proud, very proud. So, I got to my feet and dusted myself off, gazing at the reddish-orange painting in the western sky. I felt Dad's arm slide around me, so I put my arm around him— my wonderful, hardworking father—and we walked back into the warmth of our tiny trailer, where we continued celebrating the goodness of God and giving thanks for this great country.

Chapter Twenty-Eight

In early 1978, my mother privately broke the news to Dad. "Honey, I'm pregnant again."

"Oh, that's wonderful," he said, grabbing her shoulders in excitement. "When are you due?"

"I think September. Maybe October."

His smile faded a little. "That will make five," he said in an almost-whisper, mind calculating how much more money we would need, what with the constant demand for attorney's fees and all. Rubbing his jaw, he stared out the window. "Since the kids won't be able to work in the cotton fields until maybe March or April, I'll see if I can pick up more hours at work."

"We'll be fine," Mom said, giving him a squeeze on the arm.

Her attitude had gotten much better after we'd started going to the new church—the Gospel Mennonite Church, a part of the General Conference Church organization. Reverend Bill Stoesz led the congregation. A less conservative, more tolerant church, they allowed women to wear store-bought clothes. Mom accepted the relaxed rules and even wore a denim skirt and blouse on occasion. At times, she looked like a real-life Seminole citizen.

Dress codes weren't all that this church offered. Pastor Stoesz preached a different message to the Mennonites, one foreign to our ears. He claimed that we weren't true Christians until we were born again. "You are simply following the rules, without regard to what's in your heart. You are not having a relationship with Jesus Christ," he said to his congregation. "You might have great values and be good people, but that's not enough. If you keep living the way you are and believing what you believe, you cannot possibly know if you are saved. Instead, you shall arrive at heaven's door and only then find out if you've made it."

Mother listened intently, turning his words over.

"You tell yourself that hopefully you've done enough good deeds to make it in. But that's not what the Bible says." He paused, opening his big book to a passage. "Whoever believes in Him shall not perish but have eternal life. John Chapter three, verse sixteen."

He made a final push for Mother's soul at a revival. "God gave His Son as a sacrifice for our sins. But you must take the first step and accept His free gift. Will any of you do this?"

Mom, unable to deny his words, stood up and walked to the altar. After the last song was sung Dad took us children out to the car to wait for Mom. When she came out, we saw that Mom had been crying. But now she was smiling. She told us, "Yes, I asked for forgiveness of my sins and repented. I accepted Jesus Christ as my personal savior."

Us children couldn't believe what we were seeing. All we had heard was how her mother hated this move to Texas and becoming part of this new world. Grandma Friesen and Aunt Margaret had worked on Mom, urging her to keep with the strict Mennonite faith. Yet suddenly, Mother was something none of us were—she was truly born again.

This changed everything for her. She now decided to fully honor her husband and accept this land as her new home. There was no going back. For the rest of us, it was quite an eye-opening experience because from birth, we'd been raised with the Mennonite way—suffering makes one closer to God. All Germans knew that He would never give anything away for free. Hard work was the only way to salvation, though you wouldn't know for sure until you arrived at heaven's entrance and learned if you had worked hard enough.

Mom's changed outlook on life affected all of us, but especially me. Several months later, I sat in church listening to Pastor Stoesz preach this new "born again" philosophy. I thought of the Sunday school lesson I had gotten a few weeks earlier about how unending God's love is. She brought a golden ring to class and passed it around to each of us to look at closely and asked us if we could find a joint in the ring. We couldn't. She told us that is how God's love is—without end. I knew I was a sinner. Surely, I needed forgiveness for my sins. Pastor Stoesz had to be right. I definitely needed to be saved.

After his sermon, several of us made a beeline for him. When it was my turn, he asked if I was ready to accept Jesus Christ as my savior. I said yes, and began confessing to every sin I could think of. Pastor Stoesz held up his hand and said, "Hold on, hold on. Let me read you this." He turned to his Bible and read me 1 John 1:9: "If we confess our sins, he is faithful and just and will forgive us our sins and purify us from all unrighteousness."

I listened carefully.

"Tina, you don't have to confess to me. All you have to do is confess to God. You do one thing and He does the rest. He forgives all your sins. He fills you with the Holy Spirit to guide you. And He gives you eternal salvation so you can be with Him in heaven."

Hearing this, I was blown away. But I had to make sure, just in case it was too good to be true. "I only have to do one thing?" I asked the pastor. "And I don't even need you to do this for me?"

His eyes sparkled. "That's right. There's no middleman between you and God. He wants a direct relationship with you."

Now, there were two in our family who had been born again. I hoped and prayed everyone else would join us.

⚜

Mayor Clark's business continued to suffer as he tried his best to help us stay in this country. Bo Brown helped us on a different front. He watched over Senate Bill S 2180 – a congressional act that would give us Mennonites the right to seek citizenship—or obtain a green card. The only problem was that this bill left off 112 names. That's why Bo boarded a plane in Lubbock and flew to Washington. He just had to get those names added to the bill.

This one-two punch of Mayor Clark and Bo Brown was packed with power. Mayor Clark woke up every day talking about us to the national media, telling the reporters how tragic it was that millions of illegal aliens could stay and be assimilated while committing crimes, yet hardworking, religious people were being kicked out. Some reporters even pursued the angle that a few politicians had their eye on the Mennonites' soon-to-be-lost farmland. Words like "heartless" and "brutal" dotted these articles. This simply added to the calls, letters, and threats delivered to immigration officials and politicians. Sen. Lloyd Bentsen, a sponsor of one of the bills, told the media that thirty-one Mennonites had been certified and were not taking away jobs from Americans. He felt confident that one way or another, we would be allowed to stay.

The public's wrath was so strong, *Washington Post* reporter Bill Curry sent this letter to Mayor Clark: "The Mennonites' story touched off one of the greatest reader reactions in years: telephone calls, telegrams, and letters all over the place." This was the *Washington Post*!

Other newspapers ran editorials stating how Americans were sick and tired of allowing the welfare cases to stay but telling the hard workers to leave. The *Wichita Eagle* in Kansas wrote bluntly that not only were millions of aliens illegally holding jobs in the U.S., but mafia leaders had successfully resisted deportation to Italy and Sicily for years. It thanked the Mennonites in Kansas for bringing them the hardy Turkey Red wheat from Russia many decades earlier. All of this led to more letters and even some checks sent to Mayor Clark. He gladly turned the money over to our leadership to help with attorney fees. We needed it.

Halfway across the country was Bo Brown, hard at work in Washington, D.C., pushing the Mennonites' cause. He met with his good friend and past boss George Mahon. One day, Bo led a meeting in the Congressman's appropriations office, which was packed with immigration officials and other interested parties. The Chairman, who had a deep fondness for Bo, placed a hand on his shoulder and said, "Son, tell these gentlemen what we want them to do. I have to excuse myself to take a vote." When he returned, the Congressman asked Bo, "Did you tell them?"

"Yes, I did," Bo replied. "I made it clear that I want the immigration service to come to Seminole to fill out the application papers so the families would not have to incur the expense of going to Dallas."

This gave Mr. Chambers, the lead immigration official, a chance to break the bad news. "Mr. Chairman, we just can't do that."

George Mahon said nothing for at least a minute. After letting this news soak in, he sighed. "Mr. Chambers, if you want to, I think you can."

To everyone's surprise, they changed their mind. Perhaps not wanting to upset the man holding the purse strings to their agency factored in their decision. Whatever it was, Bo had accomplished his mission. The 112 names were added to the Senate bill and immigration officials were coming to Seminole.

This news shifted the burden to John Shepherd, the lawyer who'd supposedly received most of the legal fee money collected from the Mennonites. It was his job to fill out a form for each Mennonite and send it to the INS office in Dallas. There, the INS would create some additional longer forms, and then come to Seminole to meet with the Mennonites individually and help begin the process toward citizenship—assuming the private bill passed.

It was several weeks later—a Monday at ten o'clock—when six INS officials arrived in Seminole ready to interview the Mennonites. Hundreds of families milled around the downtown area, waiting for their turn, hopeful the end was near. Then a problem arose.

"I'm sorry," an INS official told Bo Brown, "but we can't process all of these folks. There's too many. We had no idea because you never sent the forms in. There just isn't enough time."

"Hang on," Bo said. "Let me get the lawyer who did that."

Bo located Attorney Shepherd and herded him to the immigration officials. "Oh yeah, I sent those in," he insisted. "You folks lost them."

"I'm sorry, sir, but you are wrong. We don't have them."

"Well, it's not my fault you have too big of an organization," Shepherd retorted, folding his arms.

"Let me make a call," Bo pleaded. A few moments later, he got the Chairman on the phone. "Mr. Chairman, this is a mess. The Mennonites' attorney swears he sent in the forms and INS swears they never got them. Someone's lying."

"Hmm," the Chairman said. "Make a check of the lawyer's files and see if you can confirm he sent them in. Surely he has some kind of receipt."

Bo went back to the cluster of men and discovered that Attorney Shepherd had disappeared. A quick check of his office found it locked and dark. This didn't make sense.

323

"What do we do?" one of the Mennonite leaders asked.

"I'm not going to let this chance pass us by," Bo said, determined. "Let me get the landlord and see what we can find."

Incredibly, Bo gained access to the lobby of Attorney Shepherd's building, but found the door to his private office locked. Shifting a cabinet closer to the wall, Bo sat down on the floor. As he pressed his back against the cabinet for leverage, he kicked hard at the wall, busting a large hole with a dozen kicks. After ripping some pieces free, he removed his coat and laid it over a chair. Then he got down on his belly and crawled into the lawyer's office, unlocking the door for his assistant. "Go through these files," he told her, "and look for anything that has to do with the Mennonites. I'll take one side and you take the other."

Ten minutes later, they had discovered absolutely nothing. The only thing that came close was an envelope holding a lone receipt for having paid some fee, possibly having to do with a record of one Mennonite. That was it.

"Gentlemen," Bo told the Mennonite leaders sternly, "there are no files, and no nothing. I don't think he's done anything."

The long faces told Bo all he needed to hear. "Let me see if I can find this Shepherd fellow."

Asking around the local businesses, he located the lawyer several buildings away from the nightmare now brewing. A few minutes later, Bo pushed him into a corner, where the Mennonites and INS officials grilled him. Finally, the truth made an appearance.

"I'm sorry," Shepherd said, staring at his shoes, "but I never sent them in."

The Mennonites slumped their shoulders, their disappointment too heavy to bear. From Russia, to Canada, to Mexico, and now here, it had been one problem after another. It wasn't the government abusing them, it was the local citizens. Yet through all this, the Mennonites never fired a shot. They never raised a hand. They never fought anyone for what was right. They simply took it. Today, though, they mustered up the courage to do something they should've done a long time ago. "You're fired," one of them said in clear English. The attorney gladly accepted his fate and spun on his heels, disappearing as quickly as he could.

"Listen," Bo said to the INS officials, "I'm going to work with my assistant and the few Mennonites who can read and write English, and get these forms filled out right now. We'll set up an assembly line for you."

The INS official shook his head. "I don't know. There's so many of them."

Another official stepped forward. "Well, we're here. At least we can try."

It was yet another miracle. By late in the afternoon, they had managed to fill out all the forms for all the families. It had been a mountain of work.

As the INS officials headed back to Dallas, it was now up to them to coordinate with Sen. Lloyd Bentsen to make sure everything matched the private bill. One wrong name or a misspelling would doom that person to permanent illegal alien status, likely preventing him or her from ever being able to apply for citizenship. We Mennonites were still miles away from the promised land.

⤙⬦⤚

Another hot summer arrived in Seminole, scorching the land and its inhabitants. For us children, that meant work. Our family needed the money now that we had to pay a new attorney to help us. Never mind that our previous payments had disappeared.

Like last year, we hoed weeds all day long. On the side, Mother picked up odd jobs from women in town. Susie Wickson was her first client.

"How did you do today?" we asked Mom.

She chuckled as she related her experience. "The lady placed a rag in my hand and showed me how to use this blue liquid in a spray bottle and clean the windows. Then she showed me how to use a vacuum cleaner. It was amazing! I didn't know what I was doing, but somehow, I cleaned her entire home."

With Mrs. Wickson's help, Mom was in business as an official house cleaner.

Dad picked up side work too. One of the jobs he landed was from Laura and Pappy Hoffman. Pappy Hoffman ran his own business—Hoffman's Well Servicing—and business was booming. This left Laura to run the house and get things done. She hired Dad to build a wooden shelf

325

at one of her windows, hoping these Mennonites werc the craftsmen she had heard about.

Sure enough, Dad did an excellent job. When Mrs. Hoffman learned that Mom cleaned houses, she tried her out. Soon, when I wasn't hoeing weeds, I tagged along to help.

"What is your name?" Mrs. Hoffman asked me, a fascinated expression on her face.

"Tina," I said. "I'm ten years old."

"My," she said, with the sweetest smile I had ever seen. "That's something. You sure are a hard worker. And you can speak English."

Even though I was still learning the language, I translated for Mother, doing the best I could with Mrs. Hoffman's instructions. When we were done, Mrs. Hoffman wrote Mom a check and set a date for her to return. The problem with this was the form of payment. We couldn't have bank accounts because we weren't citizens. So, what to do with this piece of paper?

We walked into Gandy's, a convenience store that we heard cashed checks. However, the cashier said we had to buy something. For me, that was no problem.

"I'm getting this," I told Mother, showing her the ice cream mud pie in my hand. When we checked out, Mom received the change back from the check as I worked fast to devour my dessert before someone changed their mind. You could never be too careful.

From that day forward, we cashed our checks at Gandy's or the Pick and Pack on 11th Street. Usually, I finagled an ice cream treat from Mom. To me, having been saved *and* allowed to eat ice cream meant I was already in heaven. It couldn't get much better than that.

While each of us—Mom, Dad, Elizabeth, David, and I—worked hard to pay our expenses, our neighbor lady watched Nancy. Mom didn't let her pregnancy slow her down. She picked up more clients, which eased Dad's money fears.

As usual, hoeing weeds was hot and brutal work. But each day, I got up in darkness and did it. When I came home, if Mom needed help cleaning a house, I'd go with her. If not, I'd water my tree and see if I could help it grow. It was about two feet high now, surprising all of us. Of course, getting apricots off it one day was another story.

One Friday—July 14—we came home from the fields to find Mother crying hard. She held Nancy for comfort.

"What's the matter?" Elizabeth asked.

"Your Grandma Friesen just passed away."

I started crying and hugged my mother. I could not imagine the pain involved in losing any relative, much less your mother. Just seeing Mom in pain hurt me.

"Are we going to Mexico for the funeral?" I asked.

"I don't know," she replied. It was obvious she hadn't thought about it. When she considered the possibility that she might not be able to make the trip, more tears flowed.

The next day, Dad contacted the new lawyer and discovered that Mom could leave the U.S. to attend the funeral, but there was a good chance she would not be allowed to reenter. This gave her a terrible choice. However, with her new life in Seminole, there was no decision. She would miss her mother's funeral and cry for weeks. It was a tragedy all around.

As we talked to our relatives in Mexico, we learned even more bad news. "Your mother was sick on her deathbed and kept asking us, 'Where's Anna? Where's Anna? Where's Anna?' We tried to tell her you were in the U.S., but she didn't understand."

This tore Mom into tinier pieces, especially since her mother had been so against her leaving Mexico in the first place. Dad, sensing Mom's anger, kept his distance while she grieved.

On the day of the funeral, Mrs. Plett came over and sat with Mom, bringing kringle with her. We had been attending a new church and she was the pastor's wife. For hours, the two women cried and cried. Mom was so distraught that she couldn't be in Mexico to say goodbye to her mother. It was truly a sad affair.

<hr/>

After another long, hot summer, the crops failed again. By now, the Mennonites had learned that we weren't planting the right crops. Even so, the local citizens weren't doing any better. Soaring temperatures and lack of rain made it almost impossible to make a crop. Fortunately, Elizabeth, David, and I got paid for our work hoeing weeds. An ice cream treat for me was all the payment I received, with the rest going into Dad's pocket.

We learned some good news about a new school coming to town. With the national attention on our plight, the Mennonite Evangelical Church (MEC) from Canada had decided to invest in a private school in Seminole. That meant no more public school for us.

The MEC taught an accelerated Christian Light Education curriculum, with a ratio of four teachers to seventy students. Low German was used but English was taught too, along with the usual subjects in public schools. And it was set up differently than the public school.

Instead of moving from class to class, we stayed in one room while four volunteer teachers rotated around, teaching various subjects. Two of my first teachers were Rose Dueck and Lois Penner, both from Manitoba. Later that year, Menno Penner, Menno Plett, Carol Plett, and Anna Plett joined our school as additional teachers.

At the MEC, we had all sorts of new experiences. One of them included a trip to the local jail. This was both scary and fascinating. We also had policemen come talk to us. And unlike in Mexico, boys and girls were not separated but mixed together. I liked that. However, the tuition fees were a tough pill to swallow.

Dad discovered the cost for all of us to attend this school was an outrageous $125 per month. But our education had always been his priority, and he wasn't going to let money stand in the way. That's why after school, David and I mowed lawns, while Mom and Elizabeth cleaned houses. Mom worked hard all through her pregnancy. Then, on September 30, she gave birth. All of a sudden, I had Jacob, a baby brother. Now, I had a new doll to play with—the only difference being he cried a lot and needed his diapers changed.

In another painful twist, a nurse came into the room and asked Mom and Dad if she could take baby Jacob for a bit. Not knowing enough English to understand what she was saying, they agreed. It wasn't long before the nurse returned with Jacob and all was forgotten, at least until it was time for Mom to be discharged. She was given an envelope with cute baby pictures along with a bill for them. It was money we could ill afford to part with. But at least we had photos of our new family member.

———◈———

In late 1978, we all looked anxiously toward Congress. Our current deadline for leaving was February 1, 1979, a few months away. Then, in October, we learned some depressing news. Congress had adjourned without acting on our bill. They said it died in subcommittee. I wasn't sure what that meant, but all the adults seemed worried about it.

Just when it seemed bleak, we received an extension to February 1, 1981—two years away. We celebrated the news with reckless abandon, which for Mennonites was nothing more than clapping a lot and baking more bread.

"Surely they will let us stay," Dad said.

Only time would tell.

To make more money, Mom set up a business she called Mother and Daughters Painting. She found out where to get business cards printed and gave them to us to pass out. We stuck them in storm doors and mailboxes and waited for the phone to ring. David and I picked our yard work business back up, even though that didn't fully kick in until April.

It didn't take long for Mom's new business to get a client. One of our first jobs was our good housekeeping client Laura Hoffman. By now, we considered them close friends. Mr. Hoffman really cared for me, making up nicknames for me like Teeny Weenie. Mrs. Hoffman pulled me aside one day and said, "You know, Pappy only gives nicknames to people he really likes." That made my day.

One time, Mom was cleaning Mrs. Hoffman's house when she spotted a tail sticking out from beneath the carpet. Not knowing the correct word for snake, she cried out, "Snack! Snack!"

Mrs. Hoffman ran in to see what all the commotion was and saw the tail. Tipping over the trashcan, Mrs. Hoffman ran outside screaming for her husband. "Pappy! Pappy! Help! There's a snake in the bathroom."

A few minutes and several loud noises later, he emerged victorious from battling the wild serpent. "What in the world are y'all getting so excited about?" he said, his fingers pinching the tail of a tiny lizard. A quick flick outside and the beast was gone.

Mrs. Hoffman gazed at Mom, who stared back. What could they say? They had been afraid and it had taken a big burly man to rescue them.

As word spread about Mom's quality work, she picked up more and more painting jobs. Her ability to accurately estimate the amount of paint needed for any job made it easy to make a profit. She needed a helper to keep up, and I was the usual suspect.

One day, Dad inspected one of our jobs and decided we were no longer Mother and Daughters Painting. "Your new name shall be The Three-Coat Painters."

"What does that mean?" I asked him.

"It means that on every job you do, you apply three coats: one on the wall, one on the plastic, and one on yourselves."

We ignored him, especially when we cashed the checks. As always, a mud pie made getting the paint off my skin bearable, if not pleasant.

Our important ally in Congress retired in early 1979. Bo Brown was sad. His old boss George Mahon had passed on running again, missing out on a chance to take on George W. Bush (our future president) in the general election. However, Sen. Bentsen picked up the slack and then some. In March, he added another 100 names to a bill he introduced in the Senate: S 707. Dad received a letter advising him of Sen. Bentsen's efforts.

In the meantime, the Canadian Old Colony Mennonites' large tract southwest of town was in trouble. In early 1978, they were staring at another payment and headed to foreclosure. However, the relentless pressure Mayor Clark put on the national media kept our story in the headlines. Incredibly, some generous person in Houston sent enough money—$50,000—to cover the Mennonites' mortgage payment and keep them on the land another year. Unfortunately, it was a year later and the payment was due again. The Mennonites were doubtful they could make it. Equally doubtful was another benefactor stepping forward to help.

Dad kept an eye on all of this because the buyers of our farm in Mexico did not make any payments. Dad was constantly on them trying to get some money, but was usually unsuccessful. One day, they suggested that he take some land their family owned on the large tract that was in trouble. Seeing no other way to get payment, Dad agreed. "At least I can go stand on this land," he said confidently.

Mom was less sure it could be sold for anything. Dad would have to sell that tract to get his money back before it foreclosed, or hold it and hope the buyers made a payment. It would be a tough decision.

In April 1979, Dad found a buyer for the Seminole land—a Mennonite who agreed to pay $2,000. Dad was thrilled.

The next morning, the man called Dad with panic in his voice. "Mr. Rempel, did you cash that check yesterday?"

Dad felt for the $2,000 in his overalls pocket. "Yes, I did. Why?"

"Oh no!" the man cried. "A few minutes ago, the land was foreclosed on. I have lost it all!"

Dad's brow furrowed. "So you mean if I had waited until today, I would be out two thousand dollars?"

"Yes," the man replied. "That's the way it looks."

Because a lawyer had handled the transaction, Dad had been able to take the check to the lawyer's bank and cash it. It was the best decision he could've made, although it was terrible that the buyer lost all his money. At least that man could take comfort in the Mennonite belief system—*Work Sets You Free*. Sadder still were all the Mennonites who had worked so hard to clear the caliche stone and farm the land. They were soon forced to leave.

In March, Mom let us know she was pregnant again. Laura Hoffman was one of the first to congratulate her. "How many will this be?" she asked.

"Six," Mom replied.

"My goodness. You Mennonites sure work hard at everything." The two women laughed.

"You know, Tina," Mrs. Hoffman said, "you and your mother can help yourselves to the dish."

The dish she was talking about sat on the bar, full of candy and snacks. I stared at it constantly while I helped Mom clean. It was always there, tempting me. But I never took anything because Mom had instructed me not to. "We can't be taking things that aren't ours," she said.

We had heard how various Seminole citizens hired Mennonites and left quarters and dollar bills around to see if they stole them. While mowing a lawn, I'd found a quarter on a sidewalk and happily walked it up to the owner. I didn't know if it was a trick, and I didn't care. Of course, I knew full well that the quarter could have bought a delicious mud pie.

We spent a lot of time at Laura and Pappy's house. They made us feel like family, not hired workers. When they sat down for lunch, they always invited us. A few times Mom agreed and we had lunch with them. It was delicious—a welcome change from our bread and pork and beans.

David, Elizabeth, and I continued working hard to make money for the family. Each week, Dad gave us $5. This was a tremendous sum for a young person like me. Because I wore pantyhose all the time, I used my funds to purchase one pair. With the leftover money, I usually sprung for a banana split at Dairy Queen. There was just something about me and ice cream.

⚬◆⚬

After another difficult labor, I had a new baby brother to play with. Henry was born November 3, 1979, and like all Rempels, he was a real cutie.

By now, Mom had figured out the ways of the new world. With Dad's blessing, she decided to stop having babies, going on birth control and shutting down the factory of little Rempels. But we still added to our family.

Uncle Jake bought a piece of our six acres and moved in with his family right next to us. The two brothers still laughed a lot at their ridiculous trip to Big Spring. If a bill could be passed, Uncle Jake would be a citizen too. So far, though, a bill wasn't anywhere close to passing.

With two babies—Jacob and Henry—Mom had her hands full. To help out, Elizabeth followed another Mennonite tradition of dropping out of school. She was only fourteen at the time. As for me and David, we kept going to school along with Nancy, who was now old enough.

Thanks to Elizabeth, Mom could still run her painting and housecleaning business. I continued to be Mom's helper.

We added more homes to our list—Lenny Maclesky, Bonnie Berger, Ruby Atkins. We also established a relationship with Mayor Clark's wife, Vicky. She hired us to clean her mother's home. Of course, I kept turning over all my money to Dad, who used it for family expenses. Really, I never thought twice about it.

When 1980 arrived, we celebrated another year in paradise. Dad had added on to the front of our trailer, giving us more room for our expanded family. I was just eleven, but felt like twenty with the extra space and privacy.

We heard Senate Bill S 707 was a bill making its way through Congress again. By now, we just assumed it would all work out. We'd been here for three years and couldn't imagine any other place we'd call home.

I spent another hard year painting and cleaning houses with Mom, and hoeing fields and mowing yards with David. Finally, the crops came in and farmers made money.

One day in October, a friend came running over to our trailer. "Did you hear the good news?" she hollered.

"You mean that Jesus saves?" I said back to her.

"No. I mean, yes to that, but no. I'm talking about the bill. It passed Congress today. We're going to become citizens!"

We hugged each other and went inside, telling Dad. He made some calls and sure enough, she was right. That same day, October 19, 1980, President Carter signed Private Law 96-63. Now, more than 500 Mennonites were on their way to citizenship. It was a true miracle from God!

The next day, Laura Hoffman presented our family with a green ivy plant to celebrate our soon-to-arrive green cards. Vicky Clark congratulated us too. Although her husband was no longer mayor, having decided to finally hang it up, this victory belonged to him if it belonged to anyone.

On November 7, 1980, the new mayor, Mickey L. Ray, declared it Mennonite Day. We all celebrated it like we had just been admitted into heaven—which we kind of had.

A day or two after our big celebration, I noticed Mom sitting at the kitchen table, a sad expression on her face. "What's the matter, Mom?" I asked. "Do you want to have a *faspa*?"

She frowned. "No, Tina, I don't."

"Then what is it?"

She sighed. "Now that I have my green card, I need to plan a trip to Mexico."

"What for?"

"I need to go and see my mother's burial place. She's waiting for me."

Chapter Twenty-Nine

1986 – Six Years Later

"Gather around, children, we need to have our picture taken." Mom motioned for us to behave, but she mostly meant the younger ones.

"Come on," I said, echoing my mother's instructions, feeling important because I was seventeen and could boss around some of my siblings. "Move in closer."

Our aunt looked at us until she was satisfied, then focused and adjusted her camera. "Cheese!" she exclaimed, and the camera snapped. "Perfect."

I glanced over at Mom, who was smiling from ear to ear. She'd been excited to have this photograph taken, because she wanted something to commemorate this week. In just two days, we would attend a ceremony to be sworn in as citizens.

It was nice to see Mom so happy. She'd had some rough times in the six years since we'd received our green cards. She finally got her chance to visit Mexico, where she planned to sit at her mother's gravesite and cry over missed goodbyes. But the trip hadn't been easy.

When my parents arrived, Mom learned that her very own sister refused her access to the cemetery, claiming she was unholy. Even though she and Dad hadn't been excommunicated, they were treated as such. Mom tried to convince Aunt Margaret to let her visit her mother's gravesite to no avail.

Then someone stole Mom's purse. It turned really bad when she realized her green card was inside that purse. When they reached the border, Dad explained what had happened to the immigration officer. The man looked into their database and discovered Mom did in fact have a green card. He gave her a temporary piece of paper and let her through. It was a close call.

Back in Seminole, Dad continued his work in construction with Mr. Ron Wickson. Ron, along with his wife, Susie, had been one of Mom's first housecleaning clients. Uncle Jake helped out as well as Ron Adams, a foreman. To our surprise, Dad made good money—more than he'd ever imagined. He soon purchased a brand new two-toned brown Silverado pickup to help him in his work, though we all knew that wasn't the only reason he saved up to buy that truck. He loved America, playing the part of a regular consumer like the rest of its citizens. With his straw cowboy hat and blue jeans (he retired his overalls), Dad was a true Texan.

One evening, he came home from work and said, "I don't think my grandfather has very long to live. I'm going to drive to Mexico and say goodbye while I have the chance."

He had just finished a large house and had a week or so before he needed to start work on the next one. It was perfect timing.

He got up one morning and left before we were even awake, traveling alone in his new pickup. When he arrived at Campo 110, there was his grandfather, sitting in the barn as if he knew Dad was coming.

"Hello, Grandfather," Dad said, embracing the man who meant so much to him. "How are you feeling?"

"Oh, not so good," Jacob said, managing a smile. "It won't be long. At least now I'll die with a smile on my face."

Dad sat next to the eighty-six-year-old man and put his arm around him. "You were right. From the very beginning, you were right."

Jacob sighed. "I know. I just wish I could've joined you. This place is still so difficult."

Dad pointed to the barn door. "I've got something to show you. Something I'm proud of."

"What is it?" Jacob asked.

Dad could barely contain himself. "It's a brand new pickup truck. You won't believe everything it has on it. Come on and get up."

Dad tried to help his grandfather up, but the old man pushed his hands away. "Let me be. I'll see it later. Right now, I just want to stay here with you and hear some stories about Texas."

With a soft sigh, Dad sat back down. "Which stories do you want to hear? Our construction work? The children's schooling? Our house?"

"All of them," Jacob said, a little bit of energy entering his voice. "I want to hear all of them. Then I'll look at your truck and take a nap."

"A nap?" Dad asked.

"Yes. And hopefully I'll dream about what my life could've been."

When Dad came home, he was melancholy. Even though his grandfather was proud of him, Dad felt sad. A month or so later, Jacob Rempel, the man who so long ago had boarded a train in Canada and brought his family down to Mexico in search of a better life, was gone.

※

It was Thursday, the day before our big citizenship ceremony, the last day of class for me and my siblings this week. Dad told us we could miss class the next day, so today was like a Friday. To make life even better, our tenth-grade class was taking the first field trip of the school year.

The bus pulled up to the Gaines County Airport. We were fascinated to see up close the smaller private airplanes, and to tour the FBO building. At the end, we posed for a class picture before heading off to our next stop.

The bus rambled along a gravel road, finding a safe spot to stop. We exited at the top of ground that gently sloped away and followed our guide, making the long walk down a narrow path. The October morning was cool on my skin, though it would likely heat up by late afternoon. I pulled my light jacket around me in case a breeze appeared.

"Children, pay attention and listen up," the guide said, clapping her hands. "These trees are hackberry. You will see them all around us."

We stared at them as if they were magical, like we'd never seen a tree before.

"And notice the slope of the draw," the guide continued. "When we entered it, we were on higher ground. But as we are walking, we are going lower, so we can't see over the edge. This is called a draw."

She was right. It was as if someone had dug out a ditch, making it shallow at one end and deep at the other. I followed the kids in front of me toward the deeper end, wondering how far down we would go.

The thirty or so students walked for ten minutes before the guide stopped us. "Gather around me," she said. "I have something to show you."

We crowded close to her, with the taller students on the outer edges straining to see what was so important. When she dropped to her knees, we bent over.

"Look at this," she said, sticking her hand through a pile of thick grass. "This is where the wells were located, the ones that were dug by Indians in the 1800s." *Oohs* and *ahhs* trickled through the group. "There are a dozen of these along a line heading deeper into the draw. It was these wells that saved the military when they were out of water and dying of thirst. I want each of you to come and look. You can walk a little farther down the draw, but don't go out of sight. When you've finished, gather back here and I'll tell you some more stories."

I moved closer to see where the wells had been, imagining the cool water on my hands. The fact that real live Indians had dug wells on this very spot made it special, like I was touching history. I moved aside and let my classmates come in closer, choosing to roam the area—but not too far from the guide. I was a rules-follower and not about to upset an adult.

It didn't take me long to see that there wasn't much else of interest, other than knee-high grass and lots of hackberry trees. When I had seen enough, I moved next to the guide and waited for the stories she'd promised.

"Okay, children, come over here and sit on the grass," the guide announced.

It took a few minutes for everyone to come back and find a place, but eventually, the group quieted down.

"Thank you," she said. "In the late 1800s, the U.S. Army was trying to chase away Indians from this area. A scout team headed by Lt. Ward came to the edge of the draw and stopped. Lt. Ward sent his Seminole scouts down to see if there were Indians. There weren't. When the scouts returned, however, they carried much-needed water. It was a huge break. The cavalry would live another day."

She gave us some background on Col. Shafter, the leader of the men in the region, before moving to other items.

"It didn't take long for this draw to be called Seminole Wells."

A student next to me raised her hand. "What does Seminole mean?"

"Good question," the guide said. "The word 'Seminole' means people set apart or runaways. It describes a collection of folks who want to be left alone from the rest of the world or maybe just don't fit in. With us being out here on the Llano Estacado, a place that's hard to survive, I suppose that description fits us well."

The guide went on to explain that with water available, a trading post was set up in 1904 by Emma and William Austin, along with a post office they named the Caput. When a town sprung up, the name was shortened to Seminole. A few years later—in 1907—B.W. Cavender started the *Seminole Sentinel* newspaper, Gaines County's oldest business. I was fascinated by all this new information.

The guide took a sip of water and cleared her throat. "I want to add this thought, which is perhaps the most important lesson you will learn today. Like the Indians who survived the harsh conditions out here, and the soldiers who survived on water from these very wells, our town has survived the loss of many things. For example, we lost the vital rail service to Midland. Then we lost a lot of crops and livestock during a terrible drought in 1917 and '18. After that came the Great Depression. We lost our bank. We lost some of our men in World War Two." Her voice cracked a little at the mention of losing men.

"And with everything else that's been thrown at us, we've not only survived, but thrived. Today, Gaines County is one of the top crop-producing counties in the nation, not to mention all the oil we bring up from the ground." She lowered her voice, drawing us in closer. "So, when you go home tonight, tell your parents that because you are from Seminole, you are one tough boy and one tough girl!"

We smiled at the thought that we were somehow tough. I couldn't wait until Dad got home so I could tell him all this.

When school let out, Mom and I went to clean Laura and Pappy Hoffman's house, starting first in their large bathroom. With Mrs. Hoffman in the other room, we took the opportunity to practice for our ceremony tomorrow. Mom started us off. "I pledge allegiance to the flag of the United States of America, and to the Republic for which it stands..."

I continued. "...one nation under God, indivisible, with liberty and justice for all."

"What's this I hear?" Mrs. Hoffman asked.

Startled, we spun around. "Uh, we were just practicing," I said. "We apologize. We'll be quiet."

"No, no, dear!" she said, hugging us. "I wouldn't think of it. Learning the pledge of allegiance is very important. Are you getting ready for something?"

"Yes," I replied. "We're getting sworn in as citizens tomorrow. We'll be just like you."

Mrs. Hoffman's eyes filled with tears. "If everyone were like you..." She couldn't finish her thought so she left.

Mom and I didn't know what to think until Mrs. Hoffman returned a few seconds later. She held a beautiful red vase filled with a green ivy. Tricolor ribbons of red, white, and blue adorned the bottom and an American flag was stuck in the middle. "We knew about your event. I was going to surprise you later, but hearing our country's pledge of allegiance made me want to give you these now."

Her eyes filled again and she hugged us. "Pappy was in on this too. We're so glad you are one of us. We would hate to think of you being anywhere else."

Tears came to us as we stood there hugging each other, grateful for a country filled with wonderful people like Pappy and Laura Hoffman.

After we had finished, Mom drove the Buick toward home, cruising past Jo's Café and the Teepee Lodge—two places that had framed our first days in Seminole. As I held our lovely plant, I saw the H&D Grocery Store, with its owner Mr. Bates and his huge heart for the German community. He'd carried the Mennonites on credit for so long, knowing they had to eat. Sadly, he hadn't gotten paid on all the accounts. Yet he'd still found it in his heart to donate a public-address system to our church. With people like him, Mayor Clark, and Bo Brown, it was hard to imagine a place on earth better than this.

⟹◦⟸

I was the first to wake. I wanted to grab the bathtub before anyone else got up. Leaning back in the hot water, I thought about the first time I had come in from the scorching fields, the red sand pasted to my skin. I couldn't ever imagine getting it all off. But a promise of ice cream was all the motivation I had needed to get moving.

I shifted my legs, which were bunched up against the bathtub. They were extra-long, my body having grown nine inches in one school year. I'd even received an award for the most growth by any student. However, the pain I'd gone through was excruciating. Mercifully, it ended, leaving me more like a woman and less like a child.

With the bath complete, I went to my room and slipped on a new pair of pantyhose. Nothing was too good for my coming citizenship. I even had a new outfit—a conservative blouse and skirt—with white leather sandals completing the look. I tied my hair with bands so that I had one long ponytail hanging down to the middle of my back. Due to my enthusiasm, I was dressed and ready before most of my family awoke.

Mom was the exception. I found her in the kitchen, preparing some of her famous fresh bread. "Can I help?" I asked her.

"Thank you for offering," she said, checking the oven, "but I think I have it all in order."

"Are you as excited as me?"

"I'm thrilled, but hardly anyone is as excited as you, Tina."

I chuckled and left her alone, searching out my younger siblings to encourage them to be ready on time.

We stepped into the junior high auditorium, the buzzing of the crowd exciting me even more. Today, the auditorium had been converted to a United States District Courtroom, with the Honorable Judge Halbert O. Woodward presiding. It was his job to swear us in.

On the stage and off to one side, really an afterthought by the organizers, was our beloved champion Mayor Bob Clark. He sat there, looking forgotten. No one really knew why he was there.

While the speeches were in progress, Judge Woodward turned to him and whispered, "How were you involved in all this?"

Mayor Clark, humble to the core, said quietly, "Well, I guess it's because I worked with George Mahon and called Sen. Bentsen to get him involved."

Judge Woodward jerked upright. "I never knew that. I was good friends with George. I really want to know more about that."

"Of course," Mayor Clark said. "After the ceremony, I'll tell you everything. But it may take a long time."

Judge Woodward grinned. "Mr. Clark, you've never seen multi-district litigation before. That takes a long time. We'll see if you can beat it."

Mayor Clark smiled and nodded as the speaker turned to the judge. "Your honor, I believe it's time."

Judge Woodward approached the podium, adjusted the microphone, and asked us to stand. "Please raise your right hand."

My heart was pounding, my pride barely containable.

"Ladies and gentlemen, please repeat the naturalization oath of allegiance to the United States of America."

The crowd grew silent as the immigrants—including the six of us—raised their right hands high and followed the judge's words.

"I hereby declare, on oath…"

I smiled at my sister Nancy, who had turned twelve six days earlier. I had no idea how close we would become in later years.

"…that I absolutely and entirely renounce and abjure all allegiance and fidelity…"

My older brother David stood to my right—my longtime hoeing and mowing partner. At nineteen, dressed in a crisp white shirt, he was nearly a man. I was so proud of him. We smiled at each other as we repeated the words.

"…to any foreign prince, potentate, state, or sovereignty, of whom or which I have heretofore been a subject or citizen…"

Introverted and sweet Elizabeth was on my left, twenty years old and ever the protector of her younger siblings. Her sacrifice of dropping out of school and going to work was so great that it had allowed me to get a good education. I was in her debt.

"...that I will support and defend the Constitution and laws of the United States of America against all enemies, foreign and domestic..."

I glanced at Mom, who was concentrating hard on the words. Her steady temperament and advice had kept all of us in line, ensuring we would be great citizens. I couldn't imagine having a better mother.

"...that I will bear true faith and allegiance to the same; that I will perform noncombatant service in the Armed Forces of the United States when required by the law..."

Dad smiled at me. All his thinking, planning, risk-taking, patience, and backbreaking hard work had the six of us seconds away from citizenship. Jacob and Henry, my two younger brothers, were already citizens, having been born in this country.

I spoke up louder, making sure my words were heard.

"...that I will perform work of national importance under civilian direction when required by the law; and that I take this obligation freely, without any mental reservation or purpose of evasion; so help me God."

Yes, so help me God! It was His good providence, His perfect plan that had brought us through the desert to a place of paradise. I promised I wouldn't disappoint Him. Someday, if I had the means, I would give back to this community the first chance I had.

Near the back of the auditorium, barely seen by anyone, stood an older lady. Next to her was her husband, an old man in bad health and supported by metal walker. Struggling with his good arm, Charles Simpson held Rose close. Each day when he awoke, he vowed to never let her go. On the other side of Rose was a younger but still old man holding a marble. Somehow, Melvin seemed to know this moment was coming.

———◆———

We drove home after a nice reception, basking in our new status. Mom prepared a wonderful supper, with me, Elizabeth, and Nancy cleaning up. As everyone scattered, I watched Dad stare out the window at the autumn sun setting fast. Pausing, as if looking for something or someone, he deliberately opened the front door and eased outside. Mom stayed at the kitchen table, staring into the cup of coffee in front of her.

"Mom, can we sit down and recollect about the joy and significance of today?" I asked her. "Maybe tell me some more stories?"

She took a deep breath as she contemplated my request. "Not right now. Why don't you go outside and spend time with your father? I don't mind being alone."

I found him wandering around in our backyard. With Uncle Jake living next door, we had a fence to give us some privacy. As my feet crunched the dry grass, Dad glanced around and saw me coming.

"Want some company?" I asked him.

"Sure."

I stood next to him for a time before speaking. "Mom sure is quiet. She wanted to be alone. Is something wrong?"

Dad fiddled with a stick he had picked up, turning it over in his rough hands. "I guess it's hit her, like it's hit me."

"I don't understand. What has hit you?"

"The dream. As long as we weren't citizens, we were still climbing that mountain. We hadn't made it to the top, so we still had a toe in Mexico. But now, the struggle is over. The weight of finally reaching the top has hit us. We know for sure we're not going back."

"I think I understand," I said. "You lived all your life in Mexico, and now, your life is here."

"That's right. My parents and grandparents lived down there. Coming here has taught me what generations of Mennonites felt, leaving a country they'd known forever and moving to a strange place."

I nodded, letting him continue.

"I guess it's even harder for me, because my great-great grandpa Johann Wiebe was the Ältester of the Old Colony in Russia back in the late 1870s. At the first sign of war, he led his people to Canada, leaving behind all the persecution and famine that the remaining Mennonites experienced. It took a lot of courage for him to do that, something I have a better understanding of." He tossed the stick away. "Our people have always been on the move."

Hearing that, I told him what I'd learned on the field trip. "You know, Dad, we're like those Seminoles—a people set apart."

"I guess so, or maybe the runaway part. Either way, I'm never going back to that life. I can't believe God wants us to live in isolation, without education, remaining ignorant to the ways of the world."

"And not out there spreading the good news about Jesus," I added. "Even Dirk Willems was able to save one man before they burned him to death."

He smiled as we walked over to the corner of the backyard.

"Tina, getting an apricot pit to become this tree was excellent work. But getting it to bear such delicious fruit is a miracle."

"I guess it's in my blood, Dad. Mom said we have ten more jars of apricot jam left."

"And I'll enjoy every bit of it, because we're in the land of milk and honey *and* apricot jam."

I wrapped my arm around his waist, just enjoying the moment as the heart of fall descended around us. We never learned who took all of the land money or the attorney's fees, because we stopped caring. We were here, and it was all part of God's plan. Like my tree, we had put down roots—deep ones—and nothing could pull us out.

I guess it's true what they say.

Some people never give up.

Family Photos

Draw where the Seminole scouts of the Tenth Cavalry found the Indian wells that saved their lives. It now runs through the city of Seminole, Texas.

A typical 1950s and 60s school in Mexico.

With rubber tires forbidden, spokes/paddles made the work hard.

Judith and Jacob Rempel (David Rempel's paternal grandparents who left Canada for Mexico).

Katharina Rempel (Tina's paternal grandmother).

Jacob Rempel the preacher (Tina's paternal grandfather).

The extended Rempel family in Ontario, Canada in 1974. (counterclockwise from bottom row left) David Rempel (child), Elizabeth Rempel, Tina Rempel, Anna Rempel (pregnant with Nancy), Aunt Lisa Rempel, Aunt Elizabeth Friesen, Henry Friesen, (Anna Rempel's brother), Uncle Jacob Rempel, David Rempel (adult).

Teepee Lodge—Where Tina and her family stayed when they first arrived in Seminole. A bush where they hung out wet laundry to dry still survives.

Tina Rempel (lower right-hand corner) experiences her first evening schooling in Seminole to learn basic English. The teacher is Mrs. Reimer.

The Rempel's first mobile home (purchased) and David's brown Buick.

348

Mom and kids in trailer (*l to r*: David, Anna, Nancy, Tina).

David Rempel at work in Seminole.

For the Rempels, many new beginnings on this property. Notice the grown apricot tree in the corner.

First day of public school in Seminole, Texas 1977.

Anna Rempel baking her
famous bread.

Citizenship day for Tina
on October 31, 1986.

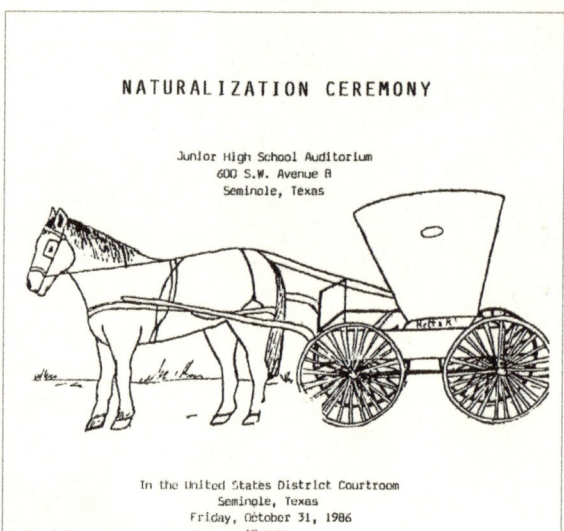

NATURALIZATION CEREMONY

Junior High School Auditorium
600 S.W. Avenue A
Seminole, Texas

In the United States District Courtroom
Seminole, Texas
Friday, October 31, 1986
12 p.m.

Presiding

U.S. District Judge-Honorable Halbert O. Woodward

Citizenship ceremony
program.

Vicky and Mayor Bob Clark with Tina between them.

Laura Hoffman and Tina Siemens.

At Tina's home, Anna Rempel teaches her two daughters Nancy (left) and Tina (right) how to make kringle.

Anna and David Rempel at home in Seminole on Christmas Day 2008. It was the last Christmas before Anna passed.

351

President Carter makes time between hospital stays in November of 2019 to visit with Tina about her book. (*l to r:* Kira Siemens, Rosalynn Carter, President Jimmy Carter, Tina Siemens, Bryleigh Siemens.) Photo by Dustin Chambers

Epilogue

In looking back at the lives of my parents in Mexico and grandparents in Canada, it seems to me that they had good intentions, but their views were clouded. Add to that the hardships of immigration, and living under the strict man-made rules, it's not hard to see why they drifted further and further away from the truth. Schools were not a priority. Without a solid understanding of the *truth*, leaders can't see it, much less teach it. Their tightly crafted bubble society began to suffer.

My mother and best friend modeled four pillars to live by: Love each other. Forgive each other. Never give up. Let's pray about it. These four are chiseled into the back of her tombstone.

As for my father, I asked him about his success and he said this: "I don't have a big wealth saved up but I live comfortably. Now, my kids can have great success." When I asked him about his grandchildren, Dad had this to say: "Our grandchildren are way smarter than me because we didn't stay in Mexico. To our grandchildren: Don't waste what we sacrificed to get you here. I wish our great-great-grandchildren a better start, and hopefully they go farther."

After reviewing my mother's and father's life advice, I thought about what I might say. I wanted future generations to know the ups and downs—a testimony as to what has been accomplished—not out of our own strength, but through God's strength. A key message I wanted our grandchildren and great-grandchildren to receive can be summed up with one word: *perseverance*. No matter what life throws at you, you can persevere. You can refuse to give up. Just put one foot in front of the other and who knows? The next step might land you exactly where you want to go, and victory will be achieved. Like an arrow on a bow—one has to pull backward before forward motion can be achieved. Life often pulls us back, but hope is always ahead, if we *persevere*.

⋙⋘

I've been interested in my family's genealogy for years and years. My dream with this project was to set down a record of the migration of my ancestors. Here's a brief summary of places our people have lived: prior to 1496 – the Netherlands (Low Country); 1530–1787 – Prussia (Poland); 1787–1874 – Russia (Ukraine); 1874 to present – Canada; 1922 to present– Mexico; 1977 to present – Seminole, Texas. As you can see, Mennonites are used to moving.

After the 1870s exodus, things looked up for the Mennonites in Russia who decided to stay behind. With so many of their fellow Mennonites gone, land was readily available for the thousands of remaining Mennonites. They built large factories and mills. They also constructed hospitals, orphanages, and prestigious schools. These Russian Mennonites began to study abroad, leading many to become physicians, lawyers, and professors. They integrated with native Russians with a few Mennonites even being elected to Russian parliament.

To fulfill their agreement with the Mennonites by not requiring them to fight, the Russian government conscripted them to serve in alternative ways like forestry and working with the Red Cross to gather the wounded from the battlefields. In this way, both the Russian government and the Mennonites could coexist in a framework that was financially successful. Owning land was the key to this prosperity. The downside of prosperity is pride because pride comes before the fall.

After WWI, Ukraine was in chaos with different armies coming and going. A few individuals like Nestor Makhno sought revenge; he brought ultimate destruction to the Mennonite villages by raping, murdering, and taking possession of their property. Thousands migrated to Canada until that exit door closed completely in 1929. For those Mennonites who didn't make it out, if they resisted Stalin's policy, they were imprisoned, executed, or exiled.

Regarding my own family's exodus, every one of my parents' siblings eventually left Mexico. Even my paternal grandparents made it out as Grandma Katharina Giesbrecht Rempel passed away in Seminole and Grandpa (Jacob the preacher) died in Manitoba, Canada, but was transported to Seminole to be buried next to his wife. As of the publication date, the following relatives are at these locations: Uncle Jake passed in Seminole; Aunt Katharina Dyck is in Bolivia; Maria Goertzen, Margaretha (Margaret) Peters, Aganetha (Nettie) Friesen, and Anita Martens are back in Manitoba, Canada; and two of Dad's sisters—Helena Hiebert and Judy Teichroeb—passed away in Mexico.

My maternal grandparents, Jacob and Elizabeth Friesen, along with Uncle Jacob Friesen, Aunt Elizabeth Peters, and Aunt Maria Wiebe passed away in Mexico. Also, Uncle Henry Friesen and Abraham Friesen both passed in Ontario, Canada. Aunt Aganetha Neufeld passed in Argentina, South America. Uncle Johan Friesen, Peter Friesen, and Isaac Friesen all passed away in Bolivia, South America.

Yet all of this migration started with one person: Menno Simons (1496 –1561). He lived a fascinating life worth examination.

Menno Simons grew up poor and had no academic education; however, he received some education when he became an ordained Catholic priest. As he educated himself to what the Bible really said, he grew disillusioned, torn between two authorities: the Bible and the church. His early life was in the Netherlands, whose citizens spoke Low German (Dutch Low Saxon as the Netherlands was known).

Once he rejected the Catholic Church, he became a hunted man with a price on his head. He wrote in 1544 that he couldn't find, in all of the countries, a cabin or a hut in which his poor wife and little children could be put safely for a year or even six months. Still, he had a following— Dutch Anabaptists—who listened to what he had to say. They gravitated toward his leadership.

At this point you need to understand that ninety-five percent of all people on earth were uneducated. No one could read or write except educated people. This consisted of the wealthy and the clergy. Thus, your average farmer needed a priest to tell him about God, and how to honor Him, and sometimes, how to think. (Sounds like many of the congregations of today.) That's why Menno Simons had such a following. His people believed his message and wanted more.

When Simons died, his followers continued with new leaders reading his sermons and writings. Decades before he died, the term "Mennonite" was derived from his first name and used to describe his followers. Five hundred years later, not much has changed.

I've often wondered if he saw the modern-day Mennonite, what Menno Simons would think. There are thousands of Mennonites who continue to do God's work. The MCC (Mennonite Central Committee) was founded in 1920 to provide food for the starving Mennonites in Ukraine, but they soon realized that they could help more than the Mennonites. Now, the MCC works in every continent except Antarctica and Australia—more than fifty countries—helping everyone. In the U.S. alone, there are forty separate Mennonite groups that differ in the way they dress or hold their church services. Then there are those who say Mennonites are an ethnic group. It was the conviction of the Anabaptist movement that started in 1525, a conviction that Menno Simons and many others preached on. It was simple: that the only foundation is Jesus Christ (1 Corinthians 3:11). Many new believers were willing to give their lives for this, like the true story in the beginning of this book about Dirk Willems. I would encourage everyone to seek the truth. It happened to my husband, John, and me. We questioned the leader of the Mennonite church we attended at the time, asking why they were enforcing rules that had no Biblical support. His answer was the timeless response borne of the ignorance that's passed down from generation to generation: "That's the way we have to do it." End of discussion. We learned that the best way to identify a counterfeit is to know the authentic—the real deal. We did and have broken the chains of inherited ignorance for our children.

If Menno Simons was alive today, I think he would say that's not what he made a sacrifice for. He would hate to see that so many are choosing to stay in the darkness, the self-imposed physical hardships, the long faces, the lack of joy or happiness, and the depression. I remember lots of families saying if they talked too loudly or laughed at the table, their father demanded total silence while they ate. There could be no family conversations at the table. That was harsh.

Mennonites are hard workers. They focus much of their attention on work. That's why it's so hard for some to believe that there's a free gift waiting for them—it's total forgiveness of sins, eternal salvation, and a journey to heaven to be with God. Many religions have created the false doctrine that you must work for it. These false religions claim that only when you are dead will you discover if you have worked hard enough.

The truth is we don't deserve anything we get for free. But God's grace *is* free. He gave it freely; you don't have to work for it. Think about it—but not too long. This offer is good for a limited time—like while you are still alive. And you never know when the end is coming. There's only one day out of the year that we can do something about it... TODAY! Yesterday is gone and we may never see tomorrow. So don't delay.

⸺◆⸺

As I explained in the book, I was so colicky as a baby I could only take milk from a cow named Rose. I decided to use that name for my special character in Seminole. Besides, I love the Victorian style, and roses were a very big part of that era.

A rose can also be a metaphor for ourselves. How? God created us in His own image. No matter who we are, we're beautiful. And the rose has two components: the beautiful flower and the nasty thorns. When we perceive events, we can choose to be negative and let the thorns come to the forefront. Or we can choose to embrace the positive and allow our inner beauty to shine. And that's just one more reason why I love the name Rose.

⸺◆⸺

The love of my life—John Siemens—and I were looking to buy some acreage north of Seminole to build a new home. I took a shovel and dug a hole because I wanted to make sure that we would have a good depth of topsoil so I could sow my plants. Really, I did one or two shovels full of dirt before John took over. Once the hole was two feet down, I was satisfied with the land and we could go forward with the purchase. I did this because on SE 5th St., where I grew up, trees had a hard time growing. Between the caliche and rocks, the little apricot tree I wrote about took years to bear fruit because there were just six to twelve inches of topsoil.

Like planting seeds, you don't have to convert every person to bear fruit. You just have to move them closer to accepting Jesus as their Savior.

When I planted that apricot pit, I started small. But with sun, water, and love, it eventually bore delicious fruit. The same is true with spreading the good news. You may be the person who planted the seed. Another person may come along and provide the sun. Still another might be the one who collects the fruit when they finally accept Jesus. It took everyone working together to save a soul—to achieve victory—not just one person. Focus on your role and let God handle the rest.

—◆—

In this book, I included a real incident that happened in Canada. I was in Sunday school awaiting a gift the teacher had for us. It was wrapped. I wondered what it could be. Then Dad ordered us to the car because we were leaving to go back to Mexico. I was devastated, always wondering what was in that package.

A few years ago I read a book on child behavior. It claimed events that happened in our childhood subconsciously shaped how we do things as adults. I believe it, because whenever I buy a gift to give, I don't like to wrap it. I will make it an open basket or tie a ribbon around the gift itself, presenting it openly so the recipient can see what it is. I believe it's due to that incident. To this day I wonder what was in the package.

Like that package, salvation is a free gift. I encourage you to unwrap the gift of knowledge and salvation and accept it. (Sorry for beating this point to death but death carries really bad news unless you have accepted Jesus Christ as your personal savior. If you truly believed it like I do, you'd be telling everyone you could.)

And be obedient by following through with the calling to be the change. Menno Simons took a bold step for change to happen. That's why I appreciate my father and his grandfather all the more. All it takes is one person.

—◆—

As for me, having the privilege to become a part of the fabric of the United States of America, enjoying the good times and enduring the difficult ones along the way, has given us a foundation to build on while the opportunities have made me and my family grateful citizens of this life. We were also shown how to secure citizenship in heaven forever through our salvation in Jesus Christ. (I had to mention it one more time.)

There are many more stories I have to tell. But they will have to wait for another book....

Faspa

aspa is an afternoon break for Mennonites. *Faspa* actually sounds like "vaspa." It's usually held at four o'clock, when the man comes in from plowing the fields and needs some refreshment. With supper not being served until eight or nine, depending on the sunset, *faspa* is a chance to relax while drinking coffee or tea, revitalizing the Mennonites so they can keep working. Remember, this tradition comes from the families who work fourteen-hour days. Because they eat at noon and supper is too far away, they need something in between.

The husband and wife will sit at their table for fifteen minutes, visiting while eating bread and kringle with butter. Usually, homemade jams are present, along with pickles, cheese, and sugar cubes. If they have been prepared, cookies are placed on a dish too.

A simple teapot is used to serve the hot liquid, and the table is set with cups and saucers.

On Sundays, *faspa* turns into a social event. Mennonites spend the day visiting family and friends. The breads and sweets served will be fresh baked on Saturday with a little extra attention to make sure that the frosting on the cake is just right and the cookies and kringle are baked to perfection. Usually, everything is prepared on Saturday so the Mennonites don't have to work on Sunday. If they have nice china, that will be used on Sundays.

For Mennonites, *faspa* is something that's second nature, like breathing. It's a break in their long day that tells them they have only four more hours to go until quitting time. With a workday that long, who wouldn't want some coffee and sweet cookies?

Baptism

Note: The information regarding baptisms contained below have been described as they were during my parents' era and are still practiced in some places today. It is not a given that all Mennonites wherever they are still practice this way.

Menno Simon was influenced by Martin Luther, who said that infant baptism was not biblical. He believed you must be baptized upon your own confession and faith, not as a child when you are under the influence of your parents. It should be of your own free will.

Mennonites get baptized in their late teens, before marriage. In many of the congregations, there is one day for baptisms each year. During this time, thirty to forty people get baptized. Baptism is a prerequisite to getting married, so the desire to marry ensures a baptism.

Four Sundays before the day of baptism, each candidate must memorize the entire catechism and recite it in church before the congregation. The girls wear brown dresses for the first two Sundays, and a black dress for the second two. The black dress is elegantly made, with pleats in the skirt and a neck tie made of the same material as the dress. It's the same dress they wear on their wedding day. Boys wear a suit but no tie.

The Sunday after the baptism, they have communion. This is a special church service to celebrate the new members. It's at this service that some couples announce they have set a wedding date.

Dating and Marriage

Note: The information regarding dating and marriage contained below have been described as they were during my parents' era and are still practiced in some places today. It is not a given that all Mennonites wherever they are still practice this way.

Dating for Old Colony Mennonites is a highly regulated process, although unlike some cultures, there are no prearranged marriages. Girls and boys are separated in school and church, but they have ample opportunity to talk to each other. Dating is allowed on Wednesdays and Sundays, but the couple should not be seen together or talk on the other days.

When a couple decides to get engaged, the marriage process has several steps. First, invitations go out. The father of the groom will sit down and write out a list of people he wants to invite. When he's done, he'll hand the list to his son, who will add the names of anyone he wants to attend. Once the son has done that, he hands the list back to his father, who sends it to the schoolteacher. The teacher makes a handwritten copy and starts the circulation by delivering it to the first name on the list. The person crosses their name off and delivers it to the next name on the list. The last person on the list crosses their name off and returns it to the groom. The same process happens on the bride's side. In this way, everyone learns of the wedding and there is written confirmation. With no mail system in the colony, it's very efficient and very German.

The circulation of the two invitation letters begins one week before the wedding, while the actual announcement is made in church on Sunday. After the service, the groom's family will ride to the bride's family home and have lunch.

During the following week, the bride and groom will travel to their friends and relatives under the pretense of making sure they know about the upcoming wedding. Of course, not only do they have a supper prepared for the happy couple, but they give them a small gift. It might be a cup, saucer, knife, fork, or spoon. This helps the couple build their inventory of essentials.

Prior to the actual ceremony, any kissing or close contact is strictly forbidden. Holding hands is all that's allowed. Maybe an arm around a shoulder, so long as it's nothing more. *Maybe*.

The day of the wedding is Sunday, and it's held at church. The couple brings a set of chairs from home and places them directly in front of the pulpit. They will sit there for the two-and-a-half-hour sermon. After that, they will be married and freed while the rest of the congregation stays for the last forty-five minutes of the service. The couple will ride to the groom's house and wait for the rest of the people to arrive. A large meal will be served. During this event, the couple will receive their wedding gifts from immediate family members.

Although most couples love each other, it's not required in a Mennonite marriage—only faith.

Funeral

Note: The information regarding funerals contained below have been described as they were during my parents' era and are still practiced in some places today. It is not a given that all Mennonites wherever they are still practice this way.

Like many aspects of Mennonite life, death was handled practically. When a member passed away, the evening of death brought together a gathering at the deceased's house. Families would arrive and sing a few songs. This was followed by prayer. The entire event would last at least an hour, depending on the popularity of the deceased.

Usually, the deceased's family would need additional seating. If so, four to six young men would go up one side of the campo or village and collect chairs and homemade benches on a flatbed trailer pulled by horses. After they had delivered the load to the deceased's house, they would travel up the other side and repeat the process. Every Mennonite had scratched and painted their names into the underside of each chair and bench, so after the gathering, the items would be returned.

The body was kept on the property of the deceased, usually in the sitting room. Sometimes it would be kept in the barn or feed room. Because embalming was not known or practiced, the body was placed on a piece of corrugated metal. The metal rested on wooden supports and tilted so the ice packed around the body would melt into a bucket. If the body was kept in the sitting room, the sleeping occupants spent several days listening to the eerie drip, drip, drip as the ice melted. If the body was kept outside in the barn, there was always the risk of a varmint getting ahold of the flesh. I guess the location of the body depended on how family wanted to deal with all of these issues: the dripping or the varmints.

The morning after the death, six to eight strong boys in the campo would begin digging the grave. They would use a pick and shovel, leaving the dirt pile next to the grave. In Mexico, this was a two-to-three-day process since the ground was extremely hard. The same group of young men would have to close up the grave when the service was over. This was done while the family stood there, watching.

The family of the deceased would be responsible for feeding the grave-diggers as well as the people attending the funeral. They would slaughter a calf. If they didn't have one, they would trade for a calf. From the calf, a lunch of vegetable soup would be prepared. The meat that flavored the soup would be removed and ground up, then mixed with salt and pepper. The mixture would be pressed flat onto cookie sheets and cooled off before being cut up into squares called *fleesch kjees*. These squares were then served with ketchup.

The soup and *fleesch kjees* would be served before the funeral. After the funeral, a *faspa* would be held. Kringle (twisted strands of white bread) and bread buns (rolls) would be served along with coffee and sugar cubes.

The women of the deceased's family, along with other village women and teenage girls, had to knead enough bread and kringle dough so that they could feed the anticipated crowd. Once the dough was prepared and stored in large containers, two girls would take the dough by horse and buggy, going door to door, giving each household a portion so they could bake some kringle. If the anticipated crowd size was to be large, many women would have to assist in preparing the funeral lunch and *faspa*.

The coffins were made of pine, just like you see in the western movies. The young men who dug the grave would act as pallbearers.

A letter or obituary notification had to be written by the Ältester or preacher, with the names of the pastors from the other campos written on the back since they were invited. If the death was a preacher or Ältester, the remaining leaders would have to carry the deceased's work load until a new leader was elected. Of course, any well-known person or leader meant the attendance would be many.

To make sure the letter or obituary notification was properly circulated, the campo's preacher would dispatch his son on horseback or buggy to deliver the letter to the neighboring preacher. That preacher would send his son to deliver the letter to the next preacher. And so on until everyone had been notified. After all, there were no phones or internet.

Throughout this process, the deceased's family did nothing but work. There was no time for mourning since they had to gather and arrange the chairs and benches, slaughter a calf, keep ice on the body, and prepare the food. It was the typical Mennonite philosophy: work makes you free.

Schooling

Note: The information regarding schooling contained below have been described as they were during my parents' era and are still practiced in some places today. It is not a given that all Mennonites wherever they are still practice this way.

Teaching for Mennonites was very limited. All the children in a campo attend a school designated for that campo. There are usually fifty to eighty children to one teacher, with the younger students sitting at the back of the room and older ones in front. Instead of individual desks, there are long benches and tables with an aisle down the middle. The girls are on one side of the aisle and boys on the other.

The teacher, always male, is given free housing in the campo for him and his family. With so many students, the teacher doesn't have time for everyone so he spends the most time with his favorites.

The children start at six with the ABC book. The kids learn to read usually by the second year. Then they memorize the catechism book. To understand the catechism, the teacher will pose a question: What is the true way to salvation? The children memorize the answer: Faith in Jesus Christ, our Savior and his shed blood. John 20:31.

When they master the catechism, the children start reading the New Testament. Then it's on to the Old Testament. As they go through the New and Old Testament verse by verse, the teacher tells them to overlook sections that are harder to understand or would provoke questions by the students and move on to other ones.

They never receive any instruction in biology, history, English, government, or science. There is a little instruction on basic math with an emphasis on the word "basic."

The girls stop at thirteen to work at home, learning the trade of house-wife. The boys can go to fourteen to get an extra year of math, although many quit early.

Things have improved for the majority of Mennonites, but there are still schools just like this in different parts of the world where more conservative Mennonites live.

Mennonite Migration

Menno Simons was a man who lived from 1496 to 1561. He rejected the teachings of the Roman Catholic Church in several areas of belief, the most notable being baptism. The Roman Catholics believed an infant should be baptized as soon as possible—as a baby. Menno Simons believed that an infant baptism was not Biblical since the baby did not have a choice in the matter. He wrote that an individual—when he or she is capable of making a conscious decision—should be able to decide on being baptized. His followers were part of a growing movement called "Anabaptists" or "Again-Baptists," meaning those who are baptized again. His motto was, "No other foundation can anyone lay than that which is laid, which is Jesus Christ" (1 Corinthians 3:11). At this time in all of Europe, religious intolerance was acted upon, which led to persecution.

Another facet of Menno Simons's beliefs was pacifism. Because he and his followers refused to fight their persecutors, they were forced to flee. This trend established a pattern of migration that affected three continents over a 400-year period.

The genesis of the Mennonite movement was in Friesland, which was part of the Netherlands, also called Lower Saxon. Thus, the Germans who lived there spoke Low German. They worked the low-lying lands on the coast, using their ingenuity to reclaim the land for much of Friesland. In exchange for doing this work, the ruler granted them an exemption from military service. However, as soon as the land was made productive, the deal changed, and the ruler forced them to stay. By limiting their freedoms and turning them into a lower class, the persecution intensified. The Mennonites had no choice but to flee. Their first stop was Prussia (present-day Poland). King Sigismund Augustus invited them to come, working to drain the marshlands for farming. By the 1770s, the Mennonites had to pay annually in exchange for military exemption, and could no longer buy new acreage for their growing families.

In the late 1780s, the Russians had a large amount of land that needed developing in what today is Ukraine. Because the Mennonites were hard workers and known for getting the land to produce, Catherine the Great invited and granted them military exemption and religious freedom in exchange for working the land. The Mennonites agreed and in 1787–1789 formed the first colony, which was called the Chortitza Colony. The second colony in 1803–1804 was called the Molotschna Colony. About one hundred years later, with crops aplenty, manufacturing equipment in use, and other trades like silk weaving being practiced, the Mennonite population swelled to 45,000. Unfortunately, the original manifesto did not permit the sixty-five dessiatines of land given to each family to be subdivided. Since only one son could inherit the farm, this resulted in a shortage of land.

In the 1850 to1860 era, political events threatened the privileges given to the Mennonites when they were first invited to Russia. When changes appeared such as the requirement to teach the Russian language in their schools, and military service, the first group sold all they had and went in search of a new homeland.

Between 1874 and 1880, large groups of Mennonites fled to Canada and the United States. Seven thousand went to the Manitoba province of Canada and nine thousand went to Kansas, Minnesota, and Nebraska. In Canada, the Mennonites requested and were granted their privileges: religious freedom and military exemption. These privileges established a very familiar pattern. Then World War I came.

In Russia (present-day Ukraine), the families who stayed behind, not leaving in the 1874 migration, were living a lavish lifestyle, and excelled in education. Now, with Germany and Russia at war, because the Mennonites spoke German, they faced new challenges. They were considered disloyal and a threat to the state. Suddenly, speaking German was forbidden. The Mennonites faced a steady decline on all fronts.

Unfortunately, it got worse. There were many brutal and horrific scenes. This became the new normal for Mennonites living in Russia. Thousands were killed or sent to prison. They asked for help from the Canadian Mennonites who had migrated in the 1870s and thus, the Mennonite Central Committee (MCC) was born. The MCC brought many of the Russian Mennonites to Canada and Paraguay in South America.

After the war, in the early 1920s, once again there were differences in the local congregations in Canada. The Canadian government asked for a public-school tax from all Mennonites, which was the first step in driving them away.

In the early 1920s, thousands of Mennonites fled Canada to Mexico, where once again they were promised the same things in exchange for working the land. Thousands more went to Paraguay, which eventually led to settlements in Belize, Uruguay, Bolivia, Brazil, and Argentina.

Today, Mennonites are scattered across the globe, popping up in the most unlikely of places like Seminole, Texas, in 1977. There, the Mennonites' hard work has made Gaines County one of the most productive crop farming counties in the nation. But stay tuned. The Mennonite migration is never-ending.

Author Bio

Katharina "Tina" Rempel immigrated to the U.S. from Mexico in 1977, becoming a U.S. citizen in 1986. She married her best friend, John Siemens, on April 17, 1988. She is the proud mother of two sons, both married, and Oma to four precious grandchildren. In 1989, Tina and her husband, John, started JW&T, Inc.—a company specializing in both residential and commercial construction.

Tina has served on various boards in Seminole, including the Chamber of Commerce and the hospital board. In November 2015, Tina had the great honor of being named citizen of the year of Seminole, Texas. And hardly a day goes by that she doesn't tell someone how proud she is to be an American!

This is her first book.

Tina is available to speak to your organization or book club. She can be contacted at SeminoleTheBook@gmail.com. Check out her website at SeminoleTheBook.com for more information.

Made in the USA
Monee, IL
03 June 2021